Fascism in the
Contemporary World

Other Titles of Interest

Self-Determination: National, Regional, and Global Dimensions, edited by Yonah Alexander and Robert A. Friedlander

Terrorism: Theory and Practice, edited by Yonah Alexander, Paul Wilkinson, and David Carlton

Radicalism in the Contemporary Age (3 vols.), edited by Seweryn Bialer and Sophia Sluzar

Strategies Against Violence: Design for Nonviolent Change, edited by Israel W. Charny

Nations and States: An Enquiry into the Origins of Nations and the Politics of Nationalism, Hugh Seton-Watson

The Relevance of Liberalism, edited by the Research Institute on International Change

A Westview Special Study

Fascism in the Contemporary World: Ideology, Evolution, Resurgence
Anthony James Joes

Central to this book is the assertion that fascist regimes similar in ideology and style to Mussolini's in Italy have arisen and will continue to arise in the underdeveloped world. The author views fascism as a definite response—authoritarian corporatist nationalism—to certain problems common to late-developing nations, not as an aberration that can be exorcised or explained away. He explores similarities between past and contemporary fascism and seeks to explain in what circumstances fascism develops, to whom it is attractive, and what its reemergence signifies for us. Single-factor explanatory strategies are explicitly rejected.

This is the first attempt to systematically link fascist ideology and practice in Europe to that in the Third World. Professor Joes discusses ten countries in some detail, stressing the political and economic milieu in which fascism develops an appeal. He explores the relative strengths of competing world views (liberal democracy, Leninism) and seeks to show how contemporary military dictatorships develop similarities to classical fascism.

Anthony J. Joes, associate professor of political science at St. Joseph's College, Philadelphia, holds a Ph.D. in politics from the University of Pennsylvania. Professor Joes's articles have appeared in *ORBIS, Comparative Political Studies, Worldview,* and *The Illinois Quarterly.*

Fascism in the Contemporary World:
Ideology, Evolution, Resurgence

Anthony James Joes
Foreword by A. James Gregor

Westview Press/Boulder, Colorado

A Westview Special Study

Copyright © 1978 by Westview Press, Inc.

Published in 1978 in the United States of America by
  Westview Press, Inc.
  5500 Central Avenue
  Boulder, Colorado 80301
  Frederick A. Praeger, Publisher

Library of Congress Cataloging in Publication Data
Joes, Anthony James.
  The rise of fascism in the contemporary world.
  (Westview special studies in social, political, and economic development)
  Bibliography: p.
  1. Fascism. I. Title.
JC481.J53   320.5'33   77-14141
ISBN 0-89158-159-6

Printed and bound in the United States of America

For Chris

Contents

Foreword

At some time in the not too distant future, political analysts will reflect upon the curious intellectual perversity that led the academicians of our time to imagine that the revolutions that characterize the twentieth century were somehow inspired by Marxism. They will fail to appreciate the noncognitive influences that led our pundits to accede to the conventional wisdom that they had learned as undergraduates. They will fail, in all probability, to comprehend the influence exercised by the pervasive prejudices of our epoch.

These future analysts will understand only that the Marxism of Marx and Engels predicted revolution in *advanced industrial environments*—environments afflicted with the "imbecility of overproduction," peopled by men who, in the "vast majority," were reduced to the status of "proletarians." Understanding that, they will fail to comprehend why our professional political analysts insisted on characterizing revolutions in *underdeveloped countries*, among populations anything but "proletarian," as "Marxist" or "Marxist-oriented."

The fact is that contemporary revolution has precious little to do with the Marxism left as an intellectual heritage by Marx and Engels. Engels, for his part, has insisted that socialist revolution could occur only in circumstances typified by "massive industrialization." Marx, in turn, had insisted that "no social order ever disappears before all the productive forces, for which there is room in it, have been developed; and new higher relations of production never appear before the material conditions of their existence have matured in the womb of the old society."

The twentieth century, however, has suffered a series of revolutions that pretend to introduce "new higher relations of production" on the basis of precapitalist and preindustrial economic foundations. We have experienced revolution in environments afflicted not by industrial overproduction but by preindustrial stagnation. We have witnessed not revolution by the "vast majority" of men reduced to the status of proletarians, but rather by peasant and petit bourgeois masses mobilized by an exiguous minority of declassed bourgeois leaders. Nowhere have proletarians figured prominently in revolutionary calculation. The majority of Bolsheviks were of peasant origin, although there were indeed proletarians in their ranks. Most of the former were military deserters, recently of peasant origin. Mao's revolutionaries were still less proletarians. They were displaced peasants almost to the man.

More than that, these revolutions have not brought with them a libertarian order characterized by universal suffrage, referendum and recall, the restricted political mandates, the rotation in office, and the voluntary association of productive communes promised by Marx and Engels and identified as the "dictatorship of the proletariat." Rather the revolutions of our time have delivered single-party states, heirarchical associations, centralized and bureaucratized developmental and modernizing economies, the orchestration of mass "consensus," the prevalence of "charismatic leaders," the instauration of a military style of life, closed autarchic systems, exacerbated nationalism, control of information and communications media, commitment of a vast expansion of military capabilities, and an insistence on the restoration of "lost territories" to the nation.

Almost every revolution in our time has displayed some of these traits. And as such, none of them have anything to do with classical Marxism. These characteristics are, in fact, the defining traits of fascism.

However one chooses to characterize "fascism," it is clear that modern revolutions share more affinities with the fascism of Benito Mussolini than they do with the Marxism of Karl Marx or Friedrich Engels. This is so because Mussolini's fascism was perhaps the first exemplar of the modern, mass-mobilizing, developmental dictatorship that has become so commonplace. The revolutions that preceded fascism displayed only some of the traits it fully exhibited. The revolutions that followed have shared more and more of those same traits. As such, Italian fascism remains a recommended point of departure of any contemporary analysis of revolution. Classical Marxism, on the other hand, provides little insight and still less theoretical leverage.

That the charter myths of many contemporary revolutionary movements pretend to Marxist inspiration tells us no more than that most men choose to identify with success. Stalin's Bolshevism was successful. Mussolini's fascism was not. But in the process of rendering itself successful, Stalin's Bolshevism developed what Leon Trotsky called a "deadly similarity with Fascism." As Bolshevism became more and more nationalistic, developmental, hierarchical, autarchic, and militaristic, in the effort to modernize its economy, it divested itself of whatever Marxist properties it may have at one time possessed. Similarly, there is precious little Marxism to be found in the system jerry-built by Mao to force-draft China into the twentieth century. That Castro was ever a Marxist is a delusion suffered only by those irremediably naive.

Recently Walter Laqueur reminded us that "after World War II a whole series of regimes have emerged . . . bearing at least some of the distinguishing signs of European fascism." He emphasized the presence of the secondary traits of fascism, the emphasis on community, the cult of violence, the ethic of sacrifice, dedication, and obedience, and all the instrumentalities of mass mobilization that characterize those regimes. There is talk in such systems of "populist" and "nationalist" socialism—and something called "military socialism." All of which does little to conceal the fact that the properties they share have only the most marginal relationship to anything in the socialist and Marxist traditions. Whatever they choose to call themselves, they look lamentably like some variant of fascism.

For at least these reasons, Anthony Joes has written a provocative book. He had directly addressed these problems. He attempts to probe a complex and sensitive area of contemporary political analysis. What he has done has been to draw our attention to some considerations that have become increasingly insistent over the past decade. His book is a beginning—an introduction into a vast and uncharted area of comparative analysis. That commentators will find a multiplicity of problems here—problems of definition, analysis, and interpretation—is testimony that he has launched us on a course through much troubled water, and is evidence, perhaps, that we are all freighted with timeworn prejudices and politically convenient, but mistaken, convictions.

A. James Gregor
Berkeley, California

Preface

Fascism is on the rise in the contemporary world. Recognizably fascist regimes have appeared in a number of underdeveloped countries in the past two decades, and there are good reasons for believing that their number will grow. I do not attempt here to explain fascism in any definitive sense. Not enough is known, and the interpretation of what we do know is often clouded in controversy. My purposes are more limited: to indicate similarities between fascist regimes of the present and those of the past, and to offer some suggestions as to what fascism is, why it develops, and what it will mean for all of us.

This is a work of synthesis; my indebtedness to other social scientists is obvious and total. But if the message is not totally new, it is nonetheless extremely important. That is why I have sought to address this book not primarily to specialists but to a broader audience. And it is with a broad audience in mind that I have done my best to keep social science jargon out of my text and to hold distractions like source references to a minimum. (This has not been easy. A social scientist's deepest instinct is to surround himself with a bristling wall of footnotes; this, he hopes, implicates authors more eminent than he in his enterprise and thus daunts the would-be critic.)

Because this book is first of all about fascism, the first chapter presents an overview of its nature, origins, and prospects. Then, a substantial portion is devoted to exploring the prototype fascist regime: Italy under Benito Mussolini. What did fascists promise the Italians? Why were those promises attractive? What did the fascists do with their power?

Following a look at fascism in European countries, consideration is given to the main forces shaping the contemporary Third World, and the reasons these forces are conducive to the emergence of fascism there. (For our purposes, the Third World encompasses Latin America, North Africa, the Middle East, sub-Saharan Africa, South and Southeast Asia, and prewar Japan.)

Brief case studies of fascism in a number of countries are presented. I do not pretend to be an authority on these countries; the purpose of the country profiles is to refresh the reader's memory about certain events and to relate them to the general theme of the book.

I owe much to many. First of all, to those scholars whose works, listed in the bibliography, I have ruthlessly ransacked; to the Committee on Faculty Research of St. Joseph's College and to the American Philosophical Society, both of which rendered timely financial assistance; to Professor William W. Kuhn, a generous and insightful mathematician; to Dr. Michael H. Glantz, a dear friend who made a vital connection; but most of all to my wife Christine, who typed practically the entire manuscript, made many sensible suggestions, and patiently put up with the whole thing.

I alone, of course, am responsible for any errors, shortcomings, and inadequacies.

Anthony James Joes

Fascism in the
Contemporary World

Part One

1. General Considerations on the Subject of Fascism

A common fault is not to reckon on storms in fair weather.
—Machiavelli

Why Be Concerned about Fascism?

There are basically three types of objections to a study of fascism. First, serious consideration of fascism is rejected on deeply emotional grounds. All fascisms are equated with Nazism, the only "real" fascism. The profound and understandable repugnance and revulsion felt by humane men and women for Nazism is thus passed on to all manifestations of fascism; the result is a widespread determination to ignore fascism, to consign it to a dark closet in mankind's historical chamber of horrors.

Second, there is the position that fascism is irrelevant. In this view, fascism was an important, if bizarre, phenomenon in Europe of the period 1918-1945, but has fortunately been defeated and uprooted; therefore attention should be given to more relevant and, it is hoped, more fruitful pursuits. The study of fascism can teach us little, if anything, about contemporary and future problems.

Third is the view that fascism as a generic category is without any useful meaning. Disagreement on what fascism is or was, even among scholars, is so wide and so blatant that the concept of fascism as an analytical tool is useless. The very fact that *fascist* has passed into everyday parlance as an insulting epithet demonstrates its lack of real cognitive content.

The Emotional Rejection of the Study of Fascism

Even if understandable, the refusal to come to grips with fascism because *fascist* and *Nazi* are equated is logically unacceptable. Even if it is correct to use the two terms as synonyms (which they are not, as will be argued below), it would still be an affront to common sense to ignore the phenomena these terms designate. Cancer is not usually studied because the pathologist finds it attractive, but because he believes it important to identify and explain it. Certainly a disease is not prevented by turning from its study in revulsion; neither is fascism.

In any case, it is not legitimate to equate all fascism with Nazism. Some scholars, such as Organski and Gregor, deny that Nazism is an example of fascism at all. Others argue that fascism includes regimes remarkably different from Hitler's Germany in many important ways. It is our position that the Nazis were one manifestation, and not a typical one, of a general fascist phenomenon.

The Relevance of Fascism

Although it is a widespread practice to relegate fascism to a particular geographical and historical locale (Europe, 1918-1945), many students of political and economic modernization have stressed the continuing and probably increasing importance of fascism. The view that fascism may find especially fertile soil in many parts of the Third World has been often expressed. A. James Gregor has said that "of the forms of totalitarianism developed in the twentieth century, fascism seems destined to exercise a continuing influence upon the nationalist and populist revolution of our times. The next two decades should witness the appearance of fascism, in various forms, throughout the underdeveloped world." John Weiss writes that "the greatest potential for fascism lies not in the liberal West, but rather . . . in the non-Western or underdeveloped societies." A. F. K. Organski argues that "it appears likely . . . that a considerable number of industrializing nations will adopt political systems that are neither bourgeois nor Stalinist and certainly not socialist, despite their occasional claims. Some

of these governments will closely resemble fascist governments in their structure, in their support, and in their
handling of industrialization."[1] More specifically, writing
of Japan, Donald C. Hellmann has observed that "a
breakdown of the present system as the result of economic
catastrophe or massive disenchantment with the ability of
governmental institutions to cope with domestic and foreign
problems, would indeed raise the spectre of a radical,
authoritarian, and militarily oriented movement more akin
to European fascism than to the militarism of Japan before
1941."

Thus, many scholars are convinced that fascist regimes in
Africa, Latin America, and Asia are not only a possibility,
but perhaps almost inevitable in some instances.

What Is Fascism?

There is much more disagreement than agreement about
what constitutes fascism in general, and whether this or that
movement or regime is or was fascist. For Organski, Franco's
Spain was the very model of a modern fascist system, but
Weiss states that "the rule of a Franco . . . may appear fascist.
In reality, however, it is old-fashioned and authoritarian."
Moore describes pre-1941 Japan as "possessing the fundamental features" of a fascist regime, yet Organski holds that
the Japanese system lacked the most essential elements of
fascism.

Attempts to achieve consensus on a general definition of
fascism do not yield much fruit either. Weiss uses the term
fascist to "refer to the general social movement of right-
wing revolutionary conservatism in Europe," which (apart
from any other problems) seems to exclude the Rumanian
Iron Guard. Ernst Nolte writes that "the most marked
characteristic of any fascism . . . is the combination of a
nationalist and socialist motif"; this might apply as well or
better to Tito's Yugoslavia than to Franco's Spain. Nolte
also approvingly quotes Franz Borkenau's statement that
after 1928 (the emergence of Stalin) the Soviet Union was to
be found "among the totalitarian fascist powers"; on the
other hand, in 1923 the Comintern officially branded the

German Social Democrats as a "fraction of German fascism." Obviously, something is wrong somewhere. Because of these difficulties and contradictions, and because students of fascism usually wind up employing many distinctions and subcategories to analyze fascism, one scholar has recently suggested that "it seems unwise to continue with studies that start with the assumption that there must have been such a generic phenomenon" as fascism.[2]

But difficulties of definition and lack of consensus about the nature of a phenomenon or concept are not necessarily grounds for discarding it. Consider the concept *representative democracy*. This term has been applied to systems as diverse as the United States, Costa Rica, and Switzerland, to name a few. In addition, the adjective *communist* is used without any apparent embarrassment to embrace countries as different as China, Yugoslavia, Mongolia, the Russia of Lenin, and the Soviet Union of Brezhnev. In spite of the wonderful diversity embraced by these terms and the consequent difficulties of precise consensual definition, no one seems ready to abandon them.

That there is serious lack of agreement about what fascism is or looks like is a convincing indication that we must study it all the more. Controversies about the identification of fascism certainly do not prove that it is unknowable, unimportant, or nonexistent. If anything, such controversy should spur us on to a determined effort to find—or create—a satisfactory understanding of fascism that will be useful for analyzing present and future conditions. At any rate, we will employ the term *fascist* to refer to (1) the ideology and system of government of Italy under Mussolini, and (2) all beliefs, leaders, parties, and regimes that resemble those of Italian fascism.

Explanations of Fascism: Clearing away Underbrush

Much of the confusion about fascism stems from the multitude of conflicting attempts to explain it in terms of some single factor. In the rest of this chapter, the most common or the seemingly most successful explanations of fascism will be summarized and examined. In treating these explanations, I have closely followed the thought of A. James Gregor.[3]

The most popular explanations of fascism, especially the original, Italian variety, have been fascism as: (1) the result of moral crisis; (2) the product of widespread psychological disabilities; (3) the consequence of the entrance of the "amorphous masses" into politics; and (4) the result of class struggle.

Fascism and "Moral Crisis"

The principal exponents of the "moral crisis"school have been Benedetto Croce, Peter Drucker, and Hans Kohn. For Croce, "Fascism was a consequence of a kind of 'moral or intellectual morbidity' that afflicted all classes and reflected a 'lost faith not only in rational liberalism but in Marxism as well.' The critical factor in the rise of fascism was the 'debasement of the idea of liberty' and the collective infatuation with 'heroes and supermen.' " For Kohn, fascism had its genesis in the "disillusionment . . . the social unrest and moral confusion which followed the war of 1914-1918." For Drucker, "men lost their faith in 'freedom and equality,' the 'two cornerstones' of European social order. The European masses languished in the belief that 'existence in society is governed not by rational and sensible, but by blind, irrational, and demonic forces.' "

Although all of these "moral crisis" explanations have appealing elements, they are disappointing from several standpoints. "Any interpretation that makes omnibus ascriptions of moral dispositions to millions of participants, is, on its face, suspect." Where is the evidence, where are the scientific data, to confirm such ascriptions? How do we know that the "European masses" were "languishing" in this or that belief? If, moreover, there was a widespread feeling of despair and confusion, why did fascism triumph, and not "Marxism, Zen Buddhism, drink, drugs, or suicide?" "To say, with Kohn, that 'deep social unrest' gave Mussolini his 'chance' is probably true, but trivial. 'Deep social unrest' can be generally understood to provide revolutionaries their 'chance.' The question is not whether there was a 'chance' to be had in the post–World War I environment of Italy, but rather why Mussolini was capable of exploiting it while the socialists (of whatever stamp) or the liberals were not."

It is instructive to note that fascists also ascribe the rise of fascism to moral crisis. In their view, liberalism and Marxism had brought Italy (and Europe) to the brink of despair and chaos; the "best and boldest spirits," the "healthiest elements" turned to fascism for moral salvation. There is no doubt some grain of truth in all these accounts, but one cannot avoid Gregor's conclusion that such explanations "hardly recommend themselves to serious students of complex historical or political phenomena."

Fascism as a Product of Psychological Disability

The view of fascism as the result of individual and collective psychopathy is "almost as popular as the interpretation of Fascism as the result of moral crisis." Perhaps "the most unfortunate accounts in this tradition are those that are the product of an unrestricted enthusiasm for Freudian analyses conjoined with the righteous indignation born in the years of conflict against Fascism and National Socialism." The principal works in this tradition are Peter Nathan's *Psychology of Fascism,* Wilhelm Reich's *Mass Psychology of Fascism,* and Erich Fromm's *Escape from Freedom.* All these accounts claim to explain fascism through a combination of sexual and economic arguments, though they differ in the amount of emphasis placed on each. All are essentially variations on the following themes: (1) all or most men are predisposed to be fascists because of stunting experiences in childhood; or (2) vast numbers of Western men are debilitated by the effects of sexual repression, social alienation, or "monopoly capitalism"; or (3) a combination of these and others. These interpretations all suffer from the same defects. If almost everyone is predisposed to be fascist, why does fascism surface or seize power here and not there, now and not then? If masses of men are alienated by monopoly capital, why did fascism first come to power in relatively rural Italy, and not in capitalist

Britain or America? And Gregor aptly states the most fatal flaw of all: "Fromm pretends to know how the artisans of the medieval period felt about the products of their labor—and how the wealthy nobles and burghers of the Renaissance felt. It is difficult, irrespective of Fromm's confidence, to know how the clinical study of a contemporary collection of self-selected neurotics, no matter how 'minutely' analyzed, could have produced information that could be projected over whole population categories and classes that lived in medieval or Renaissance times."

No matter how plausible or pleasing such psychoanalytical accounts of fascism may be, we are left without any real data to substantiate them, on the one hand, and with the uncomfortable awareness that psychoanalytical explanations, in explaining literally everything, really explain nothing.

The same type of criticism can be leveled against the apparently more sophisticated attempt—in studies of the "authoritarian personality"—to apply Freudian categories to political phenomena. The fascist, or potential fascist, is revealed to be brutal, latently homosexual at least, aggressive, unsophisticated, the psychologically deformed product of strict, repressive, and punitive family life. To Gregor, "it seems intuitively obvious that as complex and relatively efficient a movement as Fascism could not have been the simple product of sadomasochistic, latently homosexual personality types characterized by a lack of rational deliberation, an addiction to simple violence, and an irrepressible mysticism. If such individuals are found in fascist movements, it would seem that such movements would also require competent administrators, effective propagandists, planning personnel, and rational agents for the formulation of strategy as well." Such studies, moreover, find that the traits of the "authoritarian personality" are much more widely distributed among the working class than among the middle classes, yet few scholars concede that the working class provided anything like substantial membership in fascist movements. "When we review the efforts to explain Fascism via this interpretation we are left with a tissue of unsupported speculation that delivers only a vague sense that we are all lunatics, neurotics, and fascists, and there is little prospect of something better. Such interpretations . . . probably tell us more about the authors of such accounts than they do about Fascism."

Fascism and the "Amorphous Masses"

Ortega y Gasset's well-known *Revolt of the Masses* and Emil Lederer's *The State of the Masses* are two outstanding examples of the interpretation of fascism as the result of the intrusion onto the historical stage of the "amorphous masses." For Ortega, industrialization and liberalism have produced "mass-men," who are "ignorant, volatile, incontinent, totalitarian, violent, devoid of morality and purpose—in effect, barbarian and primitive." For Lederer, the "masses"of modern times are a true and unique psychological entity. The masses are "unsystematic, irrational, emotional"; fascism arose because mass-men provided the fertile soil, mass-men "stripped of their identification with specific economic groups and productive categories, shorn of their commitments to established loyalties, displaced by their involvement in urban industrial complexes." Mass-man is rootless, mobilizable, susceptible to the myths and brutal certainties of fascism.

The objections to this explanation of fascism, that is, as the triumph of the amorphous masses, are similar to those raised to psychosexual explanations. Where are the data to back up broad statements? "The difficulty, it would seem, lies in Ortega y Gasset's evident readiness to make wholesale and unqualified ascriptions of personality traits to entire populations—the nationalities, classes, and categories of an entire continent—if not the entire globe. It would be difficult to imagine the kind of evidence to which Ortega y Gasset might make recourse in attempting to warrant such ascriptions. Whatever evidence he does cite in the course of his exposition is fragmentary, intuitionistic and uncontrolled."

We really have no explanation of why mass-man (assuming that he existed in vast numbers) was attracted to fascism and not to socialist maximalism (in the Italian case, for instance). Certainly, a more than plausible case can be made for the irrationality and emotionalism of the extreme left in Italy in 1918-1922. We are left with the idea that mass-man was attracted to fascism because fascism was what mass-man was attracted to. This is not very satisfactory.

The theory that the amorphous masses were the recruiting ground of fascism, the soil from which and in which it grew, is contradicted by a great deal of hard evidence that certain quite specific groups supported Italian fascism (for instance) in its rise to power. Northern landlords who feared socialist violence and Po Valley smallholders who feared collectivization responded readily to the fascists' explicit words and deeds against the Red menace. Business interests contributed rather generously to the struggling fascist party in its early years; whatever we think of their motives in doing so, they were hardly "irrational and unthinking." Communists and others had made it a point to outrage the sentiments of returning war veterans, even going so far as to spit in the faces of wounded veterans in the streets. Fascists early espoused the satisfaction of the veterans' economic and social claims, and were rewarded with widespread veteran support. Policemen were attracted by the pledge of the fascists to restore "strict order" and to suppress "subversive" groups. Fascist promises to stop inflation and curb the unions appealed powerfully to numerous middle-class elements. The examples can be multiplied, but the point is clear: specific groups in Italian society viewed specific aspects of fascism as remedies for specific grievances or fears. On the other hand,

> the socialists had succeeded in alienating the entrepreneurial bourgeoisie, the landed property owners, the returning war veterans, many Catholics, and almost all liberals. The "maximalists" were transfixed by the Russian experiment remote though it was from Italian circumstances and Italian problems. It is hard to argue that Italian socialism had a more "rational" program and therefore failed to attract the "mass mind." It is harder still to argue that reasonably well-articulated groups and organized population elements found

nothing rational in the Fascist program. Their passive or active support of Fascism could hardly be construed as *totally* irrational and simply emotional.

Fascism and the Class Struggle

The explanation of fascism as an invention of the wealthy to suppress or delay the revolution of the suffering toilers was (and still is) widely popular. This approach to the origins and meaning of fascism was most attractive to those in, or allied to, the Marxian intellectual tradition. Class explanations of fascism run from the crudest Stalinist-mechanistic formula to the much more sophisticated analysis of the iconoclastic Franz Borkenau.

The Stalinist school, as exemplified by Palme Dutt's *Fascism: An Analysis* and Daniel Guerin's *Fascism and Big Business*, advances the hypothesis of the "capitalist conspiracy." Italian capitalism not only financed fascism, it invented it. That is, capitalism—in its last, "declining" stages—called fascism into existence, hoisted it into power, and then used it to do the dirty work of breaking up the institutions of the proletariat and keeping them under foot so that they might be the more easily exploited.

Serious difficulties arise with this interpretation of fascism. On one hand, there is convincing evidence that the leadership of Italian big business was wary of Mussolini from the beginning (though willing to aid him in preference to the revolutionary parties). Relations between the Mussolini regime and the great business leaders seriously degenerated in the 1930s—much to the disadvantage of the latter. This is the thesis of Roland Sarti's very interesting *Fascism and the Industrial Leadership in Italy, 1919-1940.* (Sarti's study sheds a great deal of light on a variety of aspects of the Mussolini regime and is treated in more detail later.) On the other hand, there are no reputable data to demonstrate the existence of a gigantic, long-range, and unbelievably sophisticated conspiracy of big money in Italy (not to mention the implied brute stupidity of Marxist political leaders and the working class, large elements of which had been attracted to fascism).

Furthermore, Marxists, even orthodox Marxists, disagree over exactly who or what was directing this vast and well-organized conspiracy. For Palme Dutt the principal culprits were the "finance capitalists," for Guerin they were the "industrial capitalists," for the Third Congress of the Italian Communist party they were the "industrial and agrarian oligarchy," and for Togliatti, in later years, fascism was the instrument of "financial, industrial, and agrarian capitalists." One is forced to agree with Gregor that "such diversity suggests that something is fundamentally wrong with the entire effort."

Another objection to the "capitalist conspiracy" theory of fascism arises from the internal contradictions that result from applying it to the Italian case. If Italian capitalism was powerful enough to conspire successfully against the whole nation and overthrow the constitution, then how could a working-class revolution frighten it? Italy was not one of Europe's leading industrial countries in 1918, which is another way of saying that its agrarian sector was very large. A conspiratorial capitalism skillful enough to subvert Italy's constitution was certainly skillful enough to form alliances with the agrarian sector and stifle the "revolution" with measures more subtle than fascism. And why was capitalism "in its last stages" in Italy, and not in far more industrially advanced Britain or the United States? If fascism is the highest stage of capitalism, or its final stage, or whatever, several other countries should have been fascist long before Italy. And if fascism is only the final stage of a "weak or inefficient" capitalism, then why didn't the weakness and inefficiency of Italian capitalism prevent it from successfully conspiring against the whole nation, especially against the Marxist-organized proletariat?

A much more sophisticated interpretation of fascism was offered in the 1930s by the Marxist Franz Borkenau, who argued that fascism "was a political system characteristic of countries that had not traversed the normal trajectory of industrial and political development."

For Borkenau, Italian fascism was the response of a society whose industrial development had been arrested. Italy's economic backwardness was the result of the convergence of many factors. Its late unification and entrance onto the world stage meant that the drive toward modernity had been necessarily delayed by absorption with internal political problems. Furthermore, Italy lost out in the drive for acquisition of colonial areas with abundant raw materials. This in itself was a grave blow to Italian economic development because nature had endowed Italy with precious little in the way of raw materials. Population pressure was continuing to mount in a country short on arable land, but the liberal regime had the cumulative effect of protecting and preserving the dominance of a very backward class of great landowners.

Aggravating the enormous weight of a relatively unproductive, but politically powerful, agrarian sector was the anomalous existence of a highly organized and aggressive urban working class, which was demanding a just distribution of the benefits of a society of mass production even before the groundwork for such a society had been entirely laid. A militant socialist movement had arisen in a society unready for socialism and was powerful enough to impede the accumulation of an investment surplus—which was essential if Italy were to break out of its agrarian stagnation.

Borkenau thus saw Italian fascism as a movement to break militant socialism's veto power and threat of widespread violence and thus to open up the road to a greatly increased industrialization effort. For the nationalist Mussolini, Italy would never be able to play its proper role in the world until it had acquired the might that only industrialization could provide; thorough economic modernization would require "a draconian system that controlled internal consumption." Thus the stalemate system of liberal Italy—with the progress of the economy impeded both by an ineffective parliamentary system heavily reliant on the southern landlord class and by a prematurely assertive working class—had to be and was broken to pieces.

For Borkenau, then, fascism was not the tool of capitalist magnates, because these were weak, part and parcel of Italian economic and social backwardness. No important fascist movement appeared in those countries dominated by their respective capitalist classes, such as Britain, the United States, or the Netherlands; fascism was, in part, a movement in favor of capitalism, but it was certainly not a demonstration of capitalist dominance. Indeed, Borkenau viewed Italian fascism as having "discharged an historic task" by breaking up at least some of the more important historical obstacles to Italian economic and social modernization.

Borkenau's analysis was remarkable among Marxist interpretations of fascism (and indeed among many non-Marxist ones as well). Borkenau was willing to build on observable facts rather than demand that facts be twisted to fit preexisting dogma. Consequently, his account never achieved that prominence enjoyed by the more simplistic accounts offered by some Marxists in the 1930s.

Contemporary Marxist Analysis

Although the old-school, capitalist-conspiracy theory of Stalinist vintage has not died out completely, Marxist theorists, even orthodox ones, have been producing much more realistic analyses of fascism in recent times. Instead of relying on a unified, homogeneous, and all-powerful clique of finance or monopoly capitalists pulling strings and destroying and creating regimes, Marxist analysts are more and more prepared to accept the existence of a relatively autonomous fascist movement that attracted support both from "ruling circles"and from numerous other elements in a troubled society, including many workers.

Democratic socialists have also refined their interpretations of fascism. G. D. H. Cole, in his *The Meaning of Marxism*, writes that "Fascism, though it wages war upon the working class and uses other classes as its instruments, is not fundamentally a class movement. . . . Far from controlling Fascism, the great capitalists come to be controlled by it, and are compelled to subordinate their money-making impulses to the requirements of the Fascist State as an organizer of national aggression." Gregor concludes:

Most Marxists, of whatever persuasion, are now prepared to admit . . . that Fascism was essentially a spontaneous movement of a variety of population elements (including a large minority of the industrial and agrarian proletariat) that, while financially supported by the monied and propertied classes, maintained a political independence and proceeded to construct a novel form of "bureaucratic" and "authoritarian" state that weighed heavily on *all* classes. . . . Some are also prepared to admit, with some reservations, that Fascism performed progressive and "revolutionary" functions.

In order to understand what fascism is, one must understand what it is not. Gregor has done a great service: he has subjected pseudo-explanations of fascism to revealing and searing criticism, he has exposed their greater or lesser inadequacies, and he has thereby indicated the complexities of fascism, "the most difficult and perhaps the most important . . . problem of our time."

2. Italy before Fascism

War is the chief promoter of despotism.
—Bertrand Russell

A consideration of Italian politics before Mussolini would be helpful for several reasons. First, liberal Italy was the seedbed of fascism; a look at the issues of the times should therefore provide insights into the nature of fascism. Fascist philosophy, moreover, consisted in large part of a repudiation of the doctrines and practices of liberalism as Italians had understood and experienced it. Fascism was first of all a reaction against liberal Italy. The question of why fascism, rather than socialism or communism, inherited power on the demise of Italian liberalism is also an important one. Finally, the usefulness of employing Italian fascism as a paradigm for contemporary movements in diverse places becomes more obvious to the degree that prefascist Italy suffered from many of the problems that beset developing nations today.

The Main Outlines of Italian Politics, 1861-1922

Italy's politics were shaped by the interplay of three fundamental problems. These were the relations between the Italian state and the papacy (the "Roman question"), the vast political, economic, and cultural distances between north and south (the "southern question"), and the growing (and increasingly violent) demands for a substantial improvement in the living standards of the lower socio-economic strata of Italian life (the "social question").

In many ways, each of these questions exacerbated the others. For example, unresolved problems between church and state weakened the psychological security of the state leadership, so that it tended to overreact to the demands of working men for recognition and redress. For another example, the increasingly depressed condition of most of the south retarded the economic development of the country, so that living standards at large were adversely affected. Italy was faced with too many serious problems simultaneously.

The problems confronting a new state (whose legitimacy was widely questioned) were so complex that it was difficult to make any dramatic progress in alleviating or reducing any one of them. Lack of visible progress along these fronts helped undermine the already shaky legitimacy of the state, which in turn hindered its ability to cope with its problems. It was a truly vicious circle. Thus, Italian leadership often sought to win laurels by theatrical (and, it hoped, inexpensive) triumphs in foreign policy. There was, however, no escape from the cruel but simple logic that a well-governed and content nation would have no need of foreign adventures and that a tumultuous and deeply divided nation would not be able to provide the means to achieve foreign success. Defeats and disappointments overseas (sometimes in humiliating circumstances) further reduced the public's approval of the state and the state's effectiveness in dealing with staggering domestic difficulties.

The great problems that shaped Italian politics for so many years (and even today) had their roots in the manner in which Italy had been unified.

Italy remained a geographical expression well into the middle of the nineteenth century, many years after such unified nation-states as France, Britain, and Spain had come into existence. Ironically, one of the principal reasons for Italian political disarray in the nineteenth century was that a few centuries before it had been politically and economically the most highly developed area in Europe. European civilization first emerged from the medieval period in the Italian peninsula, with its bustling, vital, and wealthy city-states. The early re-urbanization of Italy contributed to the implantation of localism, strengthened by decades and even centuries of commercial rivalry and warfare among the numerous independent states of the peninsula. Politics in Italy became balance-of-power politics, with each of the Italian states combining and recombining with others to prevent the hegemony of any single one and, thus, unification of the Italians. This situation was even more complicated because the pope ruled one of the principal states in this balance-and-warfare system. During the sixteenth century, the practice of inviting foreign monarchs to take sides in the innumerable conflicts made this pathological condition even worse. Thus the powerful French and Habsburg monarchies acquired the habit of intervening in, and a vested interest in the perpetuation of, Italian squabbles and political fragmentation. Italian politics became "colonialized"; native potentates struggled against each other with the aid of foreign imperialists.

The Early Days of the Risorgimento

The movement for Italian unification, called the *Risorgimento*, began during the upheavals of the Napoleonic wars. The germs of the Italian national idea crossed the Alps in the knapsacks of the all-conquering French. The movement quickened in the 1840s and demonstrated its seriousness in the rash of ill-fated revolutions and short-lived republican regimes that swept the peninsula in 1848.

During these exhilarating years, many schemes for the unification of Italy competed for attention. The dominant ones were those of Mazzini, Gioberti, and Cavour.

Vincenzo Gioberti (1801-1852), Piedmontese priest and politician, attempted to reconcile the independence of the papacy with the unification of Italy. His vision was a federated Italy under the presidency of the pope (who would continue to be sovereign of his own Papal State). Gioberti's plan was doomed from the outset, as indicated by the church-state controversies that would debilitate the united Italian kingdom that eventually came into being (Mazzinian and other anticlericals wanted an end to the temporal power short and simple, and the Vatican soon bitterly turned its face from Italian nationalism in any guise).

Giuseppe Mazzini (1805-1872) was one of the most influential revolutionary figures of nineteenth-century Europe. His dream was a Europe of the peoples, a continent of republics living in amity under the rule of justice and reason. Deeply hostile to throne and altar, persuaded that redemption and brotherhood could be established only through purifying violence, the Mazzinian movement was nowhere successful for very long. But it remained the terror of the established order.

Thus, through the weaknesses of his competitors and through his own genius, Camillo Cavour (1810-1861) became the grand architect of Italian unity. He was prime minister of Piedmont (the Kingdom of Sardinia) for most of the decade before 1861, and many have called him Europe's greatest statesman of the nineteenth century. (Bismarck, after all, had mighty Prussia behind him; Cavour had only Piedmont, with its five million inhabitants. The great Metternich had said, "There is only one statesman in Europe today. That is Monsieur Cavour—and he is against us!") Under Cavour's leadership, little Piedmont won recognition as a center of progress and as the best-governed state in Italy. Cavour's aim was an Italy united under Piedmont's House of Savoy and regulated by its liberal constitution. (Nineteenth-century liberalism was the party of the rising middle classes: businessmen, bankers, professionals, the generally "enlightened." It stood for Reason against Tradition, Science against Superstition, the Modern against the Decadent—all spelled with capitals! Adam Smith and Jeremy Bentham were its great spokesmen, England its model. It believed in parliamentary government, votes for those qualified—the educated and affluent—separation of church and state, and a relatively generous amount of free speech, press, and assembly. Ideas such as these were considered in many circles to be scandalously radical.)

Cavour's aims earned him the enmity of the Mazzinian party. Thus, this thread runs through the epic of how Italy was created—whether the about-to-be-created state would be monarchical, modeled on Piedmont and run by the genteel classes, or Mazzinian, modeled on the principles of 1789, ushered in by bloody revolution, and run by "the people."

Enemies of Unification

The prospect of a new state embracing all twenty-five million inhabitants of the Italian peninsula was not welcomed by all Europeans or even by all Italians. Italian unification would complicate the policies and plans of most of the chancelleries of Europe. In every corner of Italy, men of wealth, education, or conservative temperament feared that the unification of the peninsula into one state must involve war, both international and civil, and probably revolution.

Certainly the crowned heads of the various petty states in Italy did not view the rising agitation for unification (not to mention Mazzinian revolution) with equanimity. Moreover, they had their supporters: clergy, nobles, and officials, along with their families, retainers, and clients, all of whom had a stake in preserving the status quo.

Most Italians were peasants, tillers of either their own or somebody else's soil. A substantial portion of these, especially in the north, looked with disapproval on various schemes for radical changes, mainly because of the determined opposition of the church. Another large element of the peasantry, especially in the south, was too dependent on the great landlords to be able to demonstrate sympathy, or even interest, in nationalist aspirations. Everywhere, but again especially in the south, was the oppressive weight of illiteracy, poverty, and apathy. Thus the *Risorgimento* remained a movement of educated townsmen.

But by far the principal obstacles to unification were two men: Pope Pius IX and Metternich.

Pius IX had begun his long (1846-1878) pontificate with the reputation of a liberal, but the violence and anti-clericalism displayed by elements of the nationalist parties in Rome soon alienated him. After 1848 he threw the whole weight of religion against national unification, which for him assumed the proportions of a vast conspiracy of modern errors, a conspiracy not only to despoil the church but to deprive it of its independence and eventually of its very life.

As, in the view of Pius, the triumph of the *Risorgimento* would be at the expense of the church, so for Clemens von Metternich (1773-1859) it would mean the destruction of his Habsburg monarchy. The Habsburg Empire was a collection of many peoples, held together in theory by loyalty to the unifying Habsburg crown. If the lands of the church could be swept into the new Italy on the grounds of nationality, then Vienna's Italian lands could likewise be swept in; rich and populous Lombardy and Venetia would be stripped from the empire. And if the Italian subjects of the empire gave up their allegiance to Vienna in order to join a state based on the principle of nationality, could not the Czechs, the Poles, the South Slavs, even the German Austrians themselves do the same thing? The ancient monarchy would disintegrate and give way to a jumble of petty successor states, jealous and suspicious, dooming Central Europe to interminable wars and eventual domination by the Russian giant. The preservation of the Habsburg Empire, the social order, the monarchical principle, the peace and independence of central Europe—all demanded, in Metternich's view, that the *Risorgimento* be resisted and that the temporal power (the rule of the popes over central Italy) be preserved. Thus, the most influential politician in Austria and his disciples forged the fateful alliance between Roman pontiff and Viennese emperor against the rising forces of liberal reform and national self-determination.

The Creation of the Kingdom of Italy

Mazzini failed because he tried to create Italy through the unaided efforts of its own people. But the passivity of the peasantry made this impossible. Probably the only way to mobilize the peasants would have been by revolutionary war waged by the peasants themselves, and no one knew how (or dared) to bring this about. Cavour, on the other hand, realizing that Italian unification could never be achieved "from the inside," set his sights on obtaining the active support of foreign governments. France, hereditary enemy of Habsburg power, was the logical candidate to act as patron of the *Risorgimento*. Napoleon III yearned to imitate his illustrious uncle by carrying the torch of liberation over the Alps into the plain of Lombardy, thus dealing a fell blow to the Austrians, helping settle the score of Waterloo, and doubtless winning the undying gratitude (and dependence) of the Italians. Cavour persuaded Napoleon to go ahead—despite fierce opposition from French Catholics, as well as from French chauvinists who feared a united Italy on their border. He provoked the Austrians into declaring war against Piedmont, and with French aid conquered Lombardy. (Austria meant to "solve" its Italian problem through military operations against Piedmont in 1859 as it would "solve" its Slavic problem by operations against Serbia in 1914.) A political avalanche swept over all Italy; groups of patriots under Cavour's lieutenants or admirers seized control of the little states in the north and center. Garibaldi, leading his red-shirted thousand, performed the impossible deed of overthrowing the Neapolitan Bourbons. There followed plebiscites on the question of unification under the Kingdom of Piedmont. The honesty or validity of some of these elections is subject to question; in any event, between 1859 and 1861 a large, new state had come into existence against odds that had once seemed insuperable.

The Nature of the Risorgimento

The unification of Italy owed at least as much to the romanticism of Napoleon III and the benevolence of the British as it did to the efforts of Italians themselves. Indeed, probably only a minority of Italians wanted unification under the leadership of Piedmont, and only a minority of that minority was at all active in the cause. The *Risorgimento* was the work of an elite—city-bred, educated, and not very representative of the population at large. Catholics and aristocrats were conspicuously absent from the unification effort; so were workers, peasants, and craftsmen (Garibaldi's thousand did not include a single peasant). Created overnight by a handful of bourgeois anticlericals, united Italy was not to escape the consequences of the manner of its birth.

Problems of the New State

The swiftness with which the long-dreamed-of unification was finally accomplished obscured the new kingdom's difficulties for some while. The possibility that these daunting problems would be dealt with in a statesmanlike and farsighted manner was handed a fatal blow with the death, in 1861, of the fifty-one-year-old Cavour, worn out at the hour of vindication with his labors of the past decade.

Centralization, furthermore, was seen as vital to national cohesion; hence, unification turned into "Piedmontization," the imposition of the legal code and bureaucracy of the more modernized north upon areas quite different in speech, custom, legal tradition, and economic level. To these insults to southern sensitivities were added Piedmontese war debts accumulated during the *Risorgimento* struggles. There was now military conscription (hitherto unknown in the south) and that hallmark of liberalism: free trade. This last policy stripped away tariff protection from the industry that was beginning to put down a few roots in the south; southern industrialism was dealt a blow from which it has never recovered. For many, therefore, unification was more like foreign occupation. The new order was off to a bad start.

The papacy refused recognition to the new state, which had taken over territories of the church. But Rome—historical, desirable, essential Rome—still remained in the hands of the pope, denied to the Italians by the protection of Napoleon III. (Poor Napoleon. He had infuriated the pope and the powerful French Catholic party by helping the Kingdom of Italy into existence; he now infuriated the Italians by denying them access to Rome.)

In 1870, Napoleon withdrew his forces from Rome, and the armies of the Italian state finally entered the Eternal City. The excommunication of the whole Italian government followed, along with the pope's proclamation that he was now "prisoner of the Vatican." Despite the passage of a rather generous Law of Guarantees, by which the Italian government recognized the inviolable sovereignty of the pope and settled a handsome indemnity on the Vatican for the loss of its territories, Pius IX grimly awaited the day when the Catholic powers would smash the usurping Italian state into pieces. Until that happy day, the pope declared that it was *non expedit* for Catholics to participate in any way ("neither electors nor elected") in the political affairs of the impious and temporary regime.

It is perhaps not easy to sympathize with the steely determination of Pius IX to hold onto the temporal power even at the cost of international and civil war. Earthly rule over two million obstreperous subjects had often dragged the papal robes into the Machiavellian muds of Italian power politics. It is no accident that the papacy's impressive recovery of worldwide prestige really dates from the loss of the temporal power.

Vatican intransigence, nevertheless, had its justifications. As spiritual father to millions of the devout—in Ireland, in Poland, in Germany—as the leader of a flock that ranged from Budapest to Bogota, the pope had to be, and to *appear* to be, independent of any earthly pressure. A papacy stripped of territorial sovereignty, existing on Italian soil, and unilaterally guaranteed by the Italian state, could conceivably become, or be made to seem, a tool of Italian policy, at least in part. It was to avoid this—the apparent reduction of the universal pontiff to the position of grand chaplain to the House of Savoy—that Pius IX insisted that he must retain at least some of his former territory as a symbol of his sovereign independence.

Although, no doubt, the pope was sincere in insisting he remain a sovereign in order to safeguard his independence, one can understand the impatience of Italian patriots with his position. After all, after 1815 the papacy was openly dependent on Austrian military support for its survival, and for many years before 1870 papal rule over the city of Rome was made possible only by the presence of French troops. Certain sovereigns, moreover, such as those of Spain and Austria, possessed and used (as late as 1903) the right to veto the election of anyone chosen to the papal throne.

Besides, the heady atmosphere of the victorious *Risorgimento* would not have allowed giving up Italian territory to a "foreign power." The cession of even a square inch would

have outraged articulate groups of nationalists. Each side
saw itself as defending immutable and self-evident principles. Thus the Roman question festered, troubling the
consciences of many, depriving the new state of the support
and participation of numerous citizens, and forcing the
government to rely even more on anticlerical extremists.
That the Italian Kingdom was in possession of Rome only
by virtue of France's defeat by Prussia added neither to the
self-confidence nor the reasonableness of Italian leaders.

Nor was Italian unification complete with Rome's
occupation in 1870. Important areas of Italian population,
notably Trieste and Trent, remained under Austrian rule.
The existence of the "unredeemed Italy" meant that the
Risorgimento was unfinished. For many patriots, all this
was deeply humiliating.

The Triumph of the Left, 1876

The gravest blow of all to the new state was Cavour's death
in 1861. His lieutenants and heirs, known as the Historical
Right, tried to implement his policies while lacking his
genius. The Right stood for centralization and free trade,
peace abroad, and eventual reconciliation with the church at
home. Faced with the state's enormous deficits, the Right
believed in financial retrenchments. Thus, many internal
improvements that might have tied the country together
were rejected, and the search for revenue produced a savagely
regressive tax system. The latter helped convince the
peasantry, already alienated through the influence of the
clergy, that the government was nothing but organized
rapine.

Opposed to the Historical Right was the other wing of the
Liberal party, the "Left." Based on the middle and lower
classes, especially strong in the long-suffering south, it was
intransigently anticlerical, expansionist, and "Garibaldian" (i.e., romanticist). The Left has been described as not a
party but a collection of grievances. By 1876, the Right was
exhausted, unpopular, and feeling unappreciated (like the
Federalists of another time and place). The first Left cabinet,
under Agostino Deprètis, came to power. Deprètis soon

called a general election and through the application of
pork, patronage, and the police, skillfully "managed" to
produce a thumping Left majority. Inviting his opponents
to "transform themselves for the good of the country,
Deprètis became the evangel of *trasformismo*, the practice of
forming cabinets from shifting center coalitions. This tactic
destroyed any possibility of a true opposition party with
alternative policies (especially in view of the political
abstention of Catholics). Parliamentary politics became a
game of musical chairs. All this, together with electoral
manipulation in the poor and backward south, began
seriously to undermine the prestige of parliamentary
institutions.

Following Deprètis as "parliamentary dictator" was the
old Garibaldian Francesco Crispi (dominant 1887-1896). His
period of leadership was highlighted by massive employment of troops to suppress popular demonstrations, an
economically disastrous rupture with France, and the
massacre of Italian troops by Ethiopians at Adowa. After
Adowa, he was forced from office forever. Crispi—activist,
nationalist, militarist, and imperialist—has been called (and
by no less than the master himself) the "forerunner of
Mussolini," which in itself reveals how poorly parliamentary government worked.

Stung and humiliated by the French occupation of Tunis
in 1881, Italy recoiled into the Triple Alliance with
Bismarck's Germany and the Habsburg Empire. In this way
it gained final recognition of its possession of Rome by the
principal Catholic power (Austria). But the losses were
greater and became more and more evident. The weakest of
the so-called great powers, Italy found that its best strategy in
international politics was to pursue the role of balancer,
committed irrevocably to no one and open to friendship with
all—friendship with Britain especially, because Britain
ruled the seas and Italy was all coastline (a fact appreciated
by the Historical Right). By joining the Triple Alliance,
Italy lost freedom of movement, antagonized the French, and
saw its armaments expenditures rise but, in return, it got not
a square inch of "unredeemed Italy."

The Giolittian Age

The decade of Italian politics before the outbreak of World War I is named after Giovanni Giolitti (1842-1928), the most controversial figure between Cavour and Mussolini. Prime minister most of the time between 1903 and 1914, Giolitti was the master of *trasformismo;* he managed elections, dominated parliament, detested extremism, and scrupulously respected the niceties of parliamentary behavior. The period was one of industrial revolution in Italy, and along with impressive increases in all indexes of production went an impressive increase in the size and self-confidence of Italian socialism. During the first decade of the century, a vigorous contest was being waged inside the Socialist party for control of its soul and destiny; on one side was the increasingly parliament-oriented wing, and on the other, the intransigent and violence-preaching "maximalist" wing (prominent in the latter was one Benito Mussolini).

Meanwhile, the Catholics were revising their estimate of the situation. The Roman question was becoming more and more a dogma neglected in practice. Pius X (1903-1914) feared the growing strength of the socialists more than he detested liberal Italy, and in 1904 the *non expedit* was revoked to permit Catholics to use their ballots to defeat the socialists.

Giolitti's grand design was to reconcile both Catholics and socialists to the constitutional order. He believed in a gradually maturing parliamentary system and was willing to pay a good price to obtain Catholic and socialist cooperation toward the realization of that belief. As early as 1903 he offered the socialists representation in his cabinet (they refused) and imposed strict neutrality upon the organs of the state in contests between capital and labor (to the chagrin of many industrialists). Giolitti trusted to improving economic conditions and a gradual process of maturation inside socialism (along the German model) to bring this important element into the fold.

Progress in reconciling the Catholics was, on the surface, more spectacular. In 1913, Catholic voters trooped to the polls to vote for Giolitti's candidates in return for guarantees on divorce, schools, and related matters.

Giolitti's labors were bearing fruit. Nevertheless, his efforts to tame Catholics and socialists and thus place the constitutional order on a sound foundation were not successful. Parliament continued to be dominated by a liberal majority, but in the country as a whole the party was almost nonexistent (most adults could not vote; those who could usually voted liberal). The peasantry of the north was almost solidly under clerical influence, and the growing working class was more and more monopolized by socialism. Despite undeniable efforts to raise the condition of the south, that large region (with over two-fifths of the population) remained the domain of illiteracy, malaria, malnutrition, political corruption, and emigration.

The domination of parliament by Giolitti's artificial majorities was turning even convinced liberals into cynics. Gaetano Mosca was effectively criticizing parliamentary government as a huge fraud that masked the domination of self-seeking elites. The rising generation was more and more persuaded to look upon a half-century of unification as a long litany of lost opportunities. The *Risorgimento* had been betrayed, Italy had been delivered into the hands of little men of pedestrian prose rather than heroic poetry, men such as the passionless Giolitti. A dangerous mood of frustrated nationalism was taking hold.

It was Italy's misfortune to have achieved nationhood (on paper) just at a time when Europe was about to be swept by messianic doctrines that demanded and promised instant utopia. Marxism, anarchism, social Darwinism, and imperialism were the great themes of the period 1875-1914, not only in Italy but in most of Europe as well. This would have been a hostile environment for liberal and parliamentary institutions under any circumstances; but Italian institutions were young, and there had been no time to sink the deep roots necessary to withstand the buffeting by destructive storms of antiparliamentary ideologies. For healthy growth, parliamentary ways needed quiet at home, peace abroad, and above all, time; but all these things were lacking.

War with Turkey

By 1911, the thirst for glory and the demand for empire convinced even the skeptical Giolitti that the time had come to make good on Italy's long-standing claim to Tripoli and Cyrenaica (Libya). A faltering Turkish empire put up a short-lived resistance (unlike that of fanatical guerrillas), but the war had unforeseen and undesirable effects (as usual). By exposing the extent of Turkish weakness, the war precipitated struggles in the Balkans in 1912 and 1913, direct preludes to the catastrophe that would overtake Europe in 1914. It weakened Italy's ties to the Triple Alliance: Germany had been penetrating Turkey and reacted negatively to its Italian ally's aggressive policy. The short duration of the war helped convince Italian opinion that Italy was indeed one of the great powers and ready for great things. (At the same time Giolitti became aware of the woeful state of Italian military resources.) Finally, the war strengthened the hands of extremists inside the Italian Socialist party, for whom the bourgeoisie's display of wanton aggression proved the irredeemable corruption of the whole system. Giolitti's plans were wrecked.

The Outbreak of the Great War

The summer of 1914 began dramatically for Italy. June witnessed the notorious Red Week, when massive demonstration of organized labor and rioting among landless farm workers turned into general insurrection in many areas; here and there the forces of order, backed up by the army, actually lost control for several days. Thus the country was close to civil war as the prelude to the guns of August was being played. Meanwhile, Giolitti had taken one of his periodic leaves of absence from office, retiring for a while to his Piedmontese retreat to recoup his powers and demonstrate his indispensability.

The premier was Antonio Salandra, whose antipathy for Giolitti ran deeper than anyone suspected. Under Salandra, the Italian government did the intelligent thing in foreign policy for a change and declined to be drawn into the war on the German-Austrian side. The manner in which war had broken out gave Italy good reasons for remaining outside of it. Austria was obviously attacking Serbia, not vice versa; Vienna had not even informed its supposed allies in Rome of what was happening. Nor was there any mention of compensation to Italy for Austrian advances in the Balkans, as the alliance required. Thus, the letter as well as the spirit of the Triple Alliance had been violated. But in spite of all these considerations, and in spite of efforts by the British and French to obtain Italian intervention on their side, Italy's declaration of neutrality in 1914 dealt its international reputation a blow from which it has not yet fully recovered.

Neutralists vs. Interventionists

The government's declaration of neutrality pleased a large majority of Italians. True, several important groups favored a declaration of war on the side of the Entente: these included pro-French Mazzinian-type social reformers; some responsible liberals (such as Albertini, publisher of Milan's *Corriere della Sera*); irredentists, who saw a golden opportunity to take Trent and Trieste (and much else); and some elements of Italian socialism (including, after a few indecisive months, the editor of the country's socialist daily, Benito Mussolini).

Ranged against this interventionist phalanx were the most influential forces in the country: the Vatican, friendly to clericalist Austria; the bulk of the socialists, opposed to this "bourgeois bloodbath"; the masterful Giolitti himself; and the scores of parliamentarians who followed his lead. Giolitti knew well how the Libyan adventure had reduced Italy's war supplies. He knew Italy's dependence on British coal and vulnerability to the British navy. He foresaw that this great struggle would give the coup de grace to a Habsburg Empire that had been disintegrating for fifty years. Thus, Italy need but bide its time, throw its husbanded resources into the struggle against Austria at the decisive moment, and all would be well. (It was typical of Giolitti to take such a calculated and cool view of things in the emotional blast furnace of 1914.)

This combination—Catholics, socialists, and Giolittians—should have been more than enough to guarantee

Italy's neutrality. That it was *not* enough reveals to what little extent public opinion and parliamentary desires influenced affairs of great moment in "constitutional" Italy. For the decisive facts were that the king, Prime Minister Salandra, and Foreign Minister Sonnino (a great enemy of Giolitti and half English) wanted intervention on the Allied side, and they were determined to have it, church, socialists, parliament, or no.

So, from the summer of 1914 to the spring of 1915, a fascinating drama took place on two levels. On the one, Salandra was engaged in continuous bargaining with London and Paris over the price Italy would be paid for its help. On the other, public opinion was worked over by Salandra's secret service funds and propaganda efforts by the Allies, and student and hooligan mobs harassed neutralist politicians, even Giolitti himself, on the streets of Rome under the eyes of strangely inactive police. Finally, in May 1915, confronted with the impossibility of repudiating the king and his ministers, who had signed the Treaty of London, parliament voted for war. Thus an economically underdeveloped, politically fragmented, and overwhelmingly neutralist nation was dragged into the holocaust by a ruthless minority. Mussolini, himself a convert to the interventionist cause, watched all these things and learned much.

The Salandra-Sonnino leadership, blind to the larger picture and long-term consequences, cleverly (in their own eyes) declared war only on Austria-Hungary. Thus, the war, opposed by most of the Italians who would have to fight it, was not a crusade in favor of justice for small nations and the overthrow of militarism, which a declaration of war against Germany would have made it. Instead, it seemed the attack on Austria was one more move in a cynical game of *realpolitik* with Italy narrowly pursuing its own selfish advantage (this was certainly how the Allies viewed Italy's entrance into the struggle).

Italy and the Great War

World War I was a carnage not only on the western front

and in Russia but also on the Italian front. Italy had a decidedly disadvantageous military frontier with Austria. Nevertheless, most of the war in this area was fought on the Austrian side of the line, with Italian armies on the offensive. General Cadorna's offensives on the Isonzo River shed vast quantities of blood.

This depressing situation brought the fall of the Salandra cabinet in 1916. All during that year the socialists had been advocating a negotiated peace, and Benedict XV's Christmas call for a "White Peace" did Italian morale little good.

By the fall of 1917, Russia was all but out of the fighting; large numbers of Austrian troops were freed for the Italian front. The German High Command, despairing of a favorable decision in the west, became converted to the Austrian view of the psychological advantages to be gained by knocking Italy out of the war through one massive, desperate blow. Austrian armies, reinforced by select German divisions, executed brilliantly unorthodox tactics of deep penetration of the Italian lines. Taken by surprise, the Italians carried out the headlong retreat that has come to be known as Caporetto. (Ernest Hemingway immortalized this, Italy's darkest hour, in his *A Farewell to Arms,* a principal reason for the low esteem in which the English-speaking world holds Italy's efforts in World War I.) Through heroic efforts, Italy did not let its trial in 1917 turn into a French-style 1940; the Austro-Germans were soon contained and finally pushed back. When the armistice was proclaimed in November 1918, General Foch, the supreme Allied commander, was preparing an invasion of southern Germany by Italian forces through Austria. The war was over, Italy was one of the "victorious powers," and it would now receive—no doubt—great rewards.

Italy and the Peace

Italy's gains from the war were deeply disappointing. Trent and Trieste were handed over, but the rewards Italy had been promised in the Balkans and Africa were resisted by Woodrow Wilson, who seemed especially mindful of high moral principles when addressing Italian claims. Abandoned by its allies, who were too busy gobbling up German colonial territories, lectured to distraction by Wilson, the Italian government and public watched their brave new world disintegrate. In point of fact, Italy gained more than any of the Allied powers because of the destruction of its hereditary enemy Austria. After 1918, Italy's land frontiers were secure (as France's were not). But many Italians were transfixed by the territories they had been promised and then denied, and by the sight of Britain and France swallowing African and Arab territories as if the self-determination of peoples had never been heard of.

Like all great wars, World War I had revolutionary consequences. The mobilization effort had provided new experiences and had stimulated new desires in many, who were now unwilling to settle down to the old, unsatisfactory ways. Dramatic inflation and huge war profits brought about the rise and fall of many. For large numbers, the end of the war was a profound emotional letdown, especially for the elite commando units (the *Arditi*), daring youths distinguished from the mass of the soldiery by their black shirts.

Peasant soldiers returning to their villages found that the land reforms promised while they were in the trenches were largely talk. Their urban compatriots returned to prospects of unemployment and discovered that many workers in the "essential" category had been making good money and enjoying the war in safety at home. Fifty thousand demobilized officers returned to civilian life to be confronted by pacifist and production-sabotaging socialists. The latter (at least the more irresponsible elements) offended all returning soldiers by an insane program of public insult and physical humiliation of veterans. Those who had gone away to fight were fools and criminals, and stories soon filled the air that gangs of socialist militants had spat upon mutilated veterans in the streets.

During these unhappy days, the star of the poet Gabriele D'Annunzio—apostle of youth, violence, and irrational experience—was on the rise. Defying the whole world, he and his freebooter followers seized the town of Fiume, claimed by Italy but awarded to Yugoslavia. D'Annunzio's influence over Italian university youth was enormous.

Among such explosive elements, the days of the Liberal party—that institution that had held Italy together and guided it, however ineptly, through its trials and crises—were numbered. Universal suffrage and proportional representation, the minimum price the state had had to pay for the draft, became law in 1919. These would work their effects quickly on a party without real organization of its own and confronted by the Socialist and Catholic parties with their grass-roots networks. The Giolittian system was finished, though few understood that fact. The old system of compromise and accommodation was about to be swept aside.

Italy was not unique in being disappointed after its great efforts. But it was poorer, more self-conscious, more vulnerable than Britain or France, its institutions less rooted, its self-esteem more fragile. Thus the cold winds that blew over Europe after the war found less resistance in Italy and eventually blew the old order away.

The Catholic Party

Early in 1919 the Popular party, Italy's first Catholic political party, was born. The *popolari* enjoyed good leadership: their founder was a Sicilian priest, Luigi Sturzo, a man of learning, good sense, and political experience at the grass roots. Pope Benedict XV's benevolent neutrality allowed the new party to tap the power of the vote-rich and devoutly Catholic northern regions, especially Lombardy and Venetia, with their networks of Catholic rural banks, cooperatives, and labor unions. Silent on the Roman question, the party studiously avoided the word *Catholic* in its name and set itself no less a task than reconciling the church, the state, and democratic institutions. In 1919, in the first postwar elections, the *popolari* did quite well, especially for a new party, winning a fifth of the seats in parliament. A new page seemed about to be written for both church and state in troubled Italy.

But the new party suffered from fatal weaknesses. The

appeal to Catholics per se meant that the party was composed of several classes. A heterogeneous membership swelled the party's electoral totals but proved a stumbling block to a coherent program. The party was handicapped in its competition with the socialists for the allegiance of the masses; if it took too forward a position on economic and social reform, it would lose the votes of conservative Catholics.

The legacy of southern history was also debilitating for the *popolari*. The church was not strong in the south, and the habits of liberal anticlericalism were well developed. Consequently, the *popolari* maintained only a shadowy existence in half of the peninsula; in the 1921 elections, 80 percent of the party's vote came from north of Rome.

Because its leader was a priest whom church authorities had forbidden to sit in parliament, the Popular party earned the incredulous disdain of the aging, but still powerful, Giolitti, with his Cavourian suspicions of clericalism and his tendency to confuse parliament with the nation.

The most severe handicap, however, was the new attitude of the Vatican. In 1922, the archbishop of Milan, Achille Ratti, became Pope Pius XI. Conservative, canny, ultra-clericalist, Pius disdained democracy, feared social revolution, and looked upon the *popolari* as too unreliable for the church to lean on in such unpredictable times. The Vatican began to turn its back on the young party and to look to other, simpler means to attain its ends.

The Socialists in the Postwar Period

The inability of liberals, *popolari*, and socialists to come together in an antifascist front, even at the last hour, was essential to fascism's coming to power. The condition of the postwar socialist party, in turn, explains why the antifascist coalition failed to materialize.

Socialist morale had been damaged by the wartime policy of defeatism and by the numerous defections and schisms this policy had produced. Perennially handicapped by a shortage of practical leaders, the party's response to the

Russian Revolution of 1917 was typical. First, a Leninist wing split off to found the Italian Communist party. Then, the remaining majority proceeded to dissolve into two major and several minor factions.

The socialists had been fighting the middle classes, the church, and the army for decades, mostly with inflammatory rhetoric, sometimes with widespread and serious violence (as in the "Red Week" of 1914). Having taught Italians to expect bloody upheavals some day, the party wore out its followers as one year after another went by and as, amid all the fist waving, nothing happened. The great seizure of the factories in 1920 was a dramatic manifestation of the socialists' lack of seriousness. They made absolutely no sustained effort to coordinate the occupied factories with political action in parliament where they were so numerous. Meanwhile, the Giolitti government followed a policy of masterful inaction: there were no bloody clashes, no martyrs, eventually no supplies and no money—and no revolution. The whole thing collapsed in September.

The factory seizures left a grim legacy. The middle classes (indeed all who hated and feared socialist revolution) felt humiliated by the workers and betrayed by the government, which had declined to use force. After these strikes, these groups would look to others for protection.

On the parliamentary level, fresh from the electoral triumphs of 1919 (156 seats out of 500), with the liberals exhausted and the *popolari* untried, the socialists were in a position to make either a cabinet or a revolution. They made neither. They refused to form a cabinet on their own; to do so would have been to "spare" the bourgeoisie from reaping the fruits of its wicked policies. Nor would they form a coalition with the *popolari*; coalitions were not the order of the day, but rather revolution! The party frittered away its enormous advantages month by month and year by year in schisms, oratory, and strikes. Obsessed with events in Russia and the "inevitability" of revolution, it squandered its strength, embittered its well-wishers, galvanized its enemies, and set the stage for its own destruction. In the words of onetime communist leader Angelo Tasca, "it was not fascism which

defeated the revolution, but the defeat of the revolution
which determined the rise and victory of fascism."

With the largest party in the parliament committed to
obstruction and opposition, it would have required superhuman statesmanship to construct an antifascist parliamentary majority. Postwar Italy had little superhuman statesmanship.

As the socialists committed slow suicide, Mussolini's ever
more numerous squads of blackshirts embarked upon a
policy of "cleansing" Italy of socialists. Socialist newspaper
offices, party headquarters, cooperatives, and workers'
recreational establishments were systematically demolished.
The physical structure of the socialist party was literally
being destroyed. For a long time, especially in central Italy,
socialist rural unions had been flouting the authority of the
state, seizing private property, forcing merchants to lower
prices, and generally bullying anyone with any property. A
lack of firm direction from the central government paralyzed
the representatives of authority. Thus, when fascist gangs
began to operate in these areas, the local authorities were
content to believe that the socialists were simply getting
what they had long deserved. That the socialists might have
at any time put a stop to fascist depredations by forming a
cabinet (or even by supporting one in return for a policy of
suppressing fascism) only underlines their own confusion.
Thus the socialists were swallowed up in an atmosphere of
violence to which they had contributed much.

Scholars have rendered an almost unanimous verdict on
the responsibility of Italian socialism for the success of
fascism. Of all the factors that contributed to the fascist
victory, writes Angelo Tasca, "the most important were
Socialist feebleness and mistakes which were the direct
causes not of fascism, which appeared in every country after
the war, but of its success in Italy." Neufeld condemns the
"dialectical hallucinations of the maximalist and communist bigots." For Mack Smith, the socialists "positively
refused to collaborate against fascism . . . and in so doing
they made [fascist] victory almost inevitable." The socialists
"between 1919 and 1921 purged the party of its humane and

liberal leaders," in the words of Sprigge, "in order to hoist the banners of anti-patriotism and dictatorial communism over the proletarian legions." In the view of A. W. Salomone, by 1922 socialism "had proved incapable of positive action, uncertain of itself, and yet afraid to collaborate with others." Thus, as Stuart Hughes puts it, "the Socialists bear the primary responsibility" "for the collapse of Italian democracy."

Italy on the Eve of Fascism

This was the shape of things in 1922. The parliament was deadlocked. Manhood suffrage and proportional representation had broken the control of the liberals and had flooded the parliament with socialists and *popolari*. Not one of these three groups approached being a majority itself, and mutual suspicions prevented the formation of a stable coalition. Thus, between the November armistice and the March on Rome, forty-seven of the most crucial months in the nation's history, there were five prime ministers. Giolitti, now seventy-eight years old, could not control the situation and resigned the prime ministership in June 1921, never to return. The socialist leader Claudio Treves summarized everything with grim clarity in his remark to the liberals: "This is the tragedy of the present crisis: you can no longer impose your order on us, and we cannot yet impose ours on you."

Meanwhile, violence became a way of life. First the obscene hecatombs of the Great War, then D'Annunzio's egomaniacal antics at Fiume, urban and rural strikes, draftee mutinies; then, in many provinces, the clash between fascists on one side and socialists and sometimes *popolari* on the other resembled civil war. The collapse of the liberal order, so passionately proclaimed by the socialists and patiently awaited by the Vatican, came ever nearer.

As anxiety increased all over Italy, Mussolini was putting together his powerful coalition. Fascist nationalism and defense of veterans' rights caused thousands of ex-officers and servicemen to enroll in his legions. These were the backbone of fascism; through them the physical assault on

the structure of socialism was largely carried out. Landowners, great and small, frightened by socialist highhanded-
ness and threats; shopkeepers outraged at the forcible
lowering of their prices; industrialists seeking higher tariffs,
chastened unions, a tamed socialist party, lower wages, and
control of lucrative state monopolies; the whole middle
class, envious of the economic power of the unions and eaten
up by inflation; Catholics, fearful of an Italian Petrograd
and looking for a "strong man" to solve the Roman question
at last; the many who despaired of liberalism and hated
socialism—all these provided a steadily growing stream of
recruits and funds for fascism. Even Giolitti gave the fascists
the imprimatur of respectability when he allowed them to
become partners in his anticlerical coalition in the elections
of 1921 (from which the fascists emerged with thirty-five
seats). The master of *trasformismo* sought to transform
even the fascists.

By the summer of 1922, the liberals were disoriented, the
popolari disintegrating, the socialists wrecked. In contrast,
the fascists grew more brazen every day. They saw themselves
as a minority composed of the most vigorous, worthy, and
aggressive elements of the nation. They demanded power.
Thus came the plans for a great march on the capital—it
would overawe the king and his craven ministers and compel
the appointment of Mussolini as prime minister.

The March on Rome is history, but its success was by no
means preordained. The key to the whole affair was the king,
Victor Emmanuel III, fifty-three years old in 1922. The army,
though sympathetic to fascism, would in the last analysis
have obeyed the king and prevented the entrance of the
fascists into Rome. Prime Minister Luigi Facta actually
prepared the order for the king's signature proclaiming
martial law. But the king refused to sign. He feared civil war
between the army and the fascists, which would ultimately
benefit only the socialists. The fascists, furthermore, were
openly threatening that if the king attempted to resist, they
would put his cousin the duke of Aosta on the throne. The
queen mother was a fascist sympathizer; and anyway, unlike
his ancestors, Victor Emmanuel III was not made of stern

stuff. He capitulated. On the evening of October 28, 1922, as the fascist legions huddled together, cold, hungry, and rain-sodden, in the towns surrounding Rome, Benito Mussolini received the call to come to the capital and form a cabinet. During all these dramatic events, he had remained in Milan, a prudent 600 kilometers from Rome.

Thus the fascists came to power, and thus Victor Emmanuel sealed his own fate and that of his ancient house.

Some Conclusions on Pre-Fascist Italy

In reviewing the difficulties and errors that paved Mussolini's way to Rome, one cannot help noticing that the political development of prefascist Italy and that of so many of the countries of today's Third World are remarkably similar.

The two great crises of Italian development—the *Risorgimento* and the struggle over entry into World War I—were characterized by elitism: small minorities of determined men, evading or attacking prevailing institutions, laws, and beliefs, ignoring the wishes of their countrymen to bring about the millenium in which they so passionately believed. Between the end of the *Risorgimento* and the outbreak of the Great War, the minoritarian nature of Italian politics was preserved and enshrined in severely restricted suffrage (in 1876 only 2 percent of the population could vote; by 1912 this had risen to but 8½ percent) and in extreme centralization of the state.

The Italian state, controlled by a small minority, used the power of arms to enforce the will of this minority. Thus, the thread of authoritarianism supported by illegal violence runs throughout Italy's political development. The alliance between the House of Savoy, Europe's oldest dynasty, and the revolutionary Garibaldi; the rigging of plebiscites; Giolitti's electoral "management"; the violence by which the country was dragged into war in 1915; the tolerance of fascist violence in 1920-1922—all found their culmination in the legalized violence of the Mussolini regime. Mussolini did no more than erect into a doctrine what had been normal political practice, the vindication of a minority through force.

From the beginning, the unity of the kingdom was gravely undermined by large dissatisfied minorities: devout Catholics, republicans, localists, disaffected peasants. Taken together, these groups probably made up a majority. Unification had meant the imposition of modern Piedmontese values and methods on other areas, which were openly considered more or less inferior. The southern question was an early expression of the "dual society" syndrome of today's Third World countries: two "nations" coexisting inside one set of national frontiers, one modern and prosperous, the other traditional and poor.

The abstention of devout Catholics from political life greatly weakened the foundations of the state. It prevented the rise of a conservative party that could make the liberals adopt more coherent and long-range policies. It also taught great numbers of peasants to view the regime as God's enemy and hence as a temporary regime.

Italy's institutions never exerted that attraction on the minds of men that might have made up for many shortcomings in other areas. Sentiments of loyalty to the House of Savoy were confined to Piedmont and were not universal even there. For many liberals, the Savoy monarchy was a *pis aller,* especially after Victor Emmanuel III ascended the throne; his was not a charismatic figure.

Nor could parliament fill the gap; it could not even do its own work properly. Limited suffrage put parliament out of the reach and interest of most Italians. *Trasformismo* meant that there was never a real alternative to the government of the day. The absence of real parties contributed to the unhealthy concentration of power in the executive; the role of member of parliament was often reduced to that of petty ambassador of local (often malignant) interests. And where policies and programs counted for little, the influence of patronage and police counted for much.

Parliamentary life, therefore, was unedifying and difficult to understand. This was a key to the weakness of liberalism. Institutions must be understood by those who live under them. If they are not, then explanations invariably cast the practices and motives of the governors in the most unflattering light possible.

Liberal institutions were also being subjected to damaging criticism on a philosophical and sociological level by high-caliber intellectuals such as Mosca, Pareto, and Michels. Liberalism was unpopular at the grass roots because of its tangible shortcomings, but these men helped rob it of even theoretical respectability among the educated.

The group that offered the most thorough critique of the status quo and that therefore might have offered an alternative, the Socialist party, was grotesquely inadequate to the task. No pragmatic British Labour party, no self-consciously responsible German Social Democratic party, found its analogue in Italian socialism. Instead, the latter developed into an organism that was at once powerful, passionate, confused, and maladroit—a most deadly combination.

The most damning evidence of the inability of Italian institutions to command loyalty was the shallowness of support they received at the crucial hour, even among their most fervently self-proclaimed champions. By forming an electoral coalition with the fascists in 1921, Giolitti had himself thrown the cloak of parliamentary respectability (such as it was) over their naked brutality. Mussolini's accession to power as the champion of action, the foe of liberal blather and effeteness, was greeted with approbation by a long list of prominent liberals: not only Giolitti, but also Albertini, publisher of the country's most prestigious daily, and Croce, a philosopher-historian of European reputation. These liberal patriarchs applauded the arch-foe of liberalism as he swaggered toward the chair of power; they would use this Mussolini for their own purposes. In its final hour, Italian liberalism thus revealed its final bankruptcy.

What happened to the dream of the Italian liberals was a true tragedy. They had built a political system suited to a society in which the average citizen was a bourgeois with bourgeois values. But the Italian economy could not produce a powerful middle class rapidly enough; before such a class could appear, radical doctrines had won a large following among workers and peasants and got in the way of economic development and political stability. Hence the liberals were left with no alternative but repression, and that meant an alliance with Mussolini.

Italy was quite poor in natural resources. No shame need have been attached to a sober recognition of the resulting limitations on internal and external policies. The demand that Italy act as if it were a great power, however, meant that its meager resources must be squandered on a hopeless race for military parity with such wealthy and well-established competitors as Great Britain and Germany. Furthermore, the regressive taxation required to support this unrealistic effort alienated an already suspicious peasantry.

Poor economic performance was matched by reverses and frustrations in foreign affairs. The defeat in Ethiopia in 1896 bloodily underlined the fact that Britain and France had extensive colonial empires and great prestige while Italy had neither. The staggering effusion of blood from 1915 to 1918, which was to redeem the past and purchase the future, seemed after the war to have been a titanic waste. Italy could not win its place in the sun, even at the cost of 600,000 young men. To many, it was no longer debatable, it was obvious, that the scattered rods of Italian strength must be gathered together into an unbreakable bundle wielded by one ruthless gladiator.

In the following chapter we will look at the ideas with which the gladiator came to power.

3. The Ideology of Fascism

*It has been customary to accept economic power
without analysis, and this had led, in modern times,
to an undue emphasis upon economics, as opposed to war
and propaganda, in the causal interpretation of history.*
—Bertrand Russell

Many elements went into the making of Italian fascist
ideology: antiliberal currents and philosophies, both
revolutionary and conservative; the political experiences
and insights of Mussolini and others; the strategic and
tactical necessities of the pursuit of power in a time of
upheaval. The discussion that follows deals with these
disparate elements and the manner in which they were to be
combined into a pattern.

Mussolini the Socialist

Both Marxists and fascists would, for their own reasons,
seek to obscure or even deny Mussolini's socialist origins and
orthodoxy. The truth is that Mussolini was born into
socialism, that he achieved his first national prominence as a
socialist leader, and that these early formative experiences
left a decisive impression on him for life.

Benito Mussolini's father was a locally influential
socialist in the tempestuous Romagna region. Romagnole
socialism was violence-prone, populist, antireligious, and
deeply tinged with anarchist tendencies. A socialist by
birthright, Mussolini was also one by intellectual conviction. "Not only was he a convinced Marxist," writes Gregor,
"he was a knowledgeable one as well. His published
writings contain regular references to the works of Marx and
Engels. He specifically refers to every major piece of Marx's

published writings available at that time."[1] As Ernst Nolte has observed, "His Marxism, of course, is neither theoretical nor philosophical. Unlike Lenin, he never undertook extensive economic research, nor was he ever interested in the differences between Hegelian and Marxist dialectics. But the basic elements of the doctrine which have practical relevance emerge with great clarity in Mussolini's thought: the doctrine of class warfare, final goal and internationalism."[2] Journalist, orator, and party militant, dedicated to the ideas of class struggle and collectivist economics, Mussolini rose early and high in the ranks of Italian socialism. By 1912, he had become the dominant voice in the extremist wing of the party, had been named a member of the party's national executive committee, and had also been made editor of the party's national newspaper, *Avanti!* All this he achieved before reaching the age of thirty. It is not without reason, therefore, that Denis Mack Smith has referred to him as "the most outstanding personality of Italian socialism."

Anti-Parliamentary Elitism: Mosca, Pareto, Michels

The early twentieth century in Italy witnessed the widespread influence of a group of thinkers whom we will for convenience call elitists, or antiparliamentarians. Chief among these were Gaetano Mosca, Vilfredo Pareto, and Roberto Michels (the first two Italian by birth, the last Italian by choice). Although their ideas, methods, and aims were not entirely similar, the cumulative effect of their influence on educated Italian public opinion in general and on the thinking of Mussolini in particular was to be extremely important.

Gaetano Mosca was born in Palermo, Sicily, in 1858. Besides his scholarly activities, he served in parliament after 1908 and was Salandra's deputy minister of colonial affairs. Created a life senator in 1918, he lived to oppose publicly the Mussolini regime that his writings had done much, indirectly, to bring to power.

Two main ideas dominated the impressive writings of Mosca. One was that all societies were ruled by oligarchies, no matter what their formal structure. The other was that the justification for this oligarchical rule, or the "political formula," would vary from society to society and from age to age, adapting itself to such standards as a given society accepted as legitimate and meaningful. Of the ubiquity and necessity of a ruling class, Mosca wrote:

> In all societies—from societies that are very meagerly developed and have barely attained the dawning of civilization, down to the most advanced and powerful societies—two classes appear—a class that rules and a class that is ruled. The first class, always less numerous, performs all political functions, monopolizes power and enjoys the advantages that power brings, whereas the second, the more numerous class, is directed and controlled by the first, in a manner that is now more or less legal, now more or less arbitrary and violent, and supplies the first . . . with material means of subsistence and with the instrumentalities that are essential to the vitality of the political organism.[3]

Mosca's analysis, founded on the concept that parliamentary governments (like all others) conceal the domination by a minority, was devastatingly effective—because it was true, at least in the Italian case. As a Sicilian, moreover, Mosca must have had special insights into the way in which the ponderous wordiness of the law concealed and permitted the practices by which the many were organized for the benefit of the few.

Aside from being a critic of parliamentary regimes, Mosca was also a productionist. That is, he believed (as Mussolini would come to believe) that the fundamental economic problem in Italy and elsewhere was not distribution (to make it more just) but production (to make it more effective). Thus he wrote of the eight-hour day, "Such a limit on working hours may be endurable in a very rich country. It can only be fatal to a poor country. The ruling classes in a number of European countries were stupid enough and cowardly enough to accept the eight-hour day after the World War, when the nations had been terribly impoverished and it was urgent to intensify labor and productivity."[4]

Roberto Michels (1876-1936) reinforced Mosca's basic

ideas from another direction. Michels was a disciple of Max Weber, the most influential non-Marxist social thinker of the age, and was quite familiar, from intimate and extensive experience, with the socialist parties and labor unions of Germany, Switzerland, and Italy. His thoughts on this experience are found in his most famous work, *Political Parties* (1915). In it, "a synthesizing mind rather than a notably original thinker, Michels was to draw together in a coherent doctrine of political leadership elements derived from nearly all the major social theorists of the generation just prior to his own."[5] In a word, Michels concluded that, in this world of group struggle, organization is necessary for survival. Organization, however, inevitably leads to the rule of a small group of experienced and self-perpetuating activists (the famous "iron law of oligarchy"). For Michels, so pervasive was the rule of the few that even in organizations that came into existence at least partially to fight against the rule of the few—such as socialism, political parties, and unions—the ordinary member would always remain essentially an object rather than a subject, would often be reduced to the level of a pawn, and on occasion would have his best interests overlooked or even sacrificed by the leadership elite.

The last and most formidable of this elitist trio is Vilfredo Pareto (1848-1923). He, like the others, believed that all societies were divided into a ruling class ("elites") and a ruled class. In Pareto's analysis, it often happened in history that those who actually ruled, and those who were entitled to rule by virtue of superior abilities, more and more became two different groups in the population. When this gap became too wide, revolution resulted, bringing about the "circulation of elites." To Pareto's way of thinking, revolution can be socially very beneficial, since it replaces the control of a society by a ruling class that has become effete and confused by another that has demonstrated its vigor and daring.

For Pareto, even the socialist societies of the future would consist of an inert mass dominated by an elite; no large-scale social organization was conceivable without this interior dichotomy. Economics, moreover, was by no means the decisive factor in human affairs; rather, nonrational motivations were primary. Pareto presented these ideas in 1902 in a work called *Les systèmes socialistes,* which "early established itself as the classic refutation of Marxian economics and sociology. Legend has it that it caused Lenin graver worry than any other anti-Marxist writing, and that he took more than one sleepless night to work out his counter-refutation."[6]

Pareto's impressive book was reviewed in 1904 by Mussolini, who also enrolled in two of Pareto's courses at the University of Lausanne. He called Pareto's theory of elites "the most ingenious sociological conception of modern times." Pareto was later to accept appointment to the Italian Senate from Mussolini, and for the short span of time between the March on Rome and his death, Pareto can be considered at least a moderate supporter of Mussolini's regime.

The Sorelian Connection

The thinking of Georges Sorel (1847-1922) had enormous influence not only on what later became fascism, but also on the entire spectrum of radical and antiestablishment movements.[7] Both communists and fascists claim Sorel as one of their ancestors.

After an impoverished middle-class youth in Normandy, Sorel trained as an engineer at the prestigious Polytechnique. After many years of study and contemplation of social problems, he turned to serious writing, his most productive period being the decade 1898-1908. It was during this period that he produced the famous, if somewhat misnamed, *Reflections on Violence* (the only work of his to be widely known in the English-speaking world). The friend of Croce and Pareto, Sorel was to be more appreciated and influential in Italy than anywhere else.

A close student of Marx for many years, Sorel believed that world history was a struggle among minorities for dominance. He diverged from orthodox Marxism, however, in fundamental ways. He rejected Marxist pretensions to scientific unassailability; he denied economic determinism.

Adopting instead a posture based on the fluid character of the real world, he naturally moved away from the study of "inexorable underlying forces" to a study of human motivation. Here enters the concept of the historical "myth," the apocalyptic vision of deliverance in the remote future, deliverance to be attained by violent preparation in the present. Sorel viewed historical myths as the primary motivating forces in social affairs, and it was basically as a myth that he conceived of Marxism, and respected it. But it was the myth of the general strike—the cataclysmic and ultimate rising of the proletariat that would paralyze and pull down a corrupt bourgeois society—to which he gave his allegiance and that he viewed as the most effective motivating force.

Sorel was a socialist, but with a difference. He hated parliamentary socialism. It cooperated with, and thus legitimized, bourgeois democracy, which dominated France and which was struggling toward maturity in Italy. For Sorel, all this meant decadence, selfishness, corruption. Purification must come through violence.

> In the Sorelian system, violence tests the virility of people, classes and nations. The contempt in which he held the bourgeoisie of France bore little resemblance to the traditional socialist critique of the immorality of the wage system. The reverse is more nearly the truth. It was the lack of barbarism, the absence of significant appeals to violence, that Sorel considered the crisis of the bourgeois world. The bourgeoisie is castigated for accepting "the ideology of a timorous humanitarian middle class professing to have freed its thought from the conditions of its existence."[8]

Sorel hated the bourgeoisie not because it was oppressive but because it was weak.

His quest, then, was for "a renewal of human history through the restoration of archaic and heroic values." Such a moral regeneration required an agent, an instrument. "That agency need not be the proletariat. It could be any organized group of consecrated warriors bound together in exclusive solidarity. They would constitute the Homeric heroes of our decadent age; they would see life as a struggle and not as a pleasure nor the looking after pleasure."[9] The function of socialism was thus to restore men of action to power, and to establish "individual virility as a general characteristic of socialized man." Sorel wanted to resurrect Sparta, and he "shared with a number of socialists the idea that continuous social revolution could alone bring back the Spartan type into prominence." This strictly instrumental view of socialism and the proletariat, this search for the tools with which society could be remade and purified, would lead Sorel down some strange paths, and it is the key to understanding his otherwise baffling political oscillations. Like Mussolini, he was concerned with ends, not means, and was thus serenely untroubled by a concern for consistency.

Sorel had some complimentary things to say about Mussolini during the latter's march to power, and a newspaper review Mussolini wrote on the *Reflections* in 1909 shows that he was familiar with Sorel's thinking.

There is, inevitably, disagreement over the degree of Sorel's real influence on Mussolini. Stuart Hughes writes that "Mussolini did not need Sorel to teach him how to climb to power; he was a far better political tactician than his presumed master. But once he was safely installed there he found it convenient to cite Sorel's writings to rationalize and give intellectual respectability to what he had done on his own." On the other hand, Gregor writes of Sorel as one "whose ideas directly influenced the political maturation of Mussolini," and Mack Smith has maintained that Mussolini's "belief in illegal action, learned from the anarchists and republicans of his native Romagna, was now refined and formalized by reading Sorel."

Revolutionary Syndicalism

Sorel has been called the principal theorist of revolutionary syndicalism, and one historian has written that "the nationalist and subsequently fascist, 'philosophy of action,' with its glorification of will and force, owed much to syndicalism."

The Italian syndicalists rejected what they considered to

be the growing tendency toward parliamentarianism within socialism; they also developed serious doubts about the reality of international proletarian brotherhood. Their program was to boycott parliament and elections and to erect the trade unions into a kind of state within a state. Their main strength lay among the lowest-paid agricultural workers in the Emilia region, among railwaymen, and among the merchant seamen of Genoa.

The syndicalists, like Lenin's Bolsheviks, denied that class consciousness would be the spontaneous result of membership in the working class. Both syndicalists and Bolsheviks maintained that the revolution, and the revolutionary consciousness essential to it, would come only through the labors of an enlightened elite whose special talents and dedication justified their leadership of the workers. By constant agitation and violence, the class struggle would be exacerbated until the final contest, the epic, revolutionary general strike that would bring the exploiting bourgeoisie and their rotten state crashing to the dust. Thus the syndicalists organized bitter and bloody agricultural strikes that utterly failed in their objectives, but taught the landowners of central Italy to organize motorized volunteer self-defense squads, a tactic the fascists would one day employ with great success.

Whatever their failures, syndicalists and ex-syndicalists, with their synthesis of socialism, nationalism, and elitism, were to constitute an important element in Italian fascism both before and after 1922.

Nationalism

A virulent form of nationalist thought began to make itself felt in Italy during the first decade of this century. It was a hybrid, developed from a number of sources, and influenced or shaped by many of the new or newly dominant ideas of the time. Denis Mack Smith writes that Italian nationalism took over "notions on the political use of violence from Sorel and the syndicalists. From Darwin and Spencer were derived such terms as the fight for existence between nations, natural selection, and the survival of the fittest. Hegelians supplied the concept of an ethical state which was far greater than the sum of individuals who composed it."

The leading character in the unfolding drama of Italian supernationalism was Enrico Corradini (1867-1931), who has been called "the intellectual voice of nationalist sentiment in Italy prior to World War I." Corradini's basic ideas may be summarized as follows: (1) real life is the struggle between ethnocentric communities; (2) liberalism is thus unhealthy, even suicidal, because it teaches man to be egoistic; (3) Italy needs a good war, both to solidify itself internally and to obtain necessary raw materials. His especial contribution to nationalist thinking, however, was the notion of Italy as the "proletarian nation." "He appropriated the language of Marxism and transferred the class struggle to the international sphere. . . . In a world dominated by plutocracies, Italy was the proletarian nation. Nationalism would be Italy's socialism in the world, her method of redemption, which would rouse a warlike spirit in the nation as socialism roused it in the working class. War, too, would put an end to internal wrangles, create a national conscience, and bring greater riches for all."[10]

Mussolini was to imbibe deeply of such ideas, to take over many of them for himself, even to appropriate the nationalist party itself.

In the decade and a half between the turn of the century and Italy's entrance into World War I, Italian intellectual life became more and more dominated by antiparliamentary and antiliberal currents, may of which were to leave an important mark on the rising young political agitator Benito Mussolini and the movement he would eventually lead. From his Romagnole socialist environment Mussolini inherited a militant anticlericalism, contempt for law and the established order, and the concept of social life as group struggle. Mosca, Pareto, and Michels insisted that parliamentary government and democratic aspirations were a delusion and a sham: that is, parliament and democracy masked the pervasive and necessary dominance of social life by elite minorities, who would rule as long as they had vigor and nerve and who would then be replaced, through revolution, by a more daring and virile minority. Sorel and the syndicalists bequeathed the views that violence was a purgative for social corruption, that the will was primary, and that great myths had the power to mobilize men. Nationalism contributed the notion of ineluctable struggle between nations and the notion of an Italy oppressed and menaced by arrogant plutocracies. The general atmosphere was also influenced by Nietzsche (the bourgeois world is corrupt and can be saved only by supermen), Durkheim (collective consciousness is prior and superior to individual consciousness), and Bergson (intuition and instinct are better guides to reality than mere fallible reason).

Having taken a look at some of the forces that shaped the intellectual environment in which fascism was born and grew, we can now consider the ideology of Italian fascism in more specific terms. Although it is often true that ruthless men manipulate ideological symbols to serve their own purposes (one has but to give a moment's consideration to the highly developed state of this art in the Soviet Union), this is not always done in an utterly ruthless and coldblooded manner. Men believe what is convenient for them to believe; a man's beliefs are at least a partial map of the way he thinks the world is or ought to be. Political belief, or ideology, is therefore important because it provides important clues to how men may perceive their options. Most men also want to know why they are right, to know why, when others call them misguided or foolish or criminals, these accusations are false. Ideology thus provides the justification, or the license, for past as well as future actions. The wholesale dismissal, therefore, of all ideology as mere mumbo jumbo to mystify the deluded masses, is very misleading; ideology is one—if only one—of the forces that shape the political drama.

The development of the ideology of Italian fascism must be understood as the development of the political thought of Benito Mussolini. "Only in this way does its doctrine emerge in its wealth of variation, its contradictions, its insights derived from living experience, but above all in its constant interplay with concrete political situations."

Let us dispose immediately of two objections to this procedure. The first objection is that Mussolini switched from the Socialist party's line of neutrality into interventionism and antisocialism in 1914-1915 because he was bought by French gold. This objection is unacceptable, for at least two reasons. First, there is no real evidence that Mussolini received subsidies from any Allied government until *after* he had already assumed a pro-Allied line. Second, Mussolini gave up a great deal by his break with the Italian socialists. To a newspaperman as well as to a lifelong socialist such as Mussolini, "the editorship of *Avanti!* was worth more than the bourgeois prime ministership."

The second objection is that Mussolini was too ill educated, too much of an intellectual lightweight to have evolved anything to be dignified with the name of ideology. In this view, he was a brutal opportunist who slapped together some ill-fitting slogans and half-digested ideas that served his purposes one day and were discarded the next. This objection cannot be accepted either; it flies in the face of the testimony of too many distinguished scholars. In the words of Ernst Nolte, Mussolini's "command of contemporary philosophy and political literature was at least as great as that of any other contemporary European political leader. So it would seem best not to cast doubt on Mussolini's sincerity without good reasons, and not to be skeptical in our approach to his self-interpretation."[11] There are many, many grounds on which one can succesfully reproach Mussolini, but ignorance of political philosophy is not one of them.

In order to understand fascism, it is helpful to remember that men did not become fascists by accident or stumble onto a full-blown fascist doctrine. Fascism evolved as a critique, a rejection of Marxism, liberalism, and democratic equalitarianism.

Fascist Elitism

Liberalism was rejected by the fascists, as well as by many others in Italy, because it had never worked the way it was supposed to; at any rate, it was clearly at the end of its rope. Democracy, as it was evolving in the United States, Britain, France, and elsewhere, was yet another matter. Mussolini had always strongly held to a belief in the fundamental irrationality of men; thus the "quantitative" basis of democracy was rejected in favor of the elitism that was so prominent an influence in Italian thought in the first two decades of the century. Even when he was a prominent socialist leader, Mussolini publicly espoused the necessity of an elite to organize and lead the proletariat to power and in power (an idea he shared with Lenin and Sorel, among others). Hence, his shift away from official socialism did not involve a change in his conception of how society should be structured: a few would, because only a few could, lead the many. The doctrine that a manifestly superior elite had a right and a duty to impose itself on the bovine mass, as well as on the effete bourgeoisie, was to have particular appeal to the young intellectuals who had served as commandos *(arditi)* on the bitter Austrian front.

As stated previously, the notion of elitism in one form or another was very widespread at the time, but the fascists gave it a flavor peculiarly their own:

> And when the *fascisti* say "we have the right to govern Italy because we alone have the strength," they do not mean merely that "might makes right"; they mean that in the conflict of forces which characterized the years 1919 to 1922, they, and not the democratic government, proved capable of exercising effective control and re-established some sort of order and authority. And they are well aware that this ability to govern is not merely a matter of "force," but the interplay of a variety of factors which go to make up the "strength" of a movement. The *fascisti* actually underwent this experience before they theorized about it. It came as an empirical discovery.[12]

As Nasser was to say, "We reached our ideology through our experience. We extracted our ideology from the details of events we passed through."

From Class to Nation

The often contradictory positions Mussolini assumed between 1915 and 1921 are very much the result of his attempts to come to a satisfying solution of the problems involved in a synthesis of socialism and nationalism. These would eventually be the two principal legs on which all recognizably fascist movements would stand, but their reconciliation was by no means easy for a generation of men who had been schooled to think that they were and had to be opposites.

Mussolini, even as he climbed the ladder of socialism, had long been aware that men's motivations are nonrational and sentimental as well as rational (in the Marxian sense of strictly economic). Like Sorel, he believed that men could be mobilized to perform great deeds only through a "myth," a vision of a better world; the myth would justify and sustain heroic effort. For European socialists of the pre-1914 vintage, that myth was the proletarian revolution, ushering in the classless society, in which, eventually, all would be equal, altruistic, and well fed. A subordinate, but nonetheless powerful, myth that had grown up in European socialism was that of international socialist solidarity: a great war was no longer possible among the advanced states of Western Europe, because the workers, organized and educated by the Socialist party, would not participate in such a war. General war would be met by the general strike: the workers would no longer shed their blood to make profits for the bloated bourgeoisie. Such beliefs were deeply and passionately held, and even many nonsocialists were convinced, much to their chagrin, that socialist internationalism was indeed a powerful, even a debilitating, obstacle to war.

The events of 1914 showed how tragically erroneous all these calculations really were. French socialists rallied to defend the republic against German militaristic monsters. German and Austrian socialists flocked to defend the colors against Tsarist imperialism and Slavic barbarism. The great international socialist palace of pacifism that had loomed so grandly on the European horizon for so many years collapsed in a few days. Only in Russia and Italy did socialism remain true to the earlier vision.

These events had profound effects on socialists all over the world. The socialist version of reality, and the premises on which that version had been based, were shown to all the world to be shockingly inadequate. Socialists struggled to make some sense, to preserve some elements of the old structure, out of this debacle. Lenin, incredulous and outraged at Western European socialist chauvinism, drew some hard conclusions from all this. So, in a different direction but for similar reasons, did Italian socialism's most prominent personality.

Mussolini's renunciation of socialism received a major impetus from the dawning awareness of the magnitude of European socialism's miscalculations about the bases and extent of its own power and influence. Added to this was his long-standing dislike of Germany and Austria, which soon turned into a real hatred; he took to describing socialism as a subtle instrument of Pan-Germanism. Soon Mussolini and the world would see Russian socialists play an instrumental part in undermining and destroying the Russian army, with all the dreadful consequences to Russian national interest and prestige.

Mussolini's disentanglement from the Socialist party was drawn out and full of anguish. If he cut himself off from mainstream socialism while remaining—as he was to the depth of his being—an enemy of the established order, was he not condenming himself to political sterility? Such problems more than once drove Mussolini almost to despair.

The key element in the conversion of Mussolini from socialism to what came to be called fascism was the substitution of the myth of national solidarity for the myth of class solidarity. Mussolini became convinced by the events of 1914-1918 that nationalism was by far a more powerful political catalyst than the class struggle. Marxian rationalist classism touched powerful nerves on the surface, but nationalism went much deeper, reaching men in their most primal nerves. The Marxists were quite right when they held that struggle was the primary fact of human existence, but they were wrong about the nature of that struggle: the fundamental basis of division was not horizontal, among economic classes, but vertical, among nations. Those nations that were organized, united, solid, and efficient would survive the struggle; those that were rent by internecine combat would be pushed aside, conquered, exploited. Among the conclusions to be drawn from such views, two were supremely important in shaping future fascism: (1) the Socialist party, by dividing and thus weakening the nation, was a true enemy of all the people and had to be dealt with vigorously; (2) the nation obviously had to be organized for international struggle on the most efficient basis, which meant that grave and far-reaching changes were going to have to be made in Italy, in the interest not of a class, but of a nation.

Thus Mussolini's political thinking made the following progression: from internationalism and revolution before 1914 to nationalism and revolution by 1916 to nationalism and antirevolution after 1919. Saving the nation meant first of all the expansion of production; expansion of production meant class collaboration under the direction of a strong state.

Armed with these ideas, Mussolini made war on the socialists; their preachings on class war were antinational (besides, they had dared expel him in 1915). The vigor and brutality of the assault on the apparatus of socialism was, along with defense of veterans' rights, one of the principal reasons for fascism's rapid growth during 1920 and 1921. Yet Mussolini's socialist origins always remained somehow with him. From the nationalists, he took over the concept of "proletarian Italy" as perfectly summarizing his new views; working-class solidarity, which had proved so ephemeral, would be replaced by the monolithic unity of the Italian people. Again, during the summer of 1921, Mussolini proposed an alliance of all the "popular" forces: fascists, socialists, and *popolari*. By that time, however, the fascist movement had grown much bigger than just the personal following of Mussolini, and bitterly antisocialist elements within it loudly vetoed the plan. Many years later, at the end of his career, making his last-ditch stand in the German supported "Fascist Republic" of Salò, Mussolini would openly revert to his radical past and attempt to establish a working-class fascist regime. This project, too, failed, but it revealed that even after many years, the inflammatory capitalist-baiting Romagnole rhetorician who had risen to become editor of *Avanti!* still lurked behind the facade of the man of order and world statesman.

The Basic Concepts

The doctrine that provided the philosophical explanation and justification for fascism had been made clear, by word and deed, by the time of the March on Rome (October 1922), although it was to be elaborated and embellished all during the years of Mussolini's rule, especially by the competent Hegelian philosopher Giovanni Gentile (1875-1944). The essential features of Italian fascist ideology can be reduced to these:

1. *nationalism:* the highest human reality is the nation, organized and expressed by the state; politics is the struggle among nations, in which the strong survive and the weak perish; Marxist internationalism is a delusion;
2. *explicit repudiation of parliamentary liberalism,* which panders to egoism and is based on the illusion of human equality;
3. *statism:* the state is a moral entity; it is through service to the state (and thus to the nation) that men transcend their limitations;
4. *productionism:* the resources of the nation must be mobilized and developed by the state; not distribution but increased production is the key to national survival and long-term economic improvement;
5. *corporatism:* struggle within the nation is not legitimate; different social classes must harmonize their aims in the national interest under the direction of the state; class war is replaced by class cooperation;
6. *authoritarianism:* power does and must flow from the top down; this is akin to a law of nature, and will be denied only by the naive or the dishonest;

7. *elitism:* only a few are gifted enough to rule, and the many are capable (and desirous) only of submitting; the elect few manifest themselves by their success in taking and holding power.

The various features are interrelated. Elitism implies authoritarianism, productionism implies corporatism, all are implied by nationalism. (Indeed it is essential to recognize that nationalism is implicitly collectivist.) Racism, as that term came to be understood in the 1930s, was entirely absent from fascist ideology. To differentiate among members of the nation on account of some factor or factors that would make some less a part of the nation than others strikes at the very heart of nationalism. Racism clashed with the cosmopolitanism of the imperial Roman tradition, much admired by the *Duce,* and contradicted Italian history, a record of many immigrations and invasions. Biological determinism, moreover, struck directly at Mussolini's emphasis on the power of the will and individual heroism. This is one of the most fundamental ways in which Italian fascism differed from German Nazism: for Mussolini, the basic criterion for participation in the Italian nation was will; for Hitler, membership in the *Volk* was inherited. Italian fascism was thus implicitly universal: any Italian of good will could become a fascist, and anybody who really wanted to could become an Italian. Nazi racist notions were not to become an important factor in fascist ideology until the regime was already in the process of demoralization and decay. Mussolini, realizing that racialism undercut the nationalist foundations of fascism, blamed the change of direction on the political opposition of "world Jewry" to the fascist regime. And Jewish veterans of the Italian army were to be exempt from any disabilities. Fascist Italy just was not in the same league as Nazi Germany (not to mention Stalinist Russia, where whole classes, whole nations, were condemned to imprisonment or death because of their "class origin," or for the crime of having been taken prisoner by the Nazis).

A great part of the attraction of the fascist regime, especially in the early years, was its style: the parades, the balcony dialogues with the crowd, the uniforms (much of this taken over from D'Annunzio). And, too, there were highly specific inducements for certain specific groups: the vindication of the dignity of veterans, the protection of large and small landholders from seizures by socialists or Catholic radicals. Beyond all these things, however, one must recognize that any final explanation of Mussolini's seizure and retention of power must take account of the general attractiveness of radical nationalist reform promised by the fascists. Liberalism had lost its vitality, Marxism could not decide what to do, the country had gone through years of supreme effort in war and years of wasteful political stalemate. "That Italian life needed a profound renewal, that Italy must at last become a modern state, that there must be an end to bureaucratic dilatoriness, had been repeated much too often during the past thirty years for the new outlook not to have also inspired fascism." Fascism promised the restoration of law and order, but that was only the beginning. Italy was to be cleaned up and built up, economic and psychological bottlenecks were to be forced open, and new plans and new methods would modernize and rejuvenate the nation and make it respected in the world.

Even the working classes were affected. Although most of the workers remained sullenly loyal to the socialists or the communists, the fascists won over a significant minority, partly owing to impatience with socialist malaise, incompetence, and failure to produce a new world, partly in response to the vision Mussolini showed them. After all, the new dictator had spent his life and built a career among these people, and his success in attracting or at least neutralizing important elements of the working classes was attested to by contemporary communist observers. Mussolini's evolving ideas about national solidarity and productionism were to work out in practice to the disadvantage of the workers as a class, but that does not begin to mean that this was the purpose behind fascism. No one will ever understand the successes of fascism who refuses to acknowledge the testimony of history: that fascism meant many things to many persons and that its attractiveness was never confined solely to one class or one group, however defined.

4. The Mussolini Regime

For how we live is so far removed from how we ought to live, that he who abandons what is done for what ought to be done, will bring about his own ruin, rather than his preservation.
—Machiavelli

In any consideration of the first fascist regime, three questions come naturally to mind. How did Mussolini obtain and solidify his power? What did he do with it at home? What did he do with it abroad?

Mussolini was prime minister of Italy for over two decades, a period long enough to give some good answers to these questions. For purposes of analysis, the fascist regime will be divided into three phases. In the first phase, from Mussolini's appointment as premier to the beginning of 1925, serious efforts were made to preserve at least the appearances of the constitutional structure of monarchical Italy. During the second phase, from 1925 to the end of 1934, the dictatorship was consolidated and the machinery of the "corporate state" erected. Finally, in 1935, a third phase begins—a drive toward economic self-sufficiency and a growing involvement in war.

By 1918, neither the working class nor the propertied classes were interested in the compromises necessary to make a democratic constitution work. Widespread, chronic social violence ensued. The Italian parliamentary system, never a model of probity or efficiency, simply could not operate in this new situation of quasi civil war. Mussolini, promising order, continuity, and reform, was thus called to power.

Fascism's Legal Path to Power

Mussolini's rise to the position of head of government was, it must be emphasized, formally constitutional. In 1921, the electoral coalition between Giolitti's liberals and the fascists conferred upon the latter a new respectability—and thirty-five seats in the Chamber of Deputies. March on Rome or no, Mussolini was appointed prime minister by the king, in the normal way, and the new cabinet was a coalition of several parties, with fascist ministers in a distinct minority. Soon after, the parliament constitutionally voted to grant the cabinet power to rule by decree for one year. Finally, in 1923, it passed the Acerbo Law, which opened the way to Mussolini's complete control of legal power. This law declared that the leading party or coalition in the next elections, provided it had at least twenty-five percent of the vote, would be awarded two-thirds of the seats in the chamber.

The Acerbo Law was intended to set the stage for several years of "legal dictatorship" for Mussolini, since, being in control of the government, he and his followers would always be able to get at least the required twenty-five percent of the vote in any new election. The fascists, however, were only a small minority in the parliament that passed the Acerbo Law. Who, then, besides Mussolini's supporters, voted for it? Mainly three groups: those who hoped that responsibility would tame Mussolini, around whom a broad conservative coalition could then be built; those who believed in parliamentary government and suspected the fascists, but who felt drastic reforms were necessary, reforms that required the existence of a large and stable majority in parliament; finally, those who detested both the fascists and the Acerbo bill, but who feared that a rejection of the latter would provoke the fascists into ignoring or closing parliament altogether. Many non-fascists and anti-fascists, in other words, chose for their own reasons to cooperate with, rather than combat, fascism.

Armed with the new law, the fascists called elections in 1924, and, to absolutely no one's surprise, won a majority of the votes and a preponderance in parliament. Intimidation certainly played an important part in gathering this majority for the fascists, but other powerful factors were present and should not be overlooked in the search to understand how dictatorship may solidify its control step by step. The fascists were aided by the old southern habit of voting for whatever government was in power. Unmistakable signals from the Vatican alerted the Italian clergy that Pius XI had big plans for Mussolini and did not want them disturbed. Finally, there was the absurd, incredible disunity among the anti-fascist forces. For example, in this, the most crucial election in the history of united Italy, the Marxists, fatuous to the bitter end, not only refused to join with "bourgeois" anti-fascist groups in a coalition of liberty, but actually fielded three distinct and competing lists of candidates (two socialist lists and one communist). The grotesque incompetence and disarray among the other parties must surely have won votes for Mussolini all by itself.

In October 1922, nobody, of course, was in a position to know or suspect that Mussolini would remain in power for over two decades, that he would overthrow the constitution, lead his country into a disastrous war, and bring down the monarchy. Mussolini's dictatorship developed by stages, the most important being the creation of a complacent majority in parliament. Other power groups in Italian society, however, were not neglected, especially the army and the church, with both of which Mussolini soon came to an understanding.

The Italian officer corps was loyal to the king. When, by virtue of his appointment and retention of Mussolini as premier, the king became implicated in the fascist regime, the army was neutralized. The army, moreover, shared certain important beliefs with the fascists: the need for preparedness, for hierarchy, for order, for nationalist ardor. The army thus found it quite congenial to follow the lead of the monarch and cooperate with Mussolini. The Italian army would pay a heavy price for all this, even before the outbreak of war. A state-supported fascist militia would eventually compete with it for funds and attention. Fascist interference in army internal affairs would result in the promotion of the wrong kind of officer, undermining discipline and morale. Years of material and moral corruption would sap the war-making powers of the army and expose it to the ridicule and contempt of enemies and allies alike.

Though Mussolini never attended mass, Pius XI called him "a man sent to us by Providence."[1] Seen from a narrow, clerical vantage point, this was not an extreme view, for Mussolini was both willing and able to solve the sixty-year-old Roman question. The Lateran Pacts, signed in 1929 after years of careful negotiation, brought important advantages to the church: the independence of Vatican City, compulsory religious instruction in public schools, legalization of religious marriages, and great sums of money in compensation for the loss of the Papal States. Mussolini also benefited. He appeared, at home and abroad, as a statesman who had accomplished what many had tried to do and what many had yearned for: the reconciliation between the Catholic church and the kingdom of Italy. Henceforth, it would be impossible to create an antifascist Catholic opposition party. Greatest boon of all, the bulk of Italy's numerous clergy rose to new heights of enthusiasm for a regime that had restored the church to it proper place; this enthusiasm would, for the most part, remain through good times and bad, until it was almost too late.

Ringmaster of parliament, friend of the army, protector of the church, hammer of the reds, by 1930 Mussolini seemed serenely ensconced in the corridors of power.

Fascist domestic policies changed several times during the more than twenty years of Mussolini's rule. As a result, Italian fascism is often seen as a movement without a philosophy, as if fascism were nothing but Mussolini and Mussolini nothing but an opportunist. Denis Mack Smith, one of the most distinguished of contemporary historians, speaks of the "fundamental unseriousness" of a regime that "was itself essentially rhetoric and blather." In another place, however, Smith calls fascism "profoundly anti-liberal" and "revolutionary," thus implying that there was considerably more substance to the whole thing than mere "rhetoric."

This ambivalent attitude among respected scholars is in part a reflection of the ambivalence of the fascists themselves. One may recall, in considering the occasionally contradictory policies pursued by fascism between 1922 and 1943, that ambivalence and opportunism were not uncharacteristic of Roosevelt's New Deal or of the first three decades of Soviet rule. For regimes that come to power in times of upheaval, on a program of radical change, the great imperative is action, not consistency. Furthermore, although Mussolini's power may have seemed secure to admirers and enemies, he was never in complete control of Italian society (no doubt especially in his own mind). The crown, the army, big business, bureaucracy, and the church were his allies, not his creatures, and they retained the ultimate option of turning on him (which, indeed, they eventually did). This is merely another facet of the coalitionist nature of Mussolini's regime: coalition between the fascist party and other power groups, and coalition within the fascist party itself. Fascism meant different things to different people; keeping the various factions within fascism in step while balancing the party with other powerful elements in Italy was a never-ending task requiring no small investment of energy and talent. Besides, changes in policy involved means, not ends; the retention of power by the fascists, increased productivity, and the attainment by Italy of its "proper place" in world politics remained the guiding stars of the regime throughout its tenure.

Fascist Corporatism

Mussolini "made the trains run on time." He increased wheat production dramatically, improved internal transportation, drained swamplands, reduced the number of landless laborers, and increased the number of owners and tenants. Italy ceased to be predominantly rural: perhaps a million farm laborers left the countryside for the city. The centerpiece of domestic policy, however, was the erection of the "corporate state."

Corporatism was no fascist invention. Catholic corporatists, drawing on the social teachings of Leo XIII, had for
many years advocated a middle road between capitalist
individualism and Marxist collectivism. A more important
influence on fascism was the "national syndicalists"—
socialist heretics, expelled from the Italian Socialist party for
advocating a program of trade unionism, nationalism, and
class collaboration. These and similar ideas had been thick
in the Italian political air since Mussolini's youth.

Under Mussolini, corporatism was about increased
production. This was to be attained through the organization of capital and labor under the supervision of the state.
Put more crudely, corporatism meant "no strikes." The
institutions of the corporate state were largely window
dressing for the basic policy of industrial peace.

By the agreements of Palazzo Chigi (1923) and Palazzo
Vidoni (1925), Italian big business recognized fascist unions
as sole bargaining agents; most Italian industry was grouped
together with the Confederation of Industry as its recognized
spokesman. Relations between the two sides were to be
supervised by the state, with strikes and lockouts abolished.

These agreements were certainly no boon for labor,
because industry remained fairly self-directed and labor
state-directed. Labor leaders were responsible not only to
their worker constituents but to the fascist party as well.
Management, on the contrary, was free to do pretty much as
it pleased in its own sphere, provided it adhered to the
general political line laid down by the regime. Business did
not run the fascist state; rather, the state let business run
itself, at least in large measure. Fascism made Italy safe for
private property but was neither its creature nor prisoner,
and leadership of Italian industry always remained aloof and
uneasy. Fascism's industrial policies were defended on the
grounds that more production rather than fairer distribution
was the fundamental solution to Italy's social woes.
Industrial peace was the key to increased productivity—in
contrast to the countless and fruitless strikes that had helped
bring down the parliamentary regime after World War I.

Significant economic development took place. Italy

joined the select ranks of those nations with predominantly industrial economies, as the population engaged in farming and allied occupations dropped below 50 percent in 1936. Wheat production increased by half from 1921 to 1938. The death rate was greatly reduced. GNP, after stagnating between 1910 and 1920, rose rapidly (in constant lire). Important advances were made in chemicals, hydroelectricity, the merchant marine, and the electrification of railways. Shepard Clough, in his *Economic History of Modern Italy*, presents the following index of industrial production (using 1922 as a base):

1922: 100.00
1927: 163.70
1929: 204.50

Fascist economic policy sought to make up for Italian industrial backwardness by encouraging the larger and more progressive firms, such as FIAT, Olivetti, and Pirelli, in the scramble for scarce resources. The fruits of these policies would be gathered years later in the vaunted "Italian economic miracle" of the 1950s.

With all its emphasis on production, fascism never worked out a comprehensive investment policy or realized the necessity of good trade relations with other countries. Mussolini also insisted on certain policies for reasons of prestige despite their harmful economic effects; maintaining the lira at an artificially high rate, for instance, made Italian goods very costly overseas and hurt tourism. So far from being the servant of the "finance capital" of Marxist demonology, Mussolini, who knew little of economics and was not impressed by the corpulent bourgeoisie, never allowed what he viewed as mere economics to interfere with high politics.

By 1938, then, Mussolini could lay claim to a considerable record of accomplishment, especially if one did not insist on looking too far below the surface. He had stopped bolshevism in Italy, pacified the church, augmented the empire (in Ethiopia), saved Spain from communism, given Italy a stable government and industrial progress, and called forth a host of imitators abroad. The less attractive aspects of the regime—the militarization of children, the stupid outlawing of the handshake as "unfascist," the corruption of bench and army through favoritism, the shameless exploitation of religion—could be and were conveniently ignored.

In 1938-1939, however, came the great descent, the unraveling of the regime. It was to accelerate at an incredible pace and finish a few years later in utter calamity. The turn of direction was signaled by the imposition of official anti-Semitism.

As late as 1935, Mussolini had condemned Nazi racialist doctrines in an article in the *Enciclopedia Italiana.* Ideas of racial purity, superiority, and inferiority directly contradicted Mussolini's doctrines of nationalism, and he, like everybody else of any sense, well knew that "scientific racism" was claptrap. Yet Mussolini was moved to inject the satanic sickness of racism into a society where it had been unknown since the days of the Romans, where the church had spoken thunderously against Nazi racialism, where anti-Semitism in the face of all opposition, fascist and non-fascist alike, can be understood only in the context of Italian foreign policy, specifically the movement toward a German alliance.

Foreign Policy: The Downward Slide

The fascists came to power to resolve two fundamental problems (they said): internal disorder fomented by the "reds," and the theft of the fruits of Italy's victory in 1918. Given fascist bellicosity before the March on Rome, Italian foreign policy between 1922 and 1933 was fairly quiescent; there was some early trouble with Greece, but, on the other hand, the long-standing dispute with Yugoslavia over Fiume (one of the problems that had undermined pre-Mussolinian stability) was resolved by treaty. Mussolini's grudging admiration of the English, plus the unique personal influence exerted on him by Austen Chamberlain (British foreign minister 1924-1929) for many years, led the *Duce* to follow the traditional Italian policy of friendship with Great Britain. Despite the many years of surface calm, however, Mussolini's ambition to play a major role on the world stage and the widely believed fiction that Italy was a great power meant trouble. The trouble came, eventually, over Ethiopia.

Many factors converged to drive Mussolini into an assault on Ethiopia. Italy was a relative latecomer to the game of nations and thus had few colonial possessions to compensate for its serious lack of natural resources. Britain, France, Russia, and the United States had for years been carrying out territorial expansion, and Italians yearned to imitate them, if neccessarily on a far smaller scale. (Most Italians always perceived British and French opposition to their colonial aspirations, especially in Ethiopia, as the grossest hypocrisy stemming from a desire to keep Italy weak and poor.) Italian involvement in East Africa was long-standing, and as early as 1896 Italy had suffered its worst military humiliation of modern times at Ethiopian hands, at Adowa. The conquest of this, one of the last remaining independent countries on the African continent, would wipe out the pain of that disaster and also consolidate Italian holdings in the area (Eritrea, Somalia) into a compact mass.

When Italy began military operations against Ethiopia in 1935, the League of Nations, under British leadership, voted economic sanctions against it. Since the sanctions did not include an embargo on all-important oil, since many nations did not observe the sanctions (such as Germany and the United States), and since the Suez Canal was not closed to the Italians, the British-organized League effort to save Ethiopia was a complete failure. It was enough, however, to infuriate Mussolini, especially since British and French leaders had given him ample reason for believing they would make no trouble over Ethiopia, and to solidify Italian opinion around him. The Ethiopian affair marked a definite break between Italy and the Western powers and the beginning of Italy's slide into the German orbit. (Churchill, who realized all this, thundered at the folly of driving the Italians into Hitler's arms, but he was not in power.) Colonial disappointment had driven Italy into a German pact in the nineteenth century (the Triple Alliance), but it got out of it in time. Ethiopia was to force Italy toward the Germans once again; this time there would be no escape.

The influence of the Ethiopian crisis on the origins of World War II cannot be exaggerated. Italy had fought against the Central Powers in World War I, and neither the *Duce,* the king, the Vatican, nor big business liked Hitler or his regime. Indeed, when Hitler made his first move to annex Austria to the Third Reich in 1934, Mussolini sent Italian troops to the Austrian border; Hitler understood the warning and backed down. In those days, Italy, France, and Britain all had a clear interest in cooperating to keep a rising Germany from completely upsetting the European balance of power. The Ethiopian affair, however, caused a bitter split between Italy and the Western powers, thus encouraging Germany to continue violating, step by step, the provisions of the Versailles Treaty. (In the 1930s, many people thought Italy was militarily powerful—at least no one could be sure that it was not.) In 1938, Hitler was determined to move against Austria once again. This time the outcome was very different. Mussolini was isolated from the French and British; he had seen these two powers pushed and bluffed time and again by Germany. Finally, thousands of his best troops were tied down in Spain's civil war. In these conditions, it would have been unthinkable to take on Germany alone. Thus, Germany gobbled up Austria with no Italian opposition.

This event was decisive for Italian foreign policy. In 1918 the removal from Italian borders of the mighty and ancient Habsburg Empire and its replacement by little Austria had been of enormous benefit to Italy. For all practical purposes, it had secured Italy from land invasion. Hitler's annexation of Austria undid the whole thing and once again brought the military might of the Teutons right to the gates of Venice and Milan. The enormity of this catastrophe, by which Italy's military security was wiped out without a shot having been fired, was masked at the time; Mussolini chose to pretend that he and Hitler had the same enemies and therefore common interests. After 1938, the *Duce* would dance to the tune of his onetime imitator and new senior partner in the Rome-Berlin Axis. If Mussolini had stayed neutral during World War II (like Franco), he might very well have seen the day of his inclusion in Mr. Dulles's "free world" combination against communist expansionism (Mussolini would have been only seventy in 1953). Instead, after the annexation of Austria, Mussolini traveled like a sleepwalker a short path through bloodshed, the humiliation and occupation of Italy, to his own brutal death.

One can learn much from a close study of fascism in Italy; perhaps the following three points are most usefully kept in mind:

1. fascism came to power after or immediately before conciliating potent institutions that were and remained distinct from it: the crown, the army, the clergy, the industrialists. These accommodations made it possible for Mussolini to rule, but impossible for him to rule completely in ways he would have liked;
2. the fascist formula for economic development was the imposition of industrial peace and the lowering of consumption standards. These techniques have become common in contemporary developing nations in the Third World;
3. despite the fact that power tends to corrupt, that Mussolini had been in power for over two decades, and that the mass of Italians were no better off economically in 1940 than they had been in 1920, Mussolini's regime was overthrown as a result of mistakes in *foreign* policy.

The Italian War Record

Italy's performance in World War II, after twenty years of fascism, was unimpressive; in fact, it was a collapse.

When the government belatedly declared war, it did so without alerting key military commanders; thus troops in defensive positions along the French border were ordered to attack. This gross mismanagement was typical. After eighteen years of militarism, Italy was militarily unprepared. It had no naval air arm; Mussolini had considered Italy to be one huge aircraft carrier. Motor transport in the army was grotesquely inadequate. Great amounts of money appropriated for defense had found their way into the pockets of party bigwigs. Huge sums had been poured out in pursuit of glory in Ethiopia and Spain (when Italy entered World War II, it had been almost continually fighting, in Africa and in Spain, for five years).

War against Britain, not to mention the United States, would have been unpopular in Italy under any circumstances; the added consideration that Axis victory would only deepen Italian subordination to Nazi Germany made war even more distasteful. Thus, for the masses of Italian officers and enlisted men, "what was the sense of showing bravery in a futile war for a bad cause?"

Although the rapid disintegration of the regular Italian armed forces is common knowledge, the bloody and protracted struggles of Italian partisans against German occupation forces in northern Italy during 1944-1945 is little known in the English-speaking world. By June 1944, about 82,000 guerrillas were operating in those regions. Mussolini himself, of course, was executed in 1945 by some of these partisans, who had forcibly removed him from an armed German motor convoy that was supposed to protect him.

The performance of the Italians in World War II ruined their reputation for valor or even simple discipline (despite the fact that most of the troops in Rommel's triumphant first offensive in North Africa were Italians). No such harsh and lasting judgment has been made against the French, despite the rapidity of their collapse in 1940 against numerically inferior German forces. The British have completely escaped censure for abandoning their stricken allies at Dunkirk and for their performance at Singapore. The Soviet military reputation emerged bright and formidable in spite of the scandalous showing against little Finland, in spite of the colossal encirclements and surrenders of 1941 and 1942, and in spite of the Russian officers and men who not only threw down their weapons but joined German-sponsored military units to fight the Red Army.

5. European Variants: Spain

*Revolutions in democracies are generally
caused by the intemperance of demagogues.*
—Aristotle

Spain has long been one of the most backward societies in
Europe—a surrealistic contrast with the position it enjoyed
at the time of its greatness. In the sixteenth and seventeenth
centuries, when Italy and Germany were mere geographical
expressions, when Russia was a peripheral collection of
barbarisms, Spain was the most powerful and wealthy state
in the entire west, perhaps in the entire world. In the year of
the American Declaration of Independence, the empire of
Spain stretched over five continents.

The dramatic reversal of Spain's fortunes and position
took a long time and was the result of a complex process, on
which historians are not entirely agreed. The Spain that was
to be the scene in the 1930s of one of history's ugliest wars
was to a very large degree the Spain that resulted from the
long descent from the heights of world empire; it may,
therefore, be worthwhile to consider at least some of what are
generally considered the most important causes of Spain's
decay.

In the sixteenth and seventeenth centuries, the sudden,
voluminous, and apparently endless influx of precious
metals from the American empire had long-range results
that can truthfully be labeled disastrous: a secular inflation
that crippled home industries, and a speculative and get-
rich-quick atmosphere that pervaded much of the country
and undermined the inclination to hard work and rational

planning. During the same period, Castile, the geographical and political heart of the Iberian peninsula, was in effect denuded of manpower by the gigantic efforts to conquer and colonize the New World, by the constant warfare of the Habsburg kings in Europe, and the encouragement (as early as the reign of Ferdinand and Isabella) of sheep raising in place of tillage. At certain points, high-caliber and farsighted leadership might have stemmed the tide of disintegration, but such leadership was not forthcoming. The Counterreformation had assumed a particularly rigid and defensive form in Spain and succeeded in producing a stifling and conformist intellectual atmosphere; those who should have been responsible for the drafting and execution of coherent economic policies had training only in law and theology. The cumulative effect of these debilitating trends was to encourage centrifugal tendencies in the Iberian peninsula, and to plant attitudes of defeatism and cynicism deep in the national character.[1]

Spain's slow, continuous decline continued into the nineteenth century, which saw the development of two Spains: one liberal (in the Spanish context) and anticlerical, with its stronghold in the army, and the other, authoritarian and clerical, embodied in the Catholic church. Nineteenth-century Spanish politics could, with little exaggeration, be described as a contest for control between these two institutions, church and army, a contest that frequently degenerated into civil war.

The Catalan question complicated the liberal-conservative (or army-church) rivalry. Catalonia had long nursed deep grievances against the central government, grievances based on the firmly held conviction that the various races of the Iberian peninsula were dominated and exploited by backward Castile. Thus Catalan economic self-interest as well as regional pride demanded autonomy from centralizing, corrupt Castile. The fact that the Catalan question (and other regionalist difficulties) could endure well into the twentieth century underlines the fact that the various regions and kingdoms of the Iberian peninsula had never been truly integrated. The first decade of the twentieth century saw

Catalonia, with its commerce, industry, and "European" culture, draw ever farther away from impoverished, rural, "African" Castile. That Catalonia, the most energetic and modern region of Spain, should also be peripheral, secessionist, and thus suspected and resented by the army, is a key to understanding why Spanish society could not come effectively to grips with its most urgent and profound tasks.

Rural poverty was the principal characteristic of central and southern Spain. A perennial and serious shortage of rainfall in many regions and the system of latifundia (often underproductive) were the bases of economic stagnation. In many areas, the system of short leases and frequent evictions discouraged those lucky enough to rent a little farm of their own from making significant improvements on it. Those who did not work their own land were part of a vast, growing, and desperately poor army of landless rural laborers. Peasant poverty kept demand for the products of industry low; peasant migration to the cities kept wages low. Limited natural resources, governments whose limited energies were devoted mainly to corruption, and an unenterprising middle class (except in progressive Catalonia) stifled economic advance. Extreme poverty and the decline of Catholicism's appeal, especially in the south, produced what was probably Europe's largest and most dedicated anarchist movement: hundreds of thousands of incredibly deprived human beings led by some of the most utopian social reformers and some of the most murderous cutthroats in all Europe. Spanish anarchism has been well described as a revolt against everything that had happened in Spain for the previous two hundred years, a revolt against the modern age. The existence of a powerful anarchist mass movement was indisputable proof that Spain was in need of drastic, sweeping reforms; yet anarchism itself was to prove the principal obstacle to such reforms. Serious reform in Spain around, say, 1900 meant that great sums would have to be spent on education and agriculture. This in turn would have meant slashing expenditures on the bloated, unproductive civil service and the top-heavy army; in other words, it would have meant the alienation of the middle classes and the military. Such a dangerous program would have required all the progressive forces in Spain to be united, rational, moderate, and determined; but the principal component of the forces of change was the anarchist movement, by definition opposed to parties, programs, voting, even to organization itself. This is the main reason why, though most Spaniards assuredly wanted profound changes in all spheres of existence (especially after the shock and humiliation of Spain's defeat by the upstart United States in 1898), profound changes did not come about.

The decomposition of Spanish society went unchecked because the institutions of the country allowed it to do so. Neither crown nor parliament nor army nor church was able to save Spain because they were themselves afflicted with fatal disabilities. The influence of the throne had been severely weakened during the nineteenth century by a succession of unedifying monarchs; Alfonso XIII, who proved to be the last king of Spain, knew how to meddle and connive but not how to be a king. The army had become a politically dominant force in the nineteenth century, not so much because it thrust itself forward as because civil institutions were so visibly decaying. The officer corps, grotesquely swollen and underpaid, commanded one of the most poorly trained and badly equipped forces in Europe; even the Moroccan rebels were to prove too much for the Spanish army. The military was quite capable of repressing Catalan aspirations, however, and remained the stronghold of an unyielding centralism right up to the Franco rebellion. The Catholic church, stripped of its lands during one of the nineteenth century's numerous civil wars, had turned for support to the wealthy. Intellectually cramped, fanatically rigid, with a clergy relatively low in numbers and in culture, the Spanish church did not seek to hold on to the growing ranks of the impoverished through the organization of cooperatives and labor unions, as a more vital Catholicism was doing in Italy and Germany. Rather, the Spanish church looked for defense from its many enemies to the repressive powers of the state. By World War I (during which, mercifully, Spain remained neutral), whole provinces of the country had long since become de-Christianized, with an uncompromising Catholicism displaced by a grim socialism or a church-burning anarchism.

Worst of all, perhaps, was the corruption of the ballot box. For decades, ballot stealing had been reduced to a system in Spain, and the introduction of universal manhood suffrage meant only that the same sordid practices had to be carried out on a bigger scale. The corruption of the vote meant that honest and responsive government was unattainable and that no one could have much faith in parliament or party. The corruption of the electoral process undermined the parliamentary-oriented and relatively moderate socialists but gave added cogency to the uncompromising and violent negativism of the anarchists.

The Dictatorship of Primo de Rivera

It might not be too outrageous to describe General Miguel Primo de Rivera as a Spanish version of Mussolini. Primo ruled Spain as a dictator under the king for over six years; at length, his policies failed, and he voluntarily relinquished power. The circumstances of his coming to power and, even more, the reasons why his regime was a failure helped significantly to move Spain closer to the crucifixion of civil war.

After World War I, the political situation in Spain became even graver than usual, and troubles in Spanish Morocco led to humiliating massacres of Spanish troops by North African rebels. In this atmosphere, and just a few days before the issuance of a parliamentary report that would have revealed the king's unlawful interference in military affairs and direct responsibility for certain bloody reverses in Morocco, General Primo de Rivera issued a *pronunciamento* in classic style and was unconstitutionally elevated by the king to be head of the government. It was September 1923, and Primo was fifty-three years old.

Primo's advent to power was greeted with widespread good wishes. It was widely believed that he would head a ninety-day "clean-up" administration, and he was also supposed to be a friend of Catalonia. One thing led to another, as happens with dictators, and Primo held on to power for considerably more than ninety days, but there is no disputing that he did in fact make some serious attempts to modernize the economy and attack social injustice. The Primo dictatorship had at least three important positive features. First, he successfully ended the bloody and seemingly interminable war in Morocco. (It is interesting to reflect on the important role that Morocco has played in modern Spanish politics. It was due mainly to events there that Primo came to power in 1923, and it was also to be from Morocco that the armed forces would launch their rebellion against the Republican government in Madrid.) Second, he alleviated unemployment and built up the economic infrastructure of the country through a vast program of public works, including a number of important roads. Third, he initiated compulsory collective bargaining and compulsory arbitration in many sectors of economic life, thereby winning the covert but real support of the Socialist party (which was then in a desperate struggle with the anarchists for the allegiance of the workers).

In spite of these considerable accomplishments, Primo's regime was a failure, for personal, national, and international reasons. In a word, Primo was a drunkard, and he often wrote and issued decrees when drunk. This made him appear undignified, a fatal flaw in grave Spanish eyes.

By definition an antirevolutionary, Primo had to look to antirevolutionary groups for support, and this meant preeminently the Catholic church and the great landowners. Moreover, he had been appointed to office by the king, to whom he was more or less loyal. Thus, he could neither break up the great Andalusian estates (and thereby strike a telling blow at the roots of anarchism) nor satisfy progressive opinion by calling the constitutional convention it had long and ardently desired; this would have spelled the end of the monarchy.

Primo had to depend on the church and landowners partly because he had no support from a mass party committed to national rejuvenation and devoted to its leader, a party such as Mussolini possessed. Such a party would have had to be a party of the bourgeoisie and the intellectuals, groups still too weak to be able to take on the church and the army, the dominant groups of the status quo. The very section of the country, moreover, that would have become the stronghold of such a party of modernization, Catalonia, had been antagonized by Primo's repressive measures against Catalan regionalism. Primo had originally come to power as a friend of Catalan aspirations, but his army supporters soon made it clear that there would be no compromise with what they saw as disintegrative tendencies. Thus, the base for a real mass party did not exist, and Primo was left alone with groups willing to support him only so long as he did not attempt those very structural reforms that could have revivified Spain.

The world depression of 1929 helped wreck many of Primo's plans and made the future look bleak. By then, Primo was getting old, and he was a diabetic who did not take proper care of himself (indeed, he would be dead before the end of 1930). Ailing, disappointed, tired of power, Primo publicly (and unexpectedly) called, in January 1930, upon the army commanders to write to him expressing their degree of confidence in his administration. The results were disappointing, and the whole maneuver deeply offended the king (who was supposed to be, after all, Primo's sovereign master). Primo resigned, went off to Paris, and died a few months later. His son remained in Spain, and would soon found the Spanish fascist party, the Falange.

The departure of Primo meant the end of the monarchy; his appointment had been a violation of constitutional practice and deeply offensive even to other conservative politicians. (In the same manner, Mussolini's end meant the end of the House of Savoy, which had been so implicated with his regime for so many years.) In 1931 public insistence on a republic had reached such a crescendo that Alfonso XIII abdicated (all was done peacefully, for no one would have raised a hand to defend the king had he chosen to make a stand). The coming of the Second Republic meant one last chance for a more or less peaceful and orderly resolution of Spain's staggering problems. In other words, the coming of the republic meant the inevitability of civil war.

The Republic

The Second Republic, born in hope in 1931, was to die by violence in 1936. Indeed, violence was perhaps the principal characteristic of the republican years. There was actually physical violence on a large scale, such as a halfhearted antirepublican rising in 1932 and a much more serious workers' rebellion in 1934. This latter had been provoked when the Catholic party, the largest in the parliament, was admitted into the republican cabinet, and it indicated that support for republican principles was tenuous, to say the least, even among ostensible republicans.

Another kind of endemic violence was characteristic, the violence of rhetoric and of faction. The divisions within the republican ranks—between Trotskyites and communists, between socialists and anarchists, between radicals and moderates, and even between hostile wings of the Socialist party—were deep, bitter, and almost paralyzing. The consequences of republican disarray were to be decisively negative. Just about the only thing the various elements of the republican coalition could agree upon was an exhilarating assault upon the Catholic church. Without doubt, the Catholic church in Spain had sunk to a low estate (and this had been so for many, many years) and was in desperate need of reform, even surgery. The republican attack on the church was so vindictive, petty, and heavy-handed, however, that it drove most middle-class Catholics, who were not originally unfriendly to the republic, into a mood of sullen opposition. The onslaught against Catholic education, however satisfying it was to doctrinaire anticlericals, left Spanish education sadly deteriorated, at least in the eyes of those who believed that Catholic schools are better than no schools at all. Following an old custom, the republicans persecuted the Jesuits, perhaps the only religious order in all Spain ready to accept the republic. Most dangerous of all for the life of the regime, however, was the failure of doctrinaire, anticlerical, republican cabinets to safeguard the church, its property and personnel, from physical destruction. Few governments that shut their eyes to large-scale and constant arson and murder committed against a large minority of the population are long for this world.

The desire of many republicans to destroy, rather than to build, which was manifested in the predilection for antireligious crusading, had its other side in the complete inability and unwillingness of these same allegedly progressive and humanitarian forces to deal with Spain's most pressing economic and social problems, especially the land question. The agrarian problem, especially in the south, had been a cancer eating up Spanish society for generations. The republican cabinets utterly failed to carry out the meaningful and timely reforms that might have stabilized rural Spanish society and begun the healing process so desperately needed.

The elections of February 1936, owing to peculiar features of the electoral laws, exaggerated the strength of the radical parties. Immediately after the elections, the country was again plunged into civil violence (much of it, indeed, provoked by the new fascist party, the Falange, under the leadership of the young son of former dictator Primo de Rivera). As Salvador de Madariaga has written, "the country had entered into a plainly revolutionary phase. Neither life nor property was safe anywhere."

In light of the distressing record of the republic for the previous five years, and the prospect of more years of the same, the rising of the army leaders in 1936 (among whom Francisco Franco would soon emerge as dominant) is hardly surprising. Indeed, it was in the long tradition of Spain's military liberalism: when the civilian politicians provoke, through their incompetence and cupidity, an overriding national crisis, it is the duty of the armed forces to restore order and preserve the national interest.

The Spain of the 1930s was by anybody's measure a land crying out for sensible, serious, and visible reformation—political, economic, social, and psychological. The essence of the Spanish tragedy lies perhaps in this: those who wanted to change the old Spain either did not have a clear picture of where they wanted to go, or had not the faintest idea how to proceed, or else confused reform with vendettas against personal and institutional enemies.

Before the outbreak of the civil war in 1936, neither the communists nor the fascists enjoyed mass support. When the fighting began, the situation changed drastically. For a number of reasons—the growing dependence of the republican government at Madrid on Russian aid, and the confusion and fatuousness of the anarchists—the Communist party soon became the dominant element in the republican coalition, especially with regard to military affairs. This increasingly visible communist direction of the republican effort certainly did no harm to the Franco cause.

On the other side, the Falangists flourished because they were the only pro-Franco group that had even the rudiments of a twentieth-century ideology. Although Franco recognized the need for the kind of ideological infrastructure that the Falangists could provide for his assault on the Madrid government, the Falangists were never strong in the army officer corps or in the fanatically Catholic areas of the peasant north. The Falangist experience helpfully points out how dangerously simplistic it is to view "fascism" and "the Right" as if they were in any way interchangeable. The Falange was always in a state of exasperated competition with monarchist and Catholic traditionalist groups (all supporting Franco); José Antonio Primo de Rivera, moreover, the founder of the Falange, paid a visit to Hitler's Germany in 1934 and came back full of foreboding and distaste for what he had found there. There was hardly more uniformity or agreement on the Franco side than there was within the republican phalanx before or during the civil war.

The bitter complexities of the Spanish civil war are endless. The Madrid government, which relied heavily on the anarchists while falling more and more under communist direction, also enjoyed the support of the most intensely Catholic region in Spain, the Basque provinces. (The Basque front was starved of supplies and finally betrayed by Madrid on the grounds that no true Catholics could possibly be reliable republicans.) On the other hand, antediluvian monarchists and sophisticated, modernizing fascists were grouped uncomfortably together under the direction of a professional officer corps whose political attitudes (as well as military tactics) belonged to the nineteenth century. A crowning, tragic irony of the "nationalist" cause was the reliance by Franco, the ardent nationalist and Christian patriot, on Moorish as well as German and Italian troops.

The horrors of the Spanish civil war shocked a world that had not yet experienced Hitlerism nor understood Stalinism. Red terror within the republican areas was matched by white terror behind the nationalist lines. The killing went on even after the triumph of Franco's forces; the Italian foreign minister, Count Ciano, was shocked at the number of executions carried out during the summer after the end of the war. (Of course, nobody can tell what the republicans would have done to their enemies had they won.)

The vast bloodbath during and after the civil war had profound political effects. It bolstered the solidarity of the army; if the Franco cause were anything but just, then all the executions would be nothing but murders. Hence the Franco regime was by definition utterly just. The army was also politicized more than ever; in effect, it became an armed party of the elite. The numerous killings also severely thinned the ranks of the opposition and left the survivors cowed and the Spanish masses yearning for peace and quiet. The most powerful support (next to the army) for Franco came from the longing of Spaniards to avoid a repetition of one of Europe's most ghastly civil wars.

Some Conclusions

The tragic history of modern Spain seems to show that democratic institutions can be worse than authoritarianism when they are imposed on a society that is not ready for them, especially when the arts of compromise are stunted or absent. Specifically, Spain's experience shows that democratic elections are dangerous—even fatal—when the losers (the radicals of 1933 or the conservatives in 1936) are unwilling to accept the results. Franco's army and its allies did not overthrow a functioning democracy. Far from it. The short-lived republic of the 1930s was inspired primarily by anarchists, communists, revolutionary socialists, Carlists, fascists, and militarists. These and the pseudo-democratic opportunists in the Radical and Catholic parties constituted a majority of the politically active, a majority whose attitudes toward democracy ran the range from cynical manipulation to ferocious rejection.

The Franco regime, despite the vicissitudes of three and a half decades of power, corresponded to the fascist model in a number of respects, especially in its opposition to class struggle, its profound hostility to communism, its rejection of Western parliamentary democracy, and the presence of an official government party with a fascistic ideology.

Nevertheless, Franco's Spain was one of the least "fascist" of the fascist regimes. All fascist regimes are coalitions of one sort or another, but the Spanish fascist party, the Falange, remained a very junior partner in the Franco coalition. Spanish fascism never had a chance to get off the ground before it was swept up in the maelstrom of civil war and army dictation. The Spanish army was one of the most traditional forces in Europe (as was another major partner in the Franco coalition, the church). In an important sense, the regime had been frozen for years. Franco and many of his intimates had fairly well formed their political opinions in the 1920s and within a Spanish army context; they were Hispanic militarists, not fascists, as that term is used in this book. Their principal purpose was not mass mobilization but the depoliticization of the masses. In short, the Falange had the appearance rather than the substance of strength.

It is by no means certain that this generation of Spaniards has learned from the mistakes of the past any more than other peoples have learned from their mistakes. A chapter in the history of Spanish fascism has drawn to a close; it is unclear whether it will be the last chapter.

6. European Variants: Eastern Europe

*Truth does not do as much good as
the semblance of truth does evil.*
—La Rochefoucauld

Just as communism is placed on the "extreme left," fascism has often been described as a movement of the "extreme right." To the degree that such a formulation is helpful, it implies that fascism is the opposite of communism. All fascists must be conservative or reactionary (and all reactionaries must be fascist). Such dichotomies leave us completely unprepared to cope with the phenomenon of antiestablishment or revolutionary fascism.

Must Fascism Be Conservative?

It goes against the grain (and not just for Marxists) to employ concepts such as "revolutionary fascism" and "antioligarchical fascism." The difficulty probably lies in fascist attitudes toward private property in those societies in which they came to power, especially Italy and Germany: no wholesale expropriations, no confiscations (except for Jews). There are two explanations (at least) for the differences between fascist and communist attitudes toward private property. First, fascist regimes have historically come to power in coalition with some of the dominant groups in the prefascist power arrangement; thus, fascists have not always been in a position to do all that they might like to do. Second, fascists have often had a much clearer idea of the efficacy of political power per se than Marxists have had. In other words, what does it matter who "owns" the factories or the newspapers as long as the state has ultimate control over what is produced or what is printed?

This is an important consideration, because of the well-known tendency to place fascism "on the right" and therefore identify it as conservative. In reality, the identification between fascism and conservatism is very misleading. Fascists have come to power in alliance with conservative forces because both have perceived themselves to have common enemies: usually an internal revolutionary movement based on class war or regional separatism. Fascism's hostility to parties and groups emphasizing internal divisions and internal struggle—especially Marxist class war—has turned it (at least in Western Europe) to an alliance with more conservative elements. Conservatives and reactionaries, on the other hand, have often mistaken the real nature of fascism. As one scholar has put it:

> Fascism is inherently revolutionary, not conservative, although conservatives might see in it, and did see in it, various components which were attractive to them. The fascist emphasis on hierarchy, on order, on believing and obeying, induced conservatives to hope that the fascist revolution was actually nothing other than a reinforcement of the traditional order, especially when fascist movements came to the fore during a time when openly radical egalitarian movements, contemptuous of the traditional hierarchies, were challenging the status quo in several countries.[1]

The real ability of fascism to assume an antiestablishment, even a revolutionary, role is well illustrated by the less familiar fascist parties of Eastern Europe in the 1920s and 1930s. In the social systems of post–World War I Hungary and Rumania (as elsewhere in Eastern Europe with the notable and noble exception of Czechoslovakia), an educated, quasi-modernized class (landowners, middle sectors, and bureaucracy) ruled over a quite backward mass of peasants and a smaller number of workers—with the aid of an energetic police force. Corruption, exploitation, hatred, and violence were the distinguishing features of political life in these countries. The conservatives, who benefitted from and upheld this arrangement, were opposed not so much by the communists, who were small and discredited, but by radicals of another stripe: fascists, often organized and led by underemployed, romantic young intellectuals.

Anti-Semitism

Nationalism and social reform were the key elements of the Eastern European fascist formula, and a rabid anti-Semitism was the link between the two.

The relationship between Central and Eastern European Jewry and the dominant groups in their respective societies was a long and complicated one. It was also potentially explosive, and the fact that the fascists discovered the appeal of anti-Semitism is indicative of no special political acumen on their part. One historian has pointed out that "the consciousness that Jews were not merely a religious community but a people had been roused just as much by Zionism as by anti-Semitism"—a decisive factor in states such as Hungary, Poland, and Rumania, where nationality questions had for decades had a fiery intensity.

In Rumania, the communists were identified with Russian expansionism, and both of these with Jewishness, since a majority of communist leaders seemed to be Jews. Equally menacing for Rumanian Jews was the fact that by 1918 most banking and industry was in Jewish hands. In Hungary, Jews tended to dominate the professions and made up a fifth of the population of "wicked Budapest." They were also seen, with justification, as closely linked with the Hungarian aristocracy: "The conservatives needed and got Jewish capital for their enterprises and estates, Jewish loans for their speculations; they had no intention of upsetting existing property arrangements in order to confiscate Jewish property. There was no knowing the effects of such gestures. The radical right, on the other hand, were as ready to get rid of the Jews as the Communists were to get rid of the capitalists, and for the same reason: the radical right saw the Jews as barring the way."[2]

Hungary

World War I was very hard on Hungary. It was sundered from its long union with Austria, stripped of two-thirds of its former territories, and reduced to the status of a third-rate power. Nor was this all: the peace treaties placed hundreds of thousands of Hungarians inside the newly formed or newly enlarged states of Yugoslavia, Czechoslovakia, and Rumania, under the dominance of their former subjects. Many of these Hungarians caught on the wrong side of the border—teachers, soldiers, bureaucrats—left the lost territories to settle in the rump Hungarian state. These displaced persons, mainly of the middle classes, helped keep Hungarian politics volatile during the years between the world wars, and the drive to restore Hungary to its "rightful position" was a major theme of Hungarian politics during all that time.

In interwar Hungary, the landowning magnates still dominated. They ruled the countryside through such devices as the open ballot and vigorous employment of the police. Admiral Horthy established a conservative military regime, which, like its Habsburg predecessors, eschewed vulgar anti-Semitism. Indeed, Jewish entrepreneurs often married into the great landowning families and were able to exercise a share of real power. The rabid Jew-baiting of the Hungarian fascists was thus correctly understood as an implicit but profound attack on the Horthy regime, the magnates, and the whole class system. It has often been pointed out that the conflict between the Horthy establishment and the fascists was to a large degree a manifestation of class struggle. This was true not only because of the ferocious anti-Semitism of the Hungarian fascist groups. It was also true because the more "natural" class struggle—that between the aristocratic-military regime and the urban working class—was toned down considerably in postwar Hungary when the Horthy regime agreed to allow the socialists to organize trade unions and engage in collective bargaining; in exchange, the socialists restricted their activity to the cities and left government employees, railwaymen, and rural laborers alone. In fascist eyes, therefore, Hungary was ruled by an unholy alliance of aristocrats, Jews, and socialists and was obviously in need of a thorough and bloody cleaning out.

Gyula Gombos, calling his movement "national socialism" as early as 1919, was openly hostile to the upper classes; in 1932 he headed the first Hungarian cabinet to contain not a single nobleman. But the principal Hungarian fascist group was the Arrow Cross party of Ferencz Szalasi, who called for a restoration of Great Hungary, abolition of "money capitalism," and stripping privileges from the clergy. Like almost all East European fascists, he also identified capitalism with the Jews. So Byzantine were the politics of Hungary during these years that in the elections of 1940 Szalasi received the support of the communists. He finally achieved the premiership through German pressure in 1944, just before the invasion of Hungary by the Red Army; by this time, many persons were convinced that he had gone completely mad.

The various Hungarian fascist parties, especially the National Socialists, had real aspirations toward social reform and even social revolution. Their formula was anti-Semitism for the middle classes and radicalism for the workers. Many who in some other country would have become socialists or communists did not do so in Hungary because they identified those parties with Jews and internationalism. They thus turned to the fascists.

Rumania

The factors that in Western Europe produced an alliance between fascists and conservatives were not operative in Rumania. One noted scholar, regarding what became known as the Iron Guard, has emphasized

> its success in a society very different from those of the West and Central European lands where fascism first appeared and prospered: a peasant country, underdeveloped, underindustrialized, where no working class parties threatened the vested interests of the bourgeoisie, where the bourgeoisie itself in its classic industrial and commercial form was weak or absent, where nationalism was not an issue of party

politics but part of the general consensus, and where therefore a radical nationalist political movement could not succeed either by recruiting nationalists against anti-nationalists or by mobilizing social reactionaries against organized workers, because there were neither antination-alists nor organized workers to justify such appeals.[3]

Post-1918 Rumania had many problems. It had doubled its territory as a result of the war, but its population was highly unintegrated, and its territorial gains had earned it the enmity of reactionary Hungary and revolutionary Russia. The bulk of the population was a submerged peasant class, ruled by corrupt overlords. Interwar Rumanian politics was often suggestive of a comic opera as conceived by Ivan the Terrible.

In the 1930s, the principal expression of fascism in Rumania was the Iron Guard, led by young intellectuals from the provinces. It combined a particularly morose Christian pseudo-mysticism with bloodthirstiness: assassination was a specialty. The Iron Guard sought to reach and mobilize the peasantry, preaching that a new day was at hand, that a world of cynicism and corruption would be replaced by another in which men would be ranked and judged not by birth or wealth but by their souls. Its principal spokesman, C. Z. Codreanu, was a genuine radical, and he was angrily aware of how often chauvinism had been used as a screen to hide social injustice. He excoriated the "oligarchical and tyrannous class" that intoned "endless appeals to the Fatherland which it does not love, to God in Whom it does not believe, to the Church where it never sets foot, to the Army which it sends to war with empty hands." The young idealists of the Iron Guard took their program of social renewal very seriously: land reform, cleaning up corruption, and the elimination of Jews. The relations between the Guard and the Rumanian establishment often resembled civil war; in 1938 the government of King Carol had most of the leaders arrested, and almost all of them were shot "while trying to escape."

Rumanian-style fascism emphasized populism rather

than Marxism, moral reform rather than historical determinism. It clothed itself in the robes of religion and
patriotism and castigated the wealthy while rejecting
communism as foreign (Russian, Semitic). It was on a
program quite similar to this that General Rojas came
within a sword's breadth of being elected president of
Colombia in 1970. Such programs seem especially well
suited to many of those developing societies that, for one
reason or another, lack a significant indigenous Communist
party.

Part Two

In this part of the book, we will examine the main currents of Third World politics: the search for political stability and the demand for economic development. Then, in brief studies of six countries, we will look at regimes that bear an unmistakable resemblance to Mussolini's fascism. No regime will be an exact replica, of course, but the similarities in ideological orientation and exercise of authority are clear.

These are not causal analyses; not enough is known about fascism for that. But two important points, at least, emerge with great clarity. The first is that fascist beliefs and forms emerge in a diversity of circumstances—from Latin America in the 1940s to the Middle East in the 1950s to West Africa in the 1960s—and have used as a vehicle either the charismatic leader, the military junta, or a combination of these.

A second important point is that in all of these countries the prefascist period resembled prefascist Italy in notable and suggestive ways, especially in (1) pressures arising from economic modernization in a condition of competitive inferiority, (2) incomplete national integration, and (3) unsuccessful experiments with Western-type political institutions.

7. Modernization: The Challenge

Mankind needs government.
—Bertrand Russell

Most of the Third World is usually described as going through "modernization," which is defined as "the process by which historically evolved institutions are adapted to the rapidly changing functions that reflect the unprecedented increase in man's knowledge, permitting control over his environment, that accompanied the scientific revolution."[1]

Modernization can be considered in a number of respects. One is the psychological upheaval that modernization exacts. Man in premodernizing society, "traditional man," lived in a universe that was in many fundamental ways unchanging. Perhaps more accurately, his universe was a cyclical one: everything had been seen before. (That is probably one good reason why in most traditional societies the aged were held in high esteem: having seen the past, they had seen the future, and their wisdom was thus to be sought out.) Nothing could contrast more with modern man than traditional man's attitude toward change, its possibility, its desirability, and its scope. Modern man not only expects change, he tries to control it or organize it to his own good. Human events are not cyclical but move in a fairly straight path (upward or downward depending on one's quotient of pessimism), this movement can be understood, and it calls for adaptation on the part of the individual. For a traditional society to undergo modernization, then, means in no small part the disruption of traditional forms and beliefs, with all the attendant psychological consequences, most of which can only be speculated upon. Traditional forms of association and status break down under the impact of modernization; the family retreats in upon itself, and vital and fundamental social links such as those of tribe or caste or religion may be weakened. Thus, "the individual is less under the domination of his environment in modern than in traditional societies, and to this extent he is freer, but at the same time he is less certain of his purpose and in times of great unrest is prepared to surrender his freedom in the interest of purposeful leadership." Some students of society have noted that this same phenomenon, the desire for an "escape from freedom," has been characteristic even of (or especially of) "modernized" societies as well. In any case, there can be no doubt that the passing of traditional society requires a great deal of psychological reorientation; such a process is never without pain.

The Impact of the West

The process of modernization was introduced into the Third World from the West, especially Western Europe, and mainly after the middle of the nineteenth century. Some societies fell directly under the political control of more advanced countries, forming parts of the British or French empires or coming under the sway of the Netherlands, Germany, or Italy. This was the fate of India, Egypt, North Africa, and sub-Saharan Africa, and most of the Middle East and Southeast Asia. Other countries, such as Turkey, Japan, China, and Thailand, were able to preserve their political independence to a greater or lesser degree while carrying out modernization on their own. This latter group of countries exemplifies "defensive modernization," the attempt, under state control, to bring political, economic, and military structures up to par with the more advanced West in order to avoid the onrush of imperialism. Defensive modernization, an aspect of the reactive nationalism that eventually was to sweep the entire Third World, was basically an attempt to safeguard existing, premodern political arrangements through economic (and to a lesser degree social) modernization.

The concept of defensive modernization brings out two important points. First, it would be very deceptive to interpret the process of modernization as being one of Westernization; that is, it is quite possible for today's modernizing countries to adapt themselves to revolutionary economic changes without necessarily producing political forms analogous to Western constitutional democracy. Two of the most prominent examples—the Soviet Union on one hand and prewar Japan on the other—demonstrate conclusively that economic modernization can be combined with a variety of nondemocratic political structures and processes. Second, it is equally misleading to conceive of the West as completely modernized, the end of the line of the modernizing process. Rather than viewing the West as the end point to which all modernizing countries, even communist ones, are inexorably if slowly drawing near, it is probably more accurate to conceive of all this planet's societies as constantly engaged in the process of modernization, some at more advanced stages than others, but all caught up in a complex process whose end is by no means in sight.

The Meaning of Modernization

In discussing modernization, it is customary to distinguish two sets of societies, one called "modern" and the other "traditional," separated from each other by a vast gulf. Modernization is then seen as the bridge between these two different sets; it is the passage across the gulf between tradition and modernity. Such a conceptualization is not entirely false and is indeed useful, but it can also be misleading.

The terms *traditional society* and *modern society* are first of all exceedingly broad and mask a number of important divergences within each category. *Modern society,* for example, includes both the Soviet Union and the United States, as well as Switzerland. More to the point, *traditional society* includes such diverse entities as the Roman Empire, the Athens of Pericles, fifteenth-century China, present-day Somalia, Tokugawa Japan, rural Quebec, the pygmy tribe, and village India. Traditional societies have one thing in common—they are not modern—but they display striking differences among themselves as a class, differences even more striking, perhaps, than those found in the category of modern societies.

The strict dichotomy between tradition and modernity is often empirically false. Many traditional societies have had elements of modernity. Several hundred years ago, the Chinese were filling important offices through civil service examinations that were open and competitive; and the empire of Augustus displayed an ability to mobilize men and materiel on a scale and with an efficiency that quite escape all but a handful of today's modern states. On the other hand, all "modern" societies continue to display many attributes usually labeled traditional: racial and ethnic rivalries, for instance, in the United States or in Ulster. Such ancient institutions as the Roman Catholic church seem much more influential in modernized Holland than in traditional Sicily or Andalusia. Indeed, the durability of tradition—the ability of so many aspects of traditional society to survive and adapt and even flourish in modern society—has been demonstrated in contemporary Japan, in the relationship between political mobilization and the caste system in democratic India, indeed everywhere. According to a leading student of modernization, "Modern society is not simply modern: it is modern *and* traditional. . . . In addition, one can go further and argue that not only coexistence is possible but that modernization itself may strengthen tradition; tribal and other ascriptive 'traditional' identities may be invigorated in a way which would never have happened in traditional society."[2]

The interpenetration of tradition and modernity occurs on a number of levels. Modernization is not a homogeneous experience for a society; various parts advance at various paces. Consequently, most modernizing societies today are often called "dual societies," with modern and traditional as well as transitional sectors all contained within the national borders. The economy of southeastern Brazil, for example, dominated by bustling Rio and São Paulo, could certainly not be classified as traditional. Yet a few miles from these cities can be found whole communities who live as their ancestors lived several centuries ago. And along with dusty villages suggestive of time before written history, India boasts literally millions of citizens who, in their educational, occupational, and attitudinal characteristics, are as modern as any. Even in modern societies, large areas preserve tradition to a marked degree; one thinks of parts of the American South, certain English counties, or those sections of northern Italy that preserve a nineteenth-century, rural way of life almost within sight of the air pollution over Milan.

Like societies, individuals are neither perfectly traditional nor perfectly modern. Few men living today are totally untouched by modernity; probably even fewer are completely void of traditional sentiments, aspirations, or patterns of behavior. This is of peculiar importance in modernizing societies; the process of modernization is not homogeneous in the society as a whole, nor is it homogeneous within the individuals who make up the society. Political groups in the Third World, government and opposition alike, who seek to a greater or lesser degree to modernize their countries still retain much of the traditional culture of their societies, whether they are conscious of it or not.

Poverty

For many, the most striking aspect of modernizing societies is their poverty: specifically, the poverty of the traditional areas within those societies. This is perhaps especially true of India, parts of the Middle East and sub-Saharan Africa, and most of Latin America. Indeed, the dichotomy between the modern and traditional areas of the globe is well expressed in the phrase, "the rich nations and the poor nations."

Obviously, poverty is not new. If poverty is defined as the lack of those things necessary to maintain a modest level of physical and intellectual well-being, then the Third World, indeed the whole world, has for the most part been poor since time immemorial. Even when the West was going through the first stages of modernization, its great cities contained slums that would rival all but the very worst in Third World cities. What is new, though, is the desire to escape from poverty, the spreading conception that such an escape is not only possible, but that it can be effected through political action. The revolt against poverty, a revolt that is seething throughout the Third World, is a consequence of spreading modernization, a consequence of contact between pre-modern (and therefore usually quite poor) societies and modernized societies. What has often been called the "international demonstration effect" means that poor peoples are made painfully aware of their poverty relative to large groups of persons living in unpoor—modern—societies. It is this contrast that accentuates the poverty of the Third World, and it is also this contrast that makes modernization in most Third World countries seem so terribly slow and difficult. The demand that Third World countries should traverse the road to modernity rapidly is the most important source of the political unrest that makes many Third World countries so explosive.

The frustration of being premodern in a modern world manifests itself in many ways, including the currently fashionable tendency to blame the poverty of the Third World exclusively or primarily on the West. This tendency is frequently a variation on one of two main themes: (1) Western imperialism looted the Third World and reduced it to its present poverty, or (2) the efforts of the Third World to escape from its age-old condition have been systematically stymied by Western economic exploitation (neocolonialism) backed up when necessary by the overt use of military force.

This line of thinking has many adherents, in the West as well as in the Third World, for complex reasons. First, although such arguments suffer from the weaknesses inherent in all single-factor explanations of complex phenomena, they are not without some truth. The question of whether, and to what degree, poor countries actually suffer from economic relations with rich countries is a complicated and most controversial question, but it does seem to be an inescapable conclusion that, at various times and in various places, there have been and are today clear instances of direct and blatant profiteering by some

Westerners from non-Western poverty. Moreover, traditional theories of international trade and its presumed benefits to
all involved are being revised along lines that emphasize the
built-in, increasing, and to a degree unavoidable disadvan-
tages for producers of primary products vis-à-vis suppliers of
sophisticated finished goods.

However, real, even numerous, examples of exploitation
do not justify a rigid and total explanation of Third World
poverty as the result of Western economic imperialism. The
fact that taxi drivers profit from rainstorms does not prove
that taxi drivers cause rainstorms. Economic exploitation is
often at least as much an effect as a cause of the backwardness
of many Third World countries. To blame all or most of
these countries' troubles on a handful of Western nations,
furthermore, is not only subtly demeaning of non-
Westerners; it also betrays a desire to ignore the indigenous
factors—political, cultural, and economic—that exert powerful influence in the Third World in directions counter to
economic modernization. It is also self-serving for some
Third World leaders: it exculpates dogmatic theorists,
incompetent windbags, epauleted megalomaniacs, and
"village tyrants" from all responsibility for the deplorable
condition of their suffering countrymen even after two
decades—or two centuries or two millenia—of political
independence. "The tutelary powers," in the words of C. E.
Black, "have borne a heavy burden of criticism, but since
their departure it has become increasingly clear that the
obstacles to modernization in these societies should be
sought primarily in the traditional heritage of resources and
institutions." We will now examine some of the elements in
this "traditional heritage."

Poverty: Some Internal Factors

Third World countries are poor by any standard, relative
or absolute. However, they are not poor by definition; that is,
one need only look at Denmark or Iowa to realize that rural
societies can attain a high level of well-being. Much of the
Third World is impoverished not because most of these
countries are agrarian or pastoral, but because the resources

necessary for a healthy agrarian economy are missing. For many countries (especially those on the rim of the Sahara), their climate and soil (and the absence of any known valuable mineral deposits) have damned them to poverty, in spite of any effort, or lack of effort, by the industrialized world or by these poverty-ridden countries themselves. Owing to the imperious decree of nature, some of the peoples of the planet are going to remain poor, come revolution, Marshall Plan, or whatever.

The presence or absence of natural resources, however, is but a small part of the story of poverty. Japan has few mineral resources but still has become the first (and so far the only) non-Western nation to build a modern economy. On the other hand, the untold natural riches of Indonesia have not made the Indonesians rich. Oil will not make the average Arab well to do, any more than it has made the average Venezuelan—or the average Texan—well to do. In order to come to grips with the poverty of nations, its origins, its continuance, and its prospects, one must confront the human factor. Most of the poverty of the Third World is man-made.

Important groups (almost always a landed aristocracy and an organized religion) have historically been, and in many instances still are, opposed to economic change because of the political and social consequences they foresee. No country in the world is so miserable, so poverty-stricken, that it does not have some groups that benefit from the misery and poverty. As far as these groups are concerned (and they are correct), serious changes in their environment would seriously diminish their prestige and power. Thus the mandarins of late nineteenth-century China resisted Western ways because these would bring an end to their status, which was based on their monopoly of classic Chinese culture. Similarly, chiefs and tribal elders from the Kurdish wilds to central Ghana have set their faces against the introduction of destabilizing changes from the outside.

Latin America offers us some important lessons in this matter. In a real sense, Latin America's economic difficulties have their roots in the wars of independence that were waged in the first quarter of the last century. Many of these Latin American "revolutions" were really to defend the privileges of the creoles or to place the creoles in the privileged positions to which they aspired. Quite a few of these revolutions, that is, were conservative revolutions, opposing changes imposed by or about to be imposed by Bourbon Spain. According to one student of the subject, "Bourbon policy was a great miscalculation, out of touch with the time, the people, and the place. And its social and racial liberalism, or relative liberalism, was powerless to impose itself—a kind of enlightenment without despotism— provoking the privileged without protecting the poor. This drew from America responses which outlived the colonial regime, a hardening of attitudes toward labor, race, and class, which left its imprint in the new nations for generations to come."[3]

In most instances, those who won the Latin American revolutionary wars wanted to stop change, to preserve, indeed to accentuate, the deprivations of the lower classes. They succeeded. Consequently, decades before the United States assumed the role of a great world economic power, nearly a dozen societies below the Rio Grande were ruled by those who were committed to preserving the status quo, committed to preserving mass illiteracy and poverty.

Similarly, in most African countries, including the very poorest, there is a sizable elite, composed of government figures, party leaders, high-ranking military officers, and the numerous relatives of all these, who enjoy extraordinarily large salaries and perquisites. Ruth First, in *Power in Africa,* points out that the leaders of African independence movements wasted no time in assuming the privileges of the former white colonial overlords. The consequences of all this have been unconducive, to say the least, to African economic progress. "In 1964, in the fourteen former French colonies, six times as much was spent in importing alcoholic drink as in importing fertilizer."

Cultural Obstacles to Development

Most of the Third World is dominated by religious-cultural systems (Hinduism, Hispanic Catholicism, Islam) that have not encouraged rational and sustained activity in the direction of mass literacy and the application of technology to improve the masses' consumption standards. On the contrary, whatever their other merits—theological, psychological, or social—may have been, the great religions of the Middle East, North Africa, India, and Latin America have acted as serious hindrances to economic and political modernization. Normally, they have not only accepted the socioeconomic status quo—they have also glorified it.

Clan loyalties and suspicions, as well as tribal, religious, and regional animosities, make it difficult or impossible to achieve that cooperation so necessary to serious efforts at economic development. One need not marvel at the divisions among the Latin Americans or the Africans. Europe's record of hatreds and bloodlettings among peoples of the same racial, linguistic, and religious tradition is a staggering monument to man's desire to divide and murder his own species. In the Third World, however, internal divisions of this kind are aggravated by several factors, such as the heterogeneity of the population within given state bounda- ries. It must be kept in mind that the boundaries of almost all African and most Middle Eastern states, for example, were drawn in London, Brussels, and Paris by a handful of diplomats and soldiers who cared and knew little of such things as cultural unity and diversity in the subject areas. The independent states inherited these artificial boundaries and the internal rivalries and hatreds that went with them. (In some places, of course, such as Ethiopia, internal ethnic discord is the result of imperial and repressive policies on the part of the indigenous government.) And, of course, there is a complete rejection of anything like boundary rectification: each state is too afraid it might lose something. It is as if some galactic power had carved out a new country from German, Polish, and Russian territories and then expected the peoples within it to live in cooperation and harmony. The well-publicized guerrilla and secessionist movements in such places as Iraq, Ethiopia, Chad, the former Congo, and the Sudan illustrate the failure of integrative attempts.

On the Latin American continent, the vastness of a Brazil or the difficulties of interregional communications in a Colombia are complicated by what many believe to be widespread cultural traits: rampant individualism, fatalism, an attachment to hierarchy, a belief that land is the only real wealth. One should not ignore the great gulf between Latins and Indians in Ecuador, Guatemala, or Peru. It becomes evident that the mystery is not that so many of these countries have made so little economic progress; rather, the mystery is how they have managed to make the significant progress that many of them have made in the face of so many heartbreaking obstacles.

Population Growth

Then there is the well-known population problem. The introduction of certain simple techniques has drastically lowered the death rate all over the Third World. There has not been a corresponding decline in the birthrate. Thus, significant increases in production are required just to maintain the present low standard of living for the bulk of the population. This is difficult enough in itself, but the popular demand is not for maintenance of the present standards but for their drastic improvement.

North Americans tend to have a profound faith in the possibility of overcoming all obstacles, no matter how gigantic, through education. The schoolroom and the lecture hall are the chapels of the religion of progress. One finds, however (as one might expect), that on the educational front as well as in most other places, the battle goes badly. From Lima to Delhi, Third World universities turn out primarily lawyers, philosophers, litterateurs, and social critics, many of whom are soon forced to join the ranks of the intellectual proletariat. Even those who graduate with technical skills of a high order often cannot find scope for their talents in their own countries or do not wish to practice their professions in environments they consider too unrewarding or unresponsive. Primary education also leaves something to be desired. Frequently, what the teacher passes on to the pupil are precisely the traditional values that block the road to modernization. It is not the poverty of the schoolroom but the poverty of the instruction, both in form and content, that makes a significant contribution to stagnation and even retrogression.

Agriculture: The Heart of the Matter

The great majority of Third World inhabitants earn their living from agriculture, usually under primitive and laborious conditions that produce meager results. The backwardness and poverty of the rural population make these countries poor. They also help keep them poor: because of agricultural backwardness and rural stagnation, the young pour out of the rural areas and into the slums of the great cities. Finally, they help to produce an outflow of a good part of what little wealth exists in the rural areas to economically more dynamic regions both inside and outside the national boundaries. If these countries are to modernize, therefore, profound changes must occur in the rural sector.

For most of the countries of the Third World, the only realistic strategy to deal with poverty is to improve agricultural productivity. This is so for positive and negative reasons. Positively, it is most often in agriculture that the most significant short-term and intermediate-term improvements can be made. Negatively, there are no other alternatives for most of these countries, whose economic modernization will long require the importation of materials and skills from the more advanced areas of the globe. Since massive and sustained foreign aid seems out of the question, these imports will have to be paid for—paid for out of what the importing country can produce from its own soil. In other words, economic improvement in the Third World requires investment, and investment requires a surplus of production over consumption. Consumption levels (at least for the mass of the population) are already desperately low, and long-term and intermediate-term economic improvement therefore means that the surplus for investment will have to come largely from an increase in agricultural output—which will be sold for the material and skills needed to diversify and modernize the economy. (Poor countries are obviously caught in something of a dilemma: to raise agricultural output significantly usually requires a combination of good fertilizer, mechanical equipment, efficient methods of labor, technical advice and supervision, and credit. But if the modernizing country had these things to invest in agriculture, it would already be modernized to a large degree.)

The modernization of the agricultural sector, of such crucial importance, thus runs into many obstructions. Agricultural reform is most often taken to mean land redistribution—giving ownership of the land, through one means or another, to those who have tilled it while paying rent to others, usually to a landed aristocracy. Naturally enough, landowners make the laws and administer them. Some Americans propose land redistribution in order to prevent revolution. No class is as conservative as a landowning peasantry, to be sure, but the case is that land reform would *be* the revolution.

Since the end of World War II, a number of countries have embarked upon programs of land reform that have proven more or less spurious. Less desirable lands have been transferred at high rates of compensation, and even much of this has eventually been recovered by the original owners by chicane. Such maneuverings are facilitated by the fact that, where the legislators and servants of the state are not drawn from the landed aristocracy, they are drawn from the urban middle classes, who identify with the aristocracy and disdain the peasant and everything associated with him, including the unglamorous tasks involved in making land reform a success (this is especially so in Latin America). The land and the peasant are ungenteel subjects with which gentlemen do not concern themselves overmuch.

Even in the few instances where a meaningful and bona fide land reform has been carried out, grave and innumerable problems persist. The immediate results of distributing land to peasant tillers often seems to be a drop in productivity, for a whole host of reasons, including peasant lack of sophistication and the loss of capital and contacts once supplied by the aristocrats. These disappointing short-term results seem to "prove" that land reform is a pipe dream, a dissipation of the resources of the country into the hands of the ignorant, the lazy, and the stupid. It is not enough to hand the peasant proprietor a title deed; he needs credit with which to purchase supplies, often long-term credit, while he develops some of the initiative and self-reliance that generations and generations of servitude and humiliation have taken from him and his people. He needs instruction in scientific agricultural techniques. He needs churches, schools, roads, and places of recreation and companionship to help him make progress toward a better life, to keep him from sinking back into resignation and apathy, to keep his sons from seeking escape in the direction of the colored lights of the cities. Probably few things besides the discovery of oil can start a society off toward political stability and economic modernization like a satisfied, independent peasantry; few such desirable conditions encounter so many frustrating obstacles.

Perhaps all that can be said with any degree of certitude about the agricultural problems of the Third World is that improvement is going to take a very long time. Consequently, for those numerous societies that must work themselves out of the mire of poverty through agricultural regeneration, the road ahead is discouragingly long and uncertain.

The Necessity of State Action

However difficult it may be to see the road ahead, to know what to do, it is clear that no road will be traversed, no roadblocks dismantled, no lasting accomplishments attained, without the erection of a stable political structure that can gather information, make decisions, and allocate men and material in the pursuit of rational societal goals. In the words of one distinguished scholar, "The economic aspect of modernization has been so dramatic that many have regarded it as the central and determining force in this process. In fact, however, economic development depends to a great extent on the intellectual and political aspects of the process, the growth in knowledge and the ability of political leaders to mobilize resources."[4] From a different perspective, A. F. K. Organski, though often dubbed an economic determinist, has maintained that "some foundation for national unification is necessary before economic modernization can proceed very far, and though the new governments of the underdeveloped world may talk economic development *ad nauseam,* many of their actions can best be understood if they are seen as steps toward the creation of national unity."

Obviously, economic modernization and political development are not the same thing. The political power of a stable regime will not necessarily advance economic and social modernization. More to the point, economic development very often brings political instability. "Social and economic changes—urbanization, increases in literacy and education, industrialization, mass media expansion—extend political consciousness, multiply political demands, broaden political participation. These changes undermine traditional sources of political authority and traditional political institutions." They do not necessarily point the way toward effective, more modern political institutions. Indeed, the "primary problem of politics is the lag in the development of political institutions behind social and economic change."[5]

The decline of traditional political power (exercised by king, priest, and landlord, in various combinations and guises) is in large part the result of economic and social change. Continued economic and social change—to the point of achieving those benefits known in shorthand as modernity—requires the erection of a modern state, an apparatus to maintain order, dispense justice, plan, foresee, organize, and distribute. For modernizing countries, "the primary problem is not liberty but the creation of a legitimate public order. Men may, of course, have order without liberty, but they cannot have liberty without order." One of the most distinguished students of political modernization, Samuel P. Huntington, has stated the issue with bluntness and clarity: "The most important political distinction among countries concerns not their form of government but their degree of government. The differences between democracy and dictatorship are less than the differences between those countries whose politics embodies consensus, community, legitimacy, organization, effectiveness, stability, and those countries whose politics is deficient in these qualities."[6]

To build up a politically developed state, then, one that can cope with the challenges of modernization and make cogent responses to them, is an undertaking of the highest priority.

Obstacles in the Way of Building Effective States

First among the difficulties frequently encountered in trying to establish institutions that can carry on, however minimally, the vitally important functions of government is, of course, the lack (sometimes an almost complete absence) of persons with the necessary qualifications and aptitude. Finding good men to staff a government has never been the easiest of tasks. The difficulty increases geometrically with the increase in the number and complexity of the functions performed by the state in the context of rapid social change.

Although shortages of trained manpower are the most visible handicap confronted by Third World countries in constructing viable and effective states, it should be borne in mind that any specific inadequacy is less important that the context in which modernization takes place, the context of the twentieth century. The exigencies of late modernization compel the leadership of newly emerging states to try to make rapid progress on every front, to try to accomplish in a few decades or less what has taken the West, Russia, or Japan more than a century. Erecting a state that can govern, modernizing the economy, and distributing the fruits of a modernized economy—these have to be tackled all at once, in order to lessen the perceived distance from the foreign models. Inevitably, these goals conflict. Over and above the age-old stresses and strains between security and liberty, or the necessity for the state to impose order and protect itself, on one hand, and the drive for self-expression, on the other, is an equally fundamental, and often even more irreconcilable, conflict: the conflict between the requirements of economic development and the demands for improved standards of living. Not only are these not the same thing, they are usually polar opposites.

Put very baldly, the problem is this: economic development requires savings, the investment of part of present production to create an increase in future production. Normally, this savings can only be acquired by holding down consumption levels, or even depressing them. Growing demands for health care, schools, transport, consumer goods, and a foreign policy to vindicate the national dignity or avenge historic wrongs require not a decrease, but a tremendous increase, in consumption. Third World leaders are faced with the necessity of somehow balancing these contradictory requirements. At the same time, the breakdown of traditional mores and controls, the growth of the bureaucracy, and the existence and spread of competing values provide wide scope for political corruption (or at least what is seen as corruption). This undermines the legitimacy of the modernizing regime and increases "social envy," which in turn stimulates demands for the distribution of goods and services before the economic base is able to provide them.

Owing chiefly to the international demonstration effect, the demands made upon the resources of most Third World countries are considerably greater than those made upon Britain, France, Japan, or the United States at a comparable stage of development, yet at the same time the resources available to meet these demands are grotesquely inadequate.

One aspect of the modernized West that is all too easily imported and imitated in the developing nations is political participation on a mass scale. Almost every country in the world today holds elections. In one way or another, they pay homage to the idea that citizens affirm the existence and power of the state and their attachment to it by depositing slips of paper into boxes, after having been assembled, paraded, and harangued on numerous occasions. Even in the most steely of military dictatorships, the "people" and the leadership must express their mutual esteem and confidence by visible, and often grandiose, activity. To one degree or another, political participation by the multitude has become a universal attribute of twentieth-century politics.

This fact has many negative consequences. There is often an inverse relationship between stability and participation. The reaction of the mass audience, however sophisticated or unsophisticated, becomes yet another variable in an already unwieldy equation that political leaders must try to solve. The economic modernization and political development of Britain or Japan, for instance, occurred before the age of mass participation. The multitude might indulge in inconvenient rioting now and again, but modernizing regimes in the eighteenth and nineteenth centuries had to pay serious attention to relatively few domestic voices. To a large extent, the modern economy and modern state were built before the expansion of participation. That is, when the need to respond to popular demands reached the point that it could be no longer ignored, the structures and the means with which to do so were in existence. Mass participation and political stability flourished side by side. In the Third World things are generally reversed: an interested, often clamorous, multitude alongside an unsatisfactory and deteriorating economic situation and a government constructed of cards. Political leadership in the Third World would have an immeasurably lighter burden if it had what traditional authority usually had: the uncritical acquiescence and respect of the ruled.

Mass participation specifically interferes with the modernization process in two important ways. On the one hand, it can undermine stability by stimulating demands on the government that are impossible to satisfy. This kind of participation assumes its most familiar forms in the student demonstration, the political strike, and the urban riot. Allowing for a certain degree of self-pity and self-dramatization, one cannot deny the force of the comment by Ben Bella, then the president of Algeria, who asked in 1965, "What African president has a majority behind him in his own capital?" Whatever one may think of the merits of the former Allende regime in Chile, one is forced to admit that wide suffrage in that country contributed to the stimulation of demands that were, in the Chilean context, unfulfillable and disequilibrating. Mass participation, then, often means that a modernizing regime finds itself outflanked on the left, less and less able to maintain order, and more and more vulnerable to a military coup.

Mass participation can hobble development from quite another direction. A broad electorate can be an instrument of conservatism or reaction, as was demonstrated in the England of Disraeli, the Germany of Bismarck, and the France of Napoleon III. Under certain conditions (which seem to occur frequently), common folk, above all the rural masses, can be enlisted under the banners of the status quo and antimodernization. Especially in countries that lack well-organized political parties, elections under universal or manhood suffrage will be exercises in demonstrating the power of the landlords, the clergy, or the ministry of the interior (or all three). Samuel Huntington speaks of the problem confronting those who believe in both the urgency of change and the right of the ruled to have a voice in the selection of the rulers as the dilemma of reform versus liberty: "The broadening of participation in a traditional society in the early stages of evolution benefits traditional forces." That is, it benefits those whose position would suffer from profound and large-scale changes in the life of the country. Under such circumstances, when a dependent or cowed peasantry is trooped to the polls under the benevolent gaze of landlord, priest, and police chief, elections become more than farcical. They become a weapon in defense of a traditional social order, and their net effect is to slow modernization, to increase the dichotomy between the more and the less modern sectors of society, and to inflame the impatience of those committed to rapid change. Under these very circumstances, fascists have attacked the corruption and rottenness of "democracy," elections, parliaments, and all the rest, from Italy and Rumania to Chile and Argentina.

One-Party Systems

Most of the two score African states that achieved independence between 1956 and 1960 were (usually officially) one-party states. In many cases, this was written into the constitution itself. These single parties were modeled to a large degree on the Leninist party, and sometimes employed such characteristic communist formulas as "democratic centralism." Most of them, nevertheless, departed from the Leninist model, both in structure and in ideology, both implicitly and explicitly. In fact, many of the one-party successor states resembled Leninist or Stalinist Russia less than they did liberal Italy: the politically relevant groups were quite small and culturally distinct from the mass of the population. Opposition elements, in liberal Italy as in one-party Africa, were often traditional or semitraditional groups that feared the consequences that centralization and modernization might have on their own power, status, and conceptions of the good life. The need to exclude the opposition from power and to maintain dominance by the elite already in power was, indeed, proclaimed and rationalized in strikingly similar terms in the Italy of the 1860s and the Africa of the 1960s. Opposition would be secessionist, reactionary, or particularist; to the degree, therefore, that opposition was allowed to flourish, the national interest would be undermined. Of course, neither in liberal Italy nor in independent Africa were these arguments without foundation. One has only to recall the internal heterogeneity of most of the newly independent states (a heterogeneity reflecting the artificiality of their European-imposed borders) to understand that secession was no remote possibility. Traditional power holders in the former colonial areas, especially the chiefs, had often cooperated with the imperial power to a remarkable degree and had very little in common with the urban-based, intellectual-led, and vociferously modernizing independence movements that would inherit power from the retreating Europeans. In the principal country in which more than one important political party was allowed—Nigeria—the various parties were almost immediately transformed from competitors for national power into advocates of regional, tribal, and religious self-interest and potential promoters of secession and civil war (as eventually happened). There were good reasons, then, to fear the opposition parties, aside from the naked self-interest of the capital-based politicians.

The one-party system is all the more attractive because of a cultural trait deeply imbedded in many of the newly emerging nations, especially in sub-Saharan Africa, namely, the tendency to look upon affairs of state as analogous to those of the clan or tribe, or even the extended family. In these areas, unity is highly prized in matters affecting the tribe or family. Thus (this is very disturbing to those who see Western-style democracy as a universal), some of the most fundamental attributes of parliamentary democracy seem bizarre and dangerous even to well-educated members of these communites. Regular elections involving competing parties look like the systematic insistence on dividing the community, the people, over fundamental issues involving the destiny of the whole community and thus requiring unanimity. The minority's right to exist, to criticize, and to seek to displace the majority may well seem an invitation to civil turmoil and disloyalty. The majority's right to implement its policies may well seem an invitation to coerce unconvinced elements of the community, thus ripping the social fabric perhaps beyond repair. Western democracy is more than a procedure for choosing leaders; it requires widespread agreement, at least implicitly, on a wide range of fundamental questions. Events in the United States in the 1860s and in Ulster in the 1960s demonstrate that the procedures of democracy avail little when this agreement on fundamentals has vanished or when it never existed in the first place. The situation becomes more acute in most of the states of Africa—with their internally diverse, and often mutually hostile, peoples.

On the positive side, arguments in favor of one-party monopoly seem compelling. The single party would forge the essential links between the villages and the capital, between rulers and ruled. It would serve as a two-way communications belt and short-circuit the local traditionalist power centers, especially the chiefs. The party would be the living symbol of unity and modernization; it would help raise the focus of loyalty of the inhabitants from the tribe or region to the state itself. Power would be concentrated in the hands of those committed to rapid modernization.

The philosophical justifications for a one-party regime were not long in coming forth. As might easily have been predicted, the argument was generally that the government party represented the entire people and was working to improve their lot. In this sense, the party *was* the people. To oppose the party, therefore, was to oppose the people. By definition, opposition was thus selfish, stupid, and probably treasonable.

The hollowness of these proclamations and logical exercises was demonstrated in the military coups that toppled one single-party regime after another in the mid-1960s, including that of Ghana's vaunted "Redeemer" Nkrumah. Not only were almost all of these regimes swept aside by their respective armies; there was hardly an instance of serious popular opposition to the coups. The party-as-people turned out to be the party-for-politicians, and the "people" did not think it worthwhile to protect it. As when the king dismissed Mussolini from office in 1943, not a single life was offered up in protest.

Why did the single-party systems, the heirs of the future (as many called them), fall so ingloriously by the wayside? The answer is found in the disloyalty of the armed forces. The armies had been created not by the independence movements, but rather by the departed colonialists. They had little reason to admire or trust the new civilian elite. But there is clearly more to it than that. Army disloyalty might have manifested itself in nothing more than sullen bad manners if the regimes themselves had not tossed away opportunities to build up civilian loyalties. Corruption was rampant, even colossal. The independence messiahs and their numerous hangers-on saw political power as a road to riches (and perhaps more deadly, conspicuous riches). At the same time, the accomplishments of the new order fell ludicrously short of the official rhetoric, which deified the leader, his lieutenants, and his glorious works. The chasm between what the government said and what the citizens knew yawned wider and wider. Thus, despite the heavily fascist-flavored propaganda equating people, nation, state, party, and leader, it soon became evident that many of these single-party regimes rested on an impossibly slender base.

8. Militarism: The Response

Political power grows out of the barrel of a gun.
—Mao Tse-tung

Third World Militarism: Old and New

Along with their poverty, perhaps the most striking aspect of Third World nations is that so many—a majority, in fact—are military dictatorships. Military coups and counter-coups are the normal processes for changing government and personnel. In some other countries (South Korea, the Philippines, Uruguay), civilian regimes have abrogated the constitution with the support of the military.

Why are there so many military coups in Third World nations? The answer would seem obvious: the military takes power because it is strong. But this answer is unsatisfactory: the military is strong in the United States and in the Soviet Union, yet these countries are not the victims of coups and military dictatorships. Many Third World armies, more-over, are quite small relative to their respective national populations. Coups have been carried off by French-trained, British-trained, American-trained, and locally trained forces; coup leaders have had their origins among the peasantry, among the lower middle class, among the landed aristocracy. Military coups have often had important civilian support, before and after the fact, as in Egypt in 1952, Colombia in 1953 and 1957, Brazil in 1964, and Chile in 1973. "The effort to answer the question, 'What characteristics of the military establishment of a new nation facilitate its involvement in domestic politics?' is misdirected because

121

the most important causes of military intervention in politics are not military but political and reflect not the social and organizational characteristics of the military establishment but the political and institutional structures of the society."[1]

Military coups occur not because of characteristics of the military but because of characteristics of the society. It is not that the military is strong—it is that civil institutions are weak.

Societies in which civil institutions—the processes by which leaders are selected and decisions are made—are weak and have little support from politically significant groups are "praetorian." In praetorian societies, force predominates in decision making and leader selection (riots, coups, assassinations), and political authority is ephemeral.

These praetorian systems vary according to the number of participants (and thus, also, according to the magnitude of political violence), but all share the same essential characteristic: politics is an affair of the streets and the gun rather than of the legislative chamber and the gavel. It is no surprise, then, that the military wind up in full political control.

Once a military coup occurs, it is extremely likely that there will be others. The military is not a monolithic institution; once power has been seized, disagreements over policy often cause the military to split (as in Brazil and Argentina during the 1960s). Moreover, once the chain of command has been violated, once the principle of authority and subordination has been breached, it is much easier to do it again. If generals can defy presidents, why cannot colonels defy generals, or majors defy colonels?

Sometimes coups are "veto" coups, that is, their aim is to keep some undesirable civilian group from assuming political power or to take power away from that group if it already holds power. Veto coups are especially likely to occur in "mass" praetorian societies, in which the working class (or, occasionally, organized elements of the peasantry) are attempting to have themselves admitted as legitimate actors, rather than objects, in the political process. Once a veto coup is carried out, the army must remain in power indefinitely (thus exposing itself to internal disagreement, internecine coups, and growing unpopularity), or it will have to carry out another coup, perhaps many more coups.[2]

In a veto coup, a civilian group strong enough to win power, either alone or in coalition, is prevented from reaping the fruits of its victory by military imposition, presumably because the military views it as a threat. The vetoed group is not going to disappear; at the first opportunity, it may be expected to seek (and perhaps win) power again, only this time it will have a score to settle with the military. Thus, once it deprives this group of power, the military must continue to do so or else suffer the consequences. In this way the hostilities between the Peruvian army and the APRA in the 1930s directly contributed to the coup of 1968. The case of Argentina is even more instructive. The army threw out Juan Perón in 1955 and eventually handed power back to a civilian government purged of *Peronista* elements. Perón's support in the country was still potent, however, and election results in 1962 demonstrated this fact beyond question. Hence, the army intervened again (removing non-*Peronista* President Frondizi) to prevent the *Peronistas* from being restored to power. In 1966, much the same thing happened again. Argentine politics between 1955 and 1973, then, was basically an attempt by the army to hand power over to a civilian government that was immune to capture by the *Peronistas*—and this proved impossible. (It is widely believed that the unhappy record of the Argentine army in this regard persuaded the Brazilian army to stay in power after its 1964 coup rather than hand power over to a purged civilian sector.)

Chile offers a contemporary laboratory in which this process may be studied. The Allende coalition, removed bloodily from power in 1973, and subjected to much suffering thereafter, will not turn conservative and pro-militarist, nor is it likely to forgive the army for many years to come, if ever. Even if a reconciliation should be attempted in the forseeable future, it is unlikely that the Chilean military would accept it: the risks are too great. A chastened *Allendista*-type government might try to move impercept-ibly within as well as against the officer corps to ensure that another coup does not occur; then the power of the army would be broken, and all the supporters of the coup would be exposed to the wrath of their enemies. Thus, if the Chilean military hands power back to a constitutional regime, it will have to watch the election returns closely, and it will have to move if (as would certainly happen) groups associated with former President Allende should begin to reemerge as powerful factors in Chilean politics. That is the path of the Argentine military, a bloody, humiliating, and frustrating path. The other option—the Brazilian option—is for the army to take and keep power until the situation "clarifies" itself, that is, indefinitely. This course, too, has risks, but fewer than those that would confront a Chilean military faced with a leftist coalition restored to power.

Historical Background of Latin American Militarism

Although the veto coup is a relatively recent phenomenon, as is the African military takeover, militarism itself has deep roots in the history of certain peoples and cultures, including the Arabs and the Latin Americans.[3]

Latin American militarism has its origins in the period before independence, that is, before the first quarter of the nineteenth century. The Spanish colonial system combined civilian and military authority in the same office. Spanish rule, for the most part, did not extend very effectively into the hinterlands beyond the great cities; local strongmen therefore established a rough law and order on horseback.

The wars of independence were long and bloody, and from them emerged the leaders of independent Latin America: politicians in uniform, men who had climbed to power (and wealth) by the successful combination of arms and politics. Clearly it would have been naive to expect these leaders to lay down power, or the source of that power. Besides, independence had decapitated civil legitimacy. Previously, the legitimacy of magistrates was their patent from the king in Madrid; now new rules had to be set up, and the men who set them up were victorious politicians at the heads of armies. Although civil institutions (including, usually, the Catholic church) had indeed been discredited or uprooted during the wars, the armies of independence were the creations of the rebels, their very own institutional offspring.

Therefore, army domination of politics was seen as normal. For most Latin republics in the nineteenth century, there were no real dangers of external invasion, and the armies had little else to do but play politics. Meanwhile, regionalism, clericalism, and problems with Indians or the lower classes prevented the rise of institutions, especially political parties, that could challenge and contain the unbridled power of the militarists. Once a society sets out on the slippery slide of praetorianism, it is very difficult to get off.

Brazil's experience with militarism has been different, although the results are hard to distinguish from those of its Spanish neighbors. Brazil obtained its independence from Portugal peacefully and even retained a member of the Portuguese royal house on the Brazilian throne. Thus, there was no opportunity to establish reputations and precedents by feats of arms. Equally important, the chain of civilian legitimacy was preserved.

Unlike its Spanish neighbors, Brazil was an empire, not a republic. This had at least two important consequences. First, Emperor Pedro II (1831-1889) was generally acceptable to the Brazilians, including the army officers. (When the empire came to an end, in a republican-militarist coup in 1889, it was not because of dissatisfaction with the monarch himself.) Second, not being a republic, Brazil had no elections to choose the head of state and thus no losing presidential candidate to cry fraud and lead a revolt in the highly stylized manner of Spanish America. Furthermore, the inglorious record of the Brazilian army during the savage Paraguayan War (1865-1870) did nothing to improve the standing of a military establishment that had never been regarded highly by Brazilians of whatever station.

Brazil, however, was not able to preserve civilian dominance in its political affairs—for a number of reasons treated later in this book. Today, therefore, Charles W. Anderson's suggestive insights into the military dimension of Latin American politics apply just as well to Brazil as to its Spanish neighbors. According to Anderson, new groups are admitted into the political arena when they demonstrate that they have power (wealth, numbers, influence on opinion) and are willing to use this power in accordance with the established rules of the game, the most important rule being that none of the present players are to be thrown completely out of it.[4] In this political poker game, it is the mission of the army, aside from consuming great portions of the national product, to enforce this state of affairs, to act as doorkeepers, and to see to it that nobody gets too rough with anybody else. When bickering or the threat of breakdown causes the system to totter, a strongman is called in temporarily to put things in order so that the game may continue (Odría, Rojas). If a player openly repudiates the rules or is considered too threatening by an established member of the game, the army will carry out a veto coup. Thus, President Goulart and his followers were apparently trying to change the rules of Brazil's political game (some would say: to carry out profound reforms), and the army had to throw them out into the cold. The army's willingness to play this role is reinforced (beyond the fact that many groups want the army to do this and that the army has the physical capacity to do it) by the fact that all Latin American armies consider themselves in effect the guardians of the constitutional order, the rules of the game. This has been the case in Spanish America since the revolutions against the king of Spain and in Brazil since the removal of Pedro II. Latin American armies are, in their own eyes as well as those of many, the court of last resort. They play the role of tutelary guardian. Although for most Latin American countries this situation arose when they were preindustrial (and even pre-Newtonian in many respects), it has endured into the age of the skyscraper and the supersonic fighter. Nothing could better illustrate the remarkable survivability of traditional practices and habits of thought (especially those that operate with peculiar force in an antidemocratic direction).

African Coups

Obviously, coups in independent sub-Saharan Africa do not antedate those in Latin America; before 1956 no present-day African state was independent except Liberia and Ethiopia. Nevertheless, the roots of militarism are deep in Africa, too, and will be exceedingly difficult to eradicate.

Colonial Africa, under the British, French, or Belgians, was run essentially along military lines: authority and information flowed downward. Policy was made by an unaccountable authority and backed up by veiled (and often unveiled) military force. In short, the colonial experience was an ideal preparation for military despotism.

The independence parties in Black Africa were led by European-educated intellectuals who were sometimes more at home in London or Paris than in the villages and towns of their own homelands. Most of the independence "struggles" these semi-Europeanized Africans led were not bloody. In a sense, this was unfortunate: these "struggles" did not permit close ties to be forged between the leaders of the independence parties and the peasantry, who largely remained aloof from the whole process. With few exceptions, the civilian leaders of independent Africa in the late 1950s and early 1960s had tenuous connections with the mass of the population. They often tried to overcome this difficulty by constructing one-party regimes, thus linking the power wielders with the population, but they were almost always unsuccessful. The civilian regimes with which Black Africa entered the 1960s were therefore quite fragile.

On the other hand, each of these states inherited a European-trained and European-equipped army. These forces were small, and the very top levels of command were inexperienced, but they were certainly superior organizationally to most of the one-party regimes in their respective countries. These post-independence armies had taken no part in the struggle for independence; on the contrary, they had almost to a man remained supporters of law and order (that is, of colonialism) until the very end. They obeyed their orders. Moreover, those who became army officers when the Europeans left were usually drawn from social circumstances very different from those of the leaders of the independence movements; therefore, the two groups tended to have very different values and aspirations.

Thus, in country after country, a civilian leadership clique with a foreign and elitist flavor and expensive tastes ruled over a country in which it had little grass-roots support and in which it was confronted by an army that was not only not committed to the clique's leadership but was also largely hostile. In addition, what had united the independence movements was the desire to inherit the power and perquisites of the colonial administrators. Once the latter were gone, the fight for the spoils began, splitting the civilian leadership in unedifying ways. The outcome can be quickly summarized: once the first coup occurred, and once it was demonstrated for all to see that a civilian government could be toppled with a puff of wind, coup followed coup in rhythmic succession. Between January 1963 and November 1968, civilian regimes were toppled in Togo, Congo-Brazzaville, Dahomey, Burundi, Central African Republic, Upper Volta, Nigeria, Ghana, Sierra Leone, and Mali, and mutinies in Tanzania, Uganda, Kenya, and Gabon were put down only with the intervention of European armed forces.

Progressive Coups

Not all coups are over spoils; nor are they "veto" coups primarily motivated by a desire to exclude certain groups from politics. Some coups are "progressive" coups, seizures of power by the military from an oligarchy too narrowly based and too outmoded to remain in control of the burgeoning energies of the country.

> Military officers are drawn from middle-class backgrounds and perform middle-class functions in a professionalized, bureaucratic environment. Where the basic issues of politics involve the displacement of the oligarchy and the accession to power of the middle class, the military necessarily are on the side of reform. This was also true in Latin America. In the more advanced Latin American societies—Argentina, Chile, Brazil—the military played a reforming role in the early part of the twentieth century. During and after World War II

military officers led or cooperated in middle class reform movements in Bolivia, El Salvador, Guatemala, Honduras, and Venezuela. In the early 1960's they became the center of a strong middle-class reform movement in Peru and played a progressive role in Ecuador.[5]

The role of the army officer as middle-class reformer is seen most clearly, perhaps, in the politics of the Middle East. In Egypt, for instance, the Naguib-Nasser coups were for the most part positive and progressive moves toward the modernization of a society whose energies were being drained away by a corrupt and selfish oligarchy clustered around the ample figure of the king. Thus, the difference between a "progressive" coup and a "conservative" coup is perhaps not so much the attitudes of the army officers who lead it, but the circumstances in which the coup occurs. In the progressive coup, the army may mobilize public opinion and form the link between the power holders and the public. That is, the army may play the role of a political party.

The Army as Party

As we use the term, *party* is a group of persons united for the purpose of placing leaders in power and legitimizing and popularizing their incumbency. A party may do many other things, but it must do at least these.

Under this definition, it is not hard to find examples in which the army fulfills the essential functions of a party. In the early years of the Nasser regime, for instance, Egyptian army officers made public appearances in their home villages, in factories, and in other places, stirring up grass-roots support on the theme of "the army is above the class struggle." The present leadership of the People's Republic of China grew out of the army, "the party in arms," and it appears that "the party in arms" will manifest its crucial role even more openly in the coming years. In the Japan of the 1930s (to go no further back), the army was in effect a singularly dedicated and "militant" vanguard party, the embodiment of national virtue—complete with a program of internal and external advance and leaders ready to assume command of the state itself. Certainly Oliver Cromwell's army was at least as much a party as some of the Communist parties in Eastern Europe: with deep roots in certain segments of the population, and enlightened with a superior ideology, its self-appointed mission was to purify and recast society.

The Turkish Case

An army can act not only as a party. Once in power, it can change the face of a country by putting its program into effect—as the Turkey of Mustafa Kemal demonstrates. Whatever else Kemal was, he was a professional soldier first and foremost; and he was by no means the only professional soldier to conceive of and use the army for the political mobilization and economic modernization of Turkey. Indeed, "the political modernization of Turkey occurred for the most part under military aegis."[6]

During the entire first quarter of this century, elements of the Turkish army were conceiving, clarifying, and carrying out their mission as the party of modernization. In 1908 occurred the famous "Young Turk" revolt, in which "a major political revolution was accomplished for the first time by popular pressure spearheaded by a party organization within which the military played a leading role." The reforms of the Young Turks were not enough to save Turkey from catastrophic defeat in World War I, and by 1919 the partition of the country seemed imminent. The army again took the forefront in the struggle to preserve the independence of a Turkish state—because "only the army could muster the secrecy and speed, the cohesion and physical force required for effective nationalist action"—and Kemal, a notably successful commander in a notably unsuccessful army, emerged as the embodiment of the honor of the Turkish army and the aspirations of the Turkish people. The first task was to clear Turkish soil of foreign occupation forces; then the implications of military nationalism would indicate the path of domestic reform.

Having asserted the independence of Turkey from foreign

powers, Kemal and his followers proceeded to clarify and consolidate the internal form of government. The sultanate was declared defunct (1922), a republic proclaimed (1923), the caliphate abolished (1924) and a representative constitution enacted (1924). These measures, together with the introduction of European dress, law codes, calendar, measures, and letters (1925-1928) provided the legal framework for a Westernized nation-state.[7]

Having provided leadership at the top, the army was to effect important changes in the lower levels of Turkish society as well. "A decade of warfare (1911-1922) gave the peasant recruit some vision of political entities beyond his narrow village horizon. Defense of the homeland provided for the first time in Turkish history a task around which all social classes could rally." (George Washington wrote that "a century in the ordinary intercourse" would not have accomplished for the unity of the American states "what seven years' association in arms did."[8]) Within a few years, then, the national territory had been redefined, new social classes were politically mobilized, reforms were carried out in the intimate and delicate areas of religion and relations between the sexes, and a whole new state structure had been erected, all in the name of a revived nationalism. This revolutionary political and social program was carried out by the groups that eventually formed the nucleus of the Republican People's Party, the supreme leader of which was Kemal. Kemal was by no means the only important party leader drawn from the army, and former officers were to play a key role in the state for many years after Kemal's death. Indeed, the RPP cabinet of 1948 was the first cabinet that did not include politicians of military background.

In Turkey in the 1920s, in Egypt in the 1950s, in Peru in the 1960s, the army came to power as a modernizing force. Indeed, the Peruvian army's seizure of power in 1968 has had very much the same consequences as an overwhelming national electoral victory by a party committed to Kemalist-type revolution. As modernizers pinned their hopes on enlightened despotism in the eighteenth century and on parliamentary liberalism in the nineteenth, so the army, in country after country, has emerged as the instrument of progress toward some dimly perceived, but passionately desired, vision of efficiency, abundance, and dignity. The army has become the party of the modernizers. As it has imposed its version of modernity, it has also imposed its values and methods upon the whole society: order, rule by a carefully selected and highly trained elite, subordination of personal or group desires to the good of the nation, mobilization of all energies toward the accomplishment of the national goals. In short, the modernizing army-party has imposed a regime animated by fascist principles.

9. Communism and Modernization

Men are so simple and so ready to obey present necessities, that one who deceives will always find those who allow themselves to be deceived.
—Machiavelli

It is often contended that communism is "the wave of the future," at least in the Third World. The communist revolution is the only way, it is said, to purge desperately troubled societies of the impediments to economic and political regeneration. The methods may be harsh, but they certainly bring about the desired results.

Is this true? What is the "communist model" that everyone talks about? What is the relevance of communism to the Third World, to which is it so attractive?

Any consideration of communism may as well begin with the teachings of Karl Marx (although Fidel Castro has admitted that he was never able to get beyond the first hundred pages or so of the first volume of *Kapital.* "Too dull!"). This presents any author with a great problem: Marx's writings are so voluminous that any effort to summarize them, especially in a few paragraphs, is almost necessarily an exercise in futility. It is very difficult, moreover, to say "Marx said this" or "Marx did not believe that," because Marx's studies were so wide-ranging that it is not hard to produce evidence that he supported this or that side of a given issue.

There is also the temptation to look good at Marx's expense. Marx was so willing to take stands, so eager to make predictions, that any interested individual can easily poke holes in his work. Although it is necessary to dwell upon

those fundamental points of Marx's teachings that history
has refuted and although it is possible to marvel at or regret
the strange transformations his teachings have undergone in
order to serve the political purposes of lesser men, we
nevertheless owe it to ourselves, as well as to Marx, to
recognize the tremendous intellectual attraction of Marxist
thought even as we seek to learn from Marx's mistakes.

Marx was the analyst and prophet of revolution.
Revolution was the result of class struggle, and all human
history could be reduced to class struggle. The modern
revolutions, especially the French Revolution, had been the
climax of an epic battle between a decaying aristocracy and
the rising capitalist class, the bourgeoisie. The nineteenth
century was to be, in Marx's eyes, the century of the
worldwide triumph of this bourgeoisie, which would cover
the earth with its factories, its steamships and railways, its
organizational and exploitative genius. For Marx, the words
bourgeois, modern, and *progressive* were all synonyms.

The capitalist system established by the triumphant
bourgeoisie, however, contained the seed of its own
destruction. Mature capitalism provided the means for
abundant production, but instead of producing as much as
could be consumed, it produced only as much as could be
sold at a profit. Meanwhile, many persons had been reduced
to the rank of propertyless factory laborers—proletarians.
The number of proletarians was growing and would
continue to grow until they were the vast majority of the
population in capitalist society, a majority poor and
alienated from the system. One day, this vast proletariat
would rise up, overthrow the shrunken capitalist minority,
and take over the limitless productive power built up by the
capitalists. With production for human need instead of
private profit, a new social environment would be created; it
would in turn create a new, fuller humanity. Inequality of
possessions, the foundation of class differences, would be
abolished, and class struggle would come to an end.

Marx logically expected the proletarian revolution to
occur in societies in which the capitalist process was most
advanced and in which, consequently, the proletariat was

most numerous: the industrialized states of Western Europe. Whatever else we may say about Marxism, it is obvious that communist revolutions have not occurred where they were supposed to. Instead of occurring in modernized Britain and Germany, they have occurred in backward Russia and China. Communist revolutions have taken place in a variety of circumstances, but all of them in precapitalist societies. Indeed, the communist revolution has been not a result of industrialization, but its precondition.

Why were Marx's predictions about the likelihood and location of revolution so far off the mark? Why has the communist revolution become the revolution of under-development? At least part of the answer to this serious question lies in Marx's concept of class. Class struggle was the fundamental concept for Marx, and it was also to be the source of the greatest difficulty for the coherence of the communist movement and Marxist ideology.

Marx assumed that the mass of the population would develop class consciousness, that this consciousness would form the primary identification for most people, and that their estimate of the class situation and class interests would be "objectively" correct. Aiding class consciousness, evident-ly, would be the ever-increasing tendency for classes to congeal, for class distinctions to become more and more obvious, oppressive, and rigid. Marx seems to have had little inkling that classes, especially in the most highly industri-alized countries, could well become less, rather that more, distinct, that there could be infinite gradations, rather than vast gulfs, between social levels. (Indeed, one might be tempted to say that in twentieth-century industrialized society, upward social mobility—the breakdown of commu-nity—is a much greater cause of frustration and malaise than social stratification.)

Marx was dead wrong in his estimation of the ability of the "bourgeoisie" to transform traditional society; that is why he expected the European pattern to be replicated all over the Third World. And because the bourgeoisie has failed to carry out its capitalist revolution, Marx's proletariat does not, in effect, exist in the form necessary to make Marx's predictions come true. Furthermore, where organized labor exists in any quantity, such as in certain parts of Latin America or West Africa, it is as likely to be conservative as revolutionary. Indeed, it can be argued that the term *bourgeoisie* as Marx employed it should not be used anywhere outside a nineteenth-century European context. What is called so blithely "the middle class" in the Third World is more often than not a residual category—all those who fall between the highest and lowest points on some scale of economic measurement. To speak of "the middle class," especially in a Latin American context, is to refer to a statistical, rather than a political or economic, entity.

In the Third World, *the masses* refers not to the industrial proletariat, which hardly exists in any form Marx would recognize, but to the peasantry. When one considers how many countries have a peasant majority, on one hand, and how few have had a peasant revolution (as distinguished from outbreaks of violence), on the other, one is justified in concluding that the peasant is not usually revolutionary. He is scattered throughout a constellation of small villages. His immediate physical needs are usually satisfied—however meagerly—by the land. His ability to engage in complex political analysis is limited. He is circumscribed by the physical power of the landlord and the soldier and the even more constraining influence of antique religious custom. Ties of kinship with powerful local personages often becloud class differences. The peasant population, finally, is often riven by ethnic, racial, or religious divisions, which make violence likely but revolution difficult. For a peasantry to overcome all these enormous obstacles to revolution, therefore, requires extraordinary circumstances. We will return to this idea; for the moment, let us only observe that to advocate a revolution of backward peasants against a bourgeoisie that has just begun its task of social transformation is as serious and as total a repudiation of the fundamentals of Marx's thought as can be imagined.

A primarily class analysis of politics ignores the complexity of the political struggle and the human psyche, especially the ability of individuals to pursue goals set by ideology, inherited hatred, or religion rather than purely economic interest. It ignores the power of racial or ethnic loyalties and animosities to overcome class divisions. It ignores the difficulties in the way of the identification of class, including self-identification, and assumes that everyone will have an overriding concern with class, will correctly identify his own class, will correctly identify his own class interests, and will reach agreement with most others of his class as to the best strategy and tactics for the pursuit of these interests. It ignores the irrefutable fact that in all the great struggles of recorded history, different classes have been internally divided, have supported conflicting sides. Even when classes are in violent conflict, it is always more accurate to say that *parts* of classes are in conflict. In struggles with such clear class implications as the French Revolution and the Chinese Communist Revolution, the leaders and followers of the various contesting parties came from a variety of class backgrounds. Mao and Lenin were drawn from levels considerably above the peasant and the proletarian. Does this not make the Russian and Chinese revolutionary movements "interclass," and therefore in need of explanation in other than purely class categories? In short, to reduce politics to class struggle is to ignore too much and assume too much.

By the first decade of the twentieth century, it had become clear that the proletariat, Marx's instrument for the regeneration of society, was not going to fulfill its revolutionary vocation, especially in Western Europe, where it was the most numerous and best organized. Indeed, classical Marxism was to go into eclipse precisely because of the nonrevolutionary nature of the European proletariat (and later be throttled by the utterly impossible—in Marxist terms—phenomenon of a proletarian nationalism).

Before World War I, Lenin had come to grips with the problem of the nonrevolutionary proletariat in a way that would thoroughly transform Marxism. Lenin explained the nonrevolutionary nature of the European proletariat through his theory of imperialism. According to this theory, the powerful nations of Western Europe had conquered lucrative empires in the underdeveloped world and had thrown a part of the loot from this empire to their respective proletariats, thereby bribing them out of their true revolutionary mission. In the face of this purchased proletariat, what was to be done? Lenin's answer was: the party. The leadership of the revolution would shift from a corrupted and somnolent proletariat to a dedicated, self-sacrificing, enlightened conspiratorial band that would educate and bring leading sections of the proletariat back to the true path. This vanguard of the proletariat would make revolution by seizing power in the name of the whole proletariat. Thus, the Leninist revolution would be violent by necessity (the Marxist revolution would not necessarily have been bloody, or at least not very bloody). Furthermore, revolution could be made almost anywhere, even in countries where the proletariat, as Marx understood the term, was a small minority of the population: the enlightened vanguard party would mobilize the masses to complete the work of the bourgeoisie.

Thus, for the inevitable uprising of the great proletarian majority Lenin substituted the voluntaristic coup d'etat of the dedicated hard core. For the seizure of the fruits of bourgeois industrial productivity he substituted the need to create an industrial society *after* the revolution. For Marx, the key concept had been class; for Lenin, it was the party, the forcible seizure of power by a small, organized elite. (This, not incidentally, is what Mussolini preached and practiced.)

That the "proletarian revolution" occurred in Russia under Leninist leadership was decisive for Marxism and for the history of the whole world. Leninist principles of authoritarian elitism were now in command in a country whose political tradition had been that of a police state built on the backs of a degraded peasantry. As a result, the communist state, which for Marx was to wither away, has become one of the most powerful and effective instruments for manipulation seen by the eyes of man; and communism, originally conceived as the result of economic moderni-zation, has instead become the revolution of underdevel-opment.

It can hardly be denied that Leninism has gutted Marxism and erected a completely new system out of the remaining parts. Indeed, these very innovations have made communism viable in the twentieth century. It is also these Leninist innovations—statism, elitism, developmentalism—that cause communism to resemble fascism in such striking ways and that lead some scholars to speak of totalitarianism as a genus, with fascism and communism as two species. This is not surprising; after all, both Lenin and Mussolini were Marxist heretics. Mussolini himself, as well as Leon Trotsky and others, have pointed out the important similarities between Italian fascism and Russian Bolshevism.

A few years ago, Western anticommunists almost universally despaired over the future of the Third World; communism, feeding on the brutal backwardness of the undeveloped countries, seemed as inevitable as the incoming tide. But the relationship between poverty and revolution, especially communist revolution, is much more complex. If poverty were the sole cause, or even a major cause, of revolution, this planet would, as Trotsky once observed, be wrapped in revolution all the time. In short, poverty has not led straight to revolution, let alone a communist revolution. For example, Latin American slum dwellers often support not communists but military strongmen such as Perón, Rojas, and Odría. One should not be too quick to assume, therefore, that the poor will take up the attitudes that middle-class Western observers have decided are logical or inevitable for them. As the gruesome debacle of Che Guevara in Bolivia in 1966 illustrates, peasants are quite capable of finding appeals to communist revolution unattractive.

In fact, neither the peasant masses nor the "proletariat" of the Third World finds the various models of communist revolution attractive; rather, it is the middle-class intellectuals who find it attractive. As one observer has put it, it is significant "that modernizing leaders, even those advocating extreme revolutionary programs, were almost never peasants, artisans, or laborers. From Cromwell, Washington, and Robespierre, to Lenin, Ataturk, Mao, Ho, Nehru, Nasser, and Castro, revolutionary leaders have normally

been well-educated individuals who could have made a respected place for themselves in the existing society if they
had not become alienated."[1] In the non-Western world especially, intellectuals and educated men in general find communism compelling; the vision of an enlightened, dedicated
minority mobilizing and modernizing a backward society
clearly implies that they, the intellectuals, will be in charge.
They are, in such a large degree, "Marxists," even as they dis-
card the most fundamental, the most crucial idea of the
master, namely, that the revolution follows, rather than pre-
cedes, economic and social modernization. Perhaps one of
the chief ironies of Marxism is that although Marx stressed
that ideas and philosophies merely reflected underlying
economic realities, his latter-day pseudo-disciples in developing countries have proved him wrong. They have used his
ideas to change underlying economic "realities."

Most communist regimes, of course, are not found in the
Third World but in Eastern Europe. It is a fact worth some
meditation that most communist governments came into
existence not through any proletarian uprising (much less a
peasant revolution) but through the agency of the victorious
Red Army in its pursuit of the retreating Germans.

As a matter of fact, there have been only two great
communist revolutions in history, the Russian and the
Chinese. Both resulted primarily from the breakdown of
normal governmental authority in the face of foreign
invasion, German in one case, Japanese in the other. Both
greatly benefited from the military ineptness and political
foolishness of their domestic opponents. Neither the
Russian nor the Chinese revolutions, world-shaking events
though they have been, "prove" anything at all about the
inevitability of communist triumph in the Third World or
anywhere else.

There is no denying the accomplishments of Soviet
industry and military power under Stalin, but to conclude
that the Stalinist model is the salvation of the Third World is
to deceive oneself. It is often overlooked that Russia had
made great industrial progress in the waning decades of
Tsarism. In the 1890s, it had one of the highest industrial

growth rates in the world, laying much of the foundation for later industrialization under the Stalinists. The Bolsheviks, moreover, inherited a country with a long tradition of centralized administration and a deeply ingrained sense of nationalism. In spite of these enormous advantages (which practically no country in today's Third World even begins to have), Stalin found it desirable to stamp out the lives of literally millions of little people who had committed such crimes as being born of educated parents, owning a plot of land, or belonging to a disliked ethnic group. Then there is the matter of Soviet agriculture: the colossal, historic destruction of Russian agriculture and the war waged by Stalin on a defenseless peasantry. (The great grain robberies of the 1970s are only one of its enduring effects.)

In defense of Stalinism, the Soviet performance in World War II is often cited: how could the Soviets have withstood the mighty assault of the Nazi supermen if Stalin had not lashed his countrymen at whatever cost through the bitter, necessary journey to industrial power? The truth is that Stalin would not have had to face Germany all alone in June 1941 (alone except for "decadent" Britain) if the Soviet regime had not pursued since its inception a foreign policy of paranoia. Hitler felt able, one will recall, to unleash his war machine against Poland because he and Stalin were allies. France fell in 1940, crushed by the German troops that could safely be taken away from duty in the east. It was also internally weakened by the pro-Nazi propaganda and strikes of the French Communist party. Stalin pursued his folly even to the point of supplying Hitler with badly needed war materiel, which enabled the Nazis to complete their conquest of the West. Indeed, Stalin—through the tactics he dictated to the German Communist party—had helped Hitler into power in the first place.

Similarly, one cannot fail to be impressed with the enormous strides taken by the Chinese communists to restore pride, dignity, and order to Chinese society, so abused for so long by the West (and Japan and Russia). After a quarter century of communist regimentation, however, China has not lived up to expectations in the industrial sector, even though the Peking regime inherited a highly disciplined and hardworking population. Moreover, the communist regime was militarily far more secure than that of any Chinese government in generations: the USSR was an ally, Japanese militarism had been utterly crushed, and the tide of European imperialism had dramatically receded. It is not inconceivable, therefore, that much of what has been accomplished in China over the past twenty-five years could have been done by any nationalist authoritarian regime, and perhaps without such distressing and expensive lapses as the Great Leap and those societal nervous breakdowns euphemistically called cultural revolutions.

Certainly, the example of Japan (and Taiwan and South Korea) makes it impossible to argue that backward countries can catch up with, or even surpass, the industrialized West only through imitation of one or another communist model.[2] Indeed, it is more than plausible that the Soviets and the Chinese have achieved what they have achieved not *because* of, but in *spite* of, the intellectual contortions required to pretend that all has been done in accordance with Marxist teachings.

A more recent fashion has been to concede that perhaps neither the Soviet Union nor China is the saving model for Third World nations, but that Castroite Cuba is, especially for Latin America. But admiration for the impressive Cuban achievements (and sheer survivability) is no substitute for political analysis. It is deceiving to turn the Cuban revolution into the model for Latin America as a whole—for many reasons, of which perhaps the most important are three. First, the Cuba that saw Castro come to power was dramatically different from the rest of Latin America. Cuba's history and economic development had produced a society in which the landed aristocracy, the church, and the army were unable to play the conservative and integral roles they usually played on the South American continent. The peasantry (in the usual sense of the term) was only a small minority of the population, and the middle classes provided the backbone of support as well as leadership of the Castroite movement. The social system that Castro blew down so easily was a house of cards. Second, the mystique surrounding the Castro revolution has obscured the importance of the inner rottenness and confusion of the Batista regime. The fall of Batista was not a defeat but a collapse. Third, Castro did not lead a communist revolution, but a constitutionalist one, heavily supported (as well as led) by the middle classes, who yearned for a restoration of political freedom and decency. The revolution turned communist after power had been attained.

Self-deception about the nature of the Cuban revolution and hence about its exportability to the continent explains the Guevara debacle. The paladin of the invincible guerrilla revolution and his dedicated followers were rebuffed by some of the poorest Indians, and hunted down and killed by one of the most uninspired armies, in all of Latin America.

Various models of communism are available to Third World countries in certain circumstances. They are not inevitable, nor are they the only viable models. Indeed, what makes twentieth-century communism a viable and attractive alternative to many elements in the Third World are precisely those attributes—nationalism, developmentalism, statism, authoritarianism, elitism—that are the hallmarks of fascism. This is not to deny significant, even decisive, differences between communism and fascism, both as to ends and to means. It is to say, however, that this is the age of the revolution of nationalist development. In the Third World, both communism and fascism are variants of that revolution. Whether one or the other will be adopted in this or that society has little to do with any "iron law of social development" or other types of single-factor determinism, no matter how they are dressed up. It has to do with a variety of factors, including peculiarities of historical development, courage and cowardice on the battlefield and in the streets, and the presence or absence of effective leadership at crucial points.

10. Japan: An Asian Road to Fascism

Nothing has done more to strengthen the state than the success of the principle of nationality.
—Bertrand Russell

Japan was the first non-Western society to produce a recognizably fascist regime. This regime came to power in a way quite different from that in Germany, Italy, or Spain. It lacked some of the features normally associated with fascism (or these features were present only in atrophied form). It did not burst upon the Japanese scene; rather, it solidified its hold on power by almost imperceptible increments. Fascism found the soil of Japan most congenial, and a brief examination of the composition and preparation of that soil will be helpful in understanding this Asian variant of fascism.

During the Tokugawa period (1603-1868), Japan was tightly controlled by members of the powerful and talented Tokugawa family. A look at the principal political and social characteristics of this lengthy period will shed light on two questions essential to an understanding of Japanese fascism: (1) Why was Japan, in contrast to almost all of Asia, able to modernize relatively rapidly and successfully? (2) Why did democratic ideas and practices, which once appeared to be flourishing in the country, reveal themselves to have such shallow roots and succumb to the forces of fascism?

Under the Tokugawa, the Divine Emperor was absolute ruler in theory, but the member of the Tokugawa clan who held the office of shogun (prime minister and commander in chief) was absolute ruler in practice. The primacy of the state was early established on a firm footing, and centralized control was enforced by that remarkable class of soldier-scholar-bureaucrats known to us as the samurai. The samurai were the backbone of the Tokugawa political order: steeped in the ideals of austerity, loyalty, and self-sacrifice, they gave an impressively military tone to premodern Japan.

Two other interesting features of the Tokugawa period reveal the nature of Japanese society and set the stage for what was to come. First, there was the practice of adoption, which regularly brought new blood and promising talent into the ruling class. This served a dual purpose: it refreshed a ruling class that otherwise might have become senile, and it provided upward mobility for talented members of the submerged classes, thus helping avoid the frustration that might foment revolution and stripping the lower classes of potential antiestablishment leadership. Second, there was the nearly complete absence of issues that Westerners view as "church-state controversies." No church in the Western sense existed, the state itself was endowed with religious significance, and Japan was spared the divisions and bloodbaths that religious struggles had engendered for so many centuries in Europe.

The rule of the Tokugawa came to an end in 1868, in a relatively brief and bloodless civil war known as the Meiji Restoration. This event marks the real beginnings of modernization in Japan, but the legacy of the Tokugawa was nonetheless to be impressive and decisive. The Tokugawa had kept Japan independent and united during a time when China, India, and other Asian societies were dissolving; they also provided their Meiji successor with an invaluable political package of institutions and traditions that were to smooth the path of the modernizers.

There was, first of all, a widespread loyalty to the state, a loyalty that transcended loyalty to family and province. A tradition of rigid hierarchy and the expectation of governmental paternalism supported loyalty to the state. Second, the state bureaucracy was relatively large and efficient, and the efficacy of authoritarian style and the need for rule by an elite were widely accepted. Finally, the Tokugawa's most important legacy was a pool of talented, energetic, and sensible leaders. They were leaders who recognized and evaluated the situation in which Japan found itself in its confrontation with the militarily superior West, leaders who knew how to respond. Indeed, the Meiji modernizers could reasonably be compared to that splendid and extraordinary crop of statesmen who arose to guide the American states through the treacherous beginnings of independence and nationhood between 1775 and 1825. These gifted and well-prepared Meiji statesmen did not, of course, spring up overnight, but were the product of the Tokugawa school.

Japanese Militarism

Perhaps no other characteristic of pre–World War II Japanese society is as noticeable, or was as influential in shaping the political evolution of the country, as the pervasive influence of the military. One might say that in speaking about Japanese fascism, one is actually speaking of the increasing imposition of military values on Japanese society as a whole. Somebody once wrote that "other countries had armies, but in Prussia the army had a country"; the same could be said with at least equal cogency of Japan.

The roots of modern Japanese militarism go back to the Tokugawa period, when the dominant class was the samurai, the soldier-administrator. Though the role of the samurai was to change between 1850 and 1920, the ethos of the samurai continued to permeate public affairs in Japan, the more so because many samurai found their way into positions in the government as well as in industry and commerce.

When the modern West finally obtruded itself upon Japan in the unmistakable form of Commodore Perry's warships, the most overwhelming impression made upon the leaders of Japan was their country's catastrophic military inferiority. Unless the situation were corrected as rapidly and effectively as possible, they saw clearly, Japan would go the way of China and India. Premodern Japan was indeed militarily inferior to the West, but this fact impressed itself so overwhelmingly and decisively upon its rulers precisely because they themselves were drawn from the military caste. Thus, from the very beginnings, Japan approached the problems of modernization and relations with the outside world almost exclusively in terms of national defense. The whole thrust of modernization in its many aspects—the school system, heavy industry, road building, and port improvements—was thus to mobilize the resources of the nation behind a modernized army and navy, the embodiments of national purpose and survival.

A new military establishment was urgently needed not only for external reasons. It was also necessary to establish the supremacy of the Meiji modernizers over the opposition of hostile traditionalists in the provinces. The new conscript army, organized along Western lines, won its first victory over the internal rebels: the great Satsuma Rebellion (1877) may be considered the last stand of the traditional forces in Japan, and they were defeated decisively and rapidly. Superior weapons systems and proven tactics were decisive in enabling the Meiji government to defeat its domestic opponents, who were armed not only with traditional philosophy but also, in large part, with traditional weaponry.

Other, and even more stunning, successes were soon to add luster to the already favored military establishment. The great victory over once-mighty China (1894-1895) and, even more, the humiliation of Tsarist Russia (1904-1905), a great power and a European state, filled the nation with an ecstasy of admiration for the victorious army and its almost superhuman commanders. Crowned with victory after victory, the Japanese Imperial Army encroached more and more on the allocation of resources and even on the formulation and execution of national policy. The quick triumph over German forces in China during World War I and the gobbling up of German colonial possessions in the Pacific—the results of the third successful foreign war in a generation—drove home the idea that "war pays."

The prestige and power of the armed forces were reflected

even in the structure of Japanese constitutional government. The ministries of war and navy had to be held by military men, and no cabinet could function constitutionally with these ministries vacant. Hence, the army and navy were able to exercise a real veto over the life of any cabinet simply by forbidding any of their officers from accepting appointment to the cabinet or by instructing them to resign if the cabinet opposed or ignored military wishes. Not only did the military hold these two key offices as a matter of right, but they often held political posts in the nation. Of thirty premiers between 1885 and 1945, fully half held the rank of general or admiral. Many of these militarists-in-office were men of great abilities, such as Yamagata Aritomo (1838-1922), who in his long and influential life held almost all the key positions in various cabinets at least once.

Men such as Yamagata and his numerous protégés and disciples distrusted and despised the incipient democratic features of Japanese political life, such as political parties and parliament. Grown to maturity during the nationalist labors of the early Meiji era, they looked upon all challenges to centralized authoritarianism as divisive and therefore dangerous to national survival. The leading democratic politicians, moreover, though often men of tactical skill and cunning, were unfortunately not above taking financial advantage of their official trust, much to the disedification of the public and the delight of the enemies of parliamentary and constitutional government. Labor was weakly organized, lacked self-confidence, and was often harassed by the police. More fundamentally, all the ideas that underpin functioning democracy—the right of the minority to exist and of the majority to rule, the fallibility of governments and the consequent right and duty to criticize, politics as a search for solutions rather than as a struggle between light and darkness—in short, the tenets of liberalism, were foreign imports, not widely supported and not well understood.

Edwin Reischauer explains the weakness of liberalism in Japan by pointing out constitutional defects. For instance, the Constitution of 1889 itself was not won by an aroused citizenry demanding protection of rights, but was rather a gift from the Divine Emperor to his worshipful and docile subjects. No Runnymede, no village Hampden, no Samuel Adams in Japan! The independence of the armed forces (through their monopoly of the two service ministries) was even more fateful, aggravated by the fact that as the twentieth century advanced, a greater and greater proportion of officers was drawn from the countryside, that is, from the areas least touched by modern and liberal ideas and practices.

Robert Scalapino, another distinguished student of the Far East, emphasizes the decisiveness of timing for the triumph of fascism. Japan began modernization much later than the West and had to catch up as rapidly as possible. The powerful Meiji state largely assumed the burdens of raising money and providing personnel and direction for Japan's new economy. In a word, an independent, self-confident, and self-assertive bourgeoisie never got a chance to grow up in Japan, and neither, consequently, did those political ideas usually associated with the bourgeoisie: belief in limited government, the sanctity of property, freedom of contract, governmental responsibility, those beliefs commonly called liberalism. Scalapino's thesis about the relationship between the timing of modernization and the growth of liberalism has disturbing implications for the future of democracy in most of the Third World.

What the times seemed to call for and what the Japanese knew best seemed to coincide: paternalistic authoritarianism directed by an enlightened, self-perpetuating elite, harnessing the energies of the nation for total defense against alien enemies—in short, the samurai spirit as embodied in the new and ever-victorious army. The inherent advantages that militarism enjoyed in Japan, coupled with the grave weaknesses of potentially countervailing institutions such as political parties or organized labor, completely foiled attempts to democratize Japanese political life, especially during the 1920s.

Boys began training to become officers by entering the military academy, usually at the age of fourteen. From then on, they remained in an environment totally cut off from normal civilian mores, which they were indeed taught to hold in complete disdain. One Japanese historian, describing the character of military education before World War II, speaks of the army's "dogmatic authoritarianism," "fanatical sense of mission," "unscientific attitudes," and "pathological irrationality." This educational system produced the officer-assassins who murdered dozens of high civilian politicians and businessmen (as well as some officers with whom they disagreed) during the 1920s, thus helping to decapitate the political leadership and demoralize the whole political process. This system produced the men who led Japan into a war against the United States and the British Empire after their country had become bogged down in a hopeless guerrilla war in China.

Fascism and Foreign Policy

In the eyes of most Japanese leaders, the overriding problems confronting Japan during the first three-quarters of a century after the Meiji Restoration were problems of foreign policy. The whole experience of economic and political modernization was permeated with the sense of urgency, of the necessity to build up Japan so that it could meet serious threats to its independence and to the very survival of its culture.

By the 1920s, Japan had been eminently successful in attaining these goals. It had preserved its independence, had won a place in the councils of the world powers, and had acquired—in Korea, in Formosa, and in islands whose names would one day become household words in the United States—the foundations of an overseas empire. These very successes, however, bred their own discontents and troubles. Japan had vanquished the troops of Russia and Germany, was one of the world's important industrial powers, and was building a magnificent navy—yet it was woefully lacking in the natural resources with which to keep the fires of international power and ambitions burning. Nature had endowed the Japanese with enormous human energy, but with little or none of the materials that feed a modern industrial economy. Japan was growing more dependent on imported raw materials and thus more vulnerable to interruptions in international trade, fluctuations in prices, and the potential hostility of the imperial powers that controlled so much Asian territory and Asian wealth. The obvious answer, the course that Britain and France had adopted, was to gather together potentially wealthy, but politically defenseless, territories under the flag of empire. By the time the Japanese were able to do this, however, most of East Asia had been gobbled up, or was being gobbled up, by Western or Russian imperialism. Its late entrance onto the stage of world politics shut Japan out of its share of the world's resources, just at the time, it seemed, when it needed them most. The distribution of world resources thus threatened to stifle Japan. Insignificant nations such as Holland were able to wallow in the largely untapped bounty of the Indonesians, and athwart the trade routes between Japan and the natural resources of Southeast Asia lay the Philippine Islands and their United States naval and air bases.

All of Japan's ambitions, frustrations, and problems seemed crystallized in the China question. Korea was considered absolutely vital to the defense of the home islands and thus had been taken after the Russo-Japanese war. In turn, a stable, friendly regime in China was vital to Japan's possession of Korea. Such a regime had not existed during the twentieth century, and as a result of Western depredations, social upheavals, and communist military operations, it must have seemed an impossible dream to the Tokyo government. Would the West, moreover, ever really be able to accept the Japanese as equals as long as the latter's fellow Asians in China were treated as so many inferior beings, pawns in a peripheral area of the European power game? China must be organized, therefore, and Japan would do the job. Yet the imposition of order on Manchuria in the early 1930s raised outraged protests from all the Western powers against Japanese imperialism. This, to Japan, was the quintessence of Western hypocrisy and racism. What was permitted to the British, the French, the Russians, and the Americans—even the Hollanders—was to be denied to the

Japanese. Thus the cry of "Asia for the Asians" came to have a complex and ominous meaning in Japan: the expulsion of the supercilious and patronizing whites, the opening up of Asia's untold resources to Japanese exploitation, the elevation of Japan to the place destiny had clearly marked out for it at the head of a prosperous and orderly East Asia, and the effective stamping out of Chinese communism. Such concepts and dreams were always implicit in a country ruled by a divine emperor and dedicated to samurai principles; Japan's rapid progress in material modernization seemed to make them attainable, and the spreading world depression of the 1930s seemed to make them imperative. At the same time, in the 1930s, the prestige of Western democracy (and hence the prestige of democracy within Japan) was receiving fateful blows: in Germany, in Spain, in Brazil, the constitutional and liberal order was being overthrown by men and parties committed to national regeneration, discipline, sacrifice, elitism, and the struggle for a place in the sun. All these things strengthened the advocates of these ideas in Japanese politics, where history had already given them a running start. All paths led to Pearl Harbor.

Several different fascist tendencies competed for supremacy during the 1930s, but all of them displayed the aspirations and assumptions found in the *Outline for the Reconstruction of Japan* by Kita Ikki, the outstanding theorist of Japanese fascism. His *Outline* became the "bible of the ultranationalists." It summarized the attitudes of all those who felt that Japan's talent and energies were being squandered by corrupt politicians, big businessmen, labor agitators, and perverse imitators of the decadent West instead of being harnessed to the great cause of a Greater East Asia under Japanese tutelage. Kita sought redemption for Japan in militarism, the abolition of strikes, limits on private capital, and war to redress Japan's international grievances. In adhering to the Anti-Comintern Pact in 1936, Japan cast its lot decisively with the fascist powers, and "by the end of 1940 Japan displayed the principal external traits of European fascism."

Barrington Moore points out that "Fascism emerged

much more 'naturally' in Japan" than in Germany or Italy; there was no March on Rome, no charismatic leader rising from obscurity, relatively little police terror, and no effective mass party. Instead, "the Japanese were forced to rely more on traditional elements in their culture and social structure in facing both the economic problems of industrial growth and the political problems that accompanied this growth." Unlike any other nation in East Asia, Japan had preserved its independence, modernized its economy, and forced the West to deal with it almost as an equal. This was no mean record of achievement, but "the price paid for the achievement was high. What Japan achieved was not so much the enhancement of the dignity of the individual as the creation of a strong state capable of coping with nineteenth century nationalism and expansionism. Westernization and modernization, which were carried out vigorously, were more material than spiritual and more in techniques of production than in the advancement of the well-being of the people. Impelling needs for national economic and military strength set the course for the nation."[1]

* * *

Japanese fascism had its roots in the culture of a country quite alien to Westerners, and it should therefore be approached with caution. It is at least clear that a dynamic regime appeared in a society long characterized by authoritarianism, elitism, nationalism, and developmentalism. Rapidly becoming a modern industrial society, Japan felt a need to expand overseas; expansion nourished fascist tendencies, and fascist tendencies nourished expansionism. Japan's experiences demonstrate, first, the ability of a non-Western country to modernize rapidly without the imposition of the communist model, and second, the affinity between fascism and many traditional cultural forms. Today's stable Japanese democracy is not the natural outgrowth of its traditions, but the result of the American occupation coupled with the discrediting of the forces that led Japan to disastrous defeat. The "natural" result of the contact of traditional Japan with the problems of the modern world was not democracy, it was fascism. Indeed, Japan was fascist before the word was invented.

11. Argentina: Proletarian Fascism

Say, then, my friend, in what manner does tyranny arise? That it has a democratic origin is evident.
—Plato

Juan Perón brought profound changes to his country. His regime was not an alien growth but emerged quite naturally from Argentine political soil, which had been prepared in many ways and for many years for his coming.

The Republic of Argentina has a tradition of authoritarian leadership and volatile politics going back to the legendary strongman Juan Rosas (dictator, 1829-1852). During the late nineteenth century and well into the twentieth, there was a heavy and steady immigration into Argentina, especially from Spain and Italy; whatever other contributions this immigrant stream made, it did not contribute to social stability. Foreign investors had long found Argentina attractive, and a remarkably large part of the Argentine economy, especially the modern sector, was in foreign, especially British, hands. The always wide disparity between the wealthy and powerful few (the "oligarchy") and the mass of the population became even wider during the depression of the 1930s. The deteriorating condition of the working class was made even worse by the fact that only a small proportion of Argentine labor was organized into unions. Finally, there was Argentine nationalism, which expressed itself chiefly in the twin beliefs that United States hegemony in the Southern Hemisphere should be stoutly resisted and that Argentina must play its obviously predestined role as leader and mentor of the South American continent, especially of the smaller countries along its extensive borders. (The intelligent exploitation of Argentine national touchiness with regard to the United States was to be an important card in the game played by Perón.)

In 1930, accumulating difficulties allowed the army to express its growing conviction that the civilian politicians did not know what they were doing; a military coup was followed by a brief, unsuccessful attempt to set up a military-fascist system. Free elections the next year returned power to the conservatives, whose policies for dealing with the world depression were uninspired. The high-handed, pro-Axis, reactionary President Ramon Castillo provoked another military coup on June 4, 1943; the principal result of this coup was to be the appearance of Colonel Juan Perón, one of the participants, on the broad stage of Argentine politics.

Perón to Power

The organization responsible for the 1943 coup, the GOU (Group of United Officers), had divergent personalities and aims. Some of its members apparently had no aims at all other than deposing the wicked, incompetent civilian politicians. Colonel Juan Perón, on the other hand, appointed head of the then relatively obscure Labor and Social Security Department, was quite sure of his aims. An excellent speaker and a tireless worker, he soon built up powerful support for the new military regime among hitherto unorganized workers of Buenos Aires. Because of his successes in this respect and shifts of power within the regime, he was made minister of war (February 1945) and vice-president (July 1945). Now in control of military administration, he was in a position to build up a base for himself within the officer corps, as well as in labor union circles. The foundation for what was to become the Peronist dictatorship—army officers and organized labor—began to take shape.

Born of a middle-class family predominantly of Italian origins, Perón entered the military academy in 1911, the year the training of the Argentine army was placed in the hands of German advisors. Promotion was slow for everyone: early in 1939 Perón went to Italy, where he spent the next two years and studied economics and politics in various universities. Perón undoubtedly learned quite a bit from his sojourn in Mussolini's Italy (which was then at the height of its influence), but it is important to remember that the Argentine political climate was already well suited to the sort of movement Perón would eventually launch. Nationalism, hatred of the oligarchy, resentment of the United States and Britain, and the military's sense of its own political vocation—all were deep-seated sentiments in Argentina of the 1940s, good materials for any would-be dictator to build with.

By the end of 1945, with wide influence among younger officers and an increasingly important power base in the labor unions, Perón was beginning to frighten the leaders of the military regime. Consequently, on October 9, 1945, he was arrested and forced to resign all his offices. Not for the last time, however, did the weakness, ineptitude, and divisions of his opponents save Perón. While his apparently victorious opponents delayed and disputed about what to do with Perón and with their power in general, Buenos Aires labor chieftains, galvanized by a rabble-rousing showgirl named Eva Duarte, organized a vast protest demonstration in the capital. Tens of thousands of workers packed the boulevards and plazas and demanded the release and full restoration of Perón. Surprised at the popular outpouring and fearing civil war, the army leaders gave in. With great skill, Perón avoided humiliating the army any further; rather, he promised the military many benefits and a considerable share in power if they would only accept his leadership and his program of social reforms. The army leaders (sensibly, as it seemed at the time) acquiesced in these proposals, and Perón, now the most powerful man in the country, left a restructured government in the hands of his friends while he set about his preparations for the upcoming presidential elections. He also married the fiery Eva.

The presidential election of 1946 was decisive for the future of Perón and Argentine politics. In a free contest, Perón garnered 56 percent of the vote, and his supporters won two-thirds of the seats in Congress. Perón's victory was due to a number of factors. All the anti-Peronist parties, from the communists to conservatives, formed a united front to support a lackluster conservative, Dr. Tamborini. Neither Tamborini's implausible backers nor his campaign style aroused much enthusiasm, to say the least. Then, a scant two months before voting day, the Peronist-controlled provisional government decreed general wage increases for most working Argentines. Perón's wife, the former Eva Duarte, was a political plus, for her humble origins and tough language appealed to the laboring masses. Most of all, however, Perón assured his triumph by posing as the defender of Argentine rights against Yankee imperialism. Just before the election, under the prodding of former U.S. Ambassador Spruille Braden, the U.S. State Department issued its notorious "blue book." This publication branded Perón as having been pro-Axis during the war and hence as unacceptable to the United States government. It is impossible, of course, to say how many votes this extraordinarily maladroit maneuver won for Perón, but the number must have been considerable, especially since Perón was enabled to campaign honestly as the foe of United States imperialism and its servile Argentine allies, the detested oligarchy. At any rate, Perón came to the presidency of Argentina constitutionally and as the clear choice of the nation.

Once inaugurated, Perón lost little time in consolidating and increasing his already broad powers. Like a good Latin American politician, he saw first to the army, which was courted with money and impressive appointments to important jobs in the new administration. Simultaneously, he put in motion the reorganization of his followers into a mass party, originally called the Single Party of the Revolution and later renamed the *Partido Peronista.*

Another important item on Perón's agenda was to capture or eliminate potential opposition. Very much like that of Mussolini, Perón's style in these matters was to proceed with as great an appearance of legality as possible, and never to make a head-on attack on an important institution where piecemeal tactics would suffice. Thus, Perón gained control of the supreme court by the perfectly constitutional device of impeaching recalcitrant members (made possible by the overwhelming Peronist majority elected in 1946). The Argentine universities were gradually subjected to controls and purges on a scale unparalleled in the troubled history of the republic. Perón also clamped down on the once-vigorous press, of which the most notorious instance was the shutting down of the widely respected *La Prensa.*

Perón, like all modern dictators, felt the need for an ideology to give direction, rationalization, and prestige to his policies. He came up with the concept of *Justicialismo,* a middle road between capitalism and communism (as, in foreign policy, Argentina's third position stressed its independence vis-à-vis both the United States and the Soviet Union). In practice, *Justicialismo* meant an emphasis on nationalism, increasing state control of key industries, and a bigger slice of the economic pie for organized labor.

Peronism meant economic independence; thus the regime bought control of the Argentine railways from the British. It meant ever increasing state direction in economic matters in general, with one notable exception: the large landowners in the countryside were left pretty much alone (Peronism was, after all, urban-oriented). It meant a substantial increase in social welfare programs for the urban workers, with consequent inflation and the further alienation of the middle classes. (Businessmen and professionals—along with the communists—were always in the main anti-Peronists.)

Despite the long-standing animosity of the middle and upper classes, Perón's power was impregnable as long as he had the support of the workers and the acquiescence of the army. This was shown in the national elections of 1951. Women voted for the first time, having been enfranchised by the Perón regime, which followed up this gesture by a large-scale effort to mobilize the female vote and to run numerous women candidates for Congress and other offices. (The opposition, again united behind a single ticket embracing the extremes of pre-Peronist politics, paid little attention to the new voters.) Although the opposition was allowed only the barest minimum of freedom for campaign purposes, Perón's share of the vote was so large (65 percent) that it is almost certain that he would have won another term no matter how the opposition had conducted itself.

The Downfall

Immediately after this triumph, however, things began to come unraveled. A decline in Argentine exports (partly caused by an increased consumption at home) and a series of unfortunate droughts destabilized the economy and created a growing belief in Perón's economic incompetence. Clamping down on wage hikes, Perón informed an astounded union leadership that if they wanted more money, they must work harder. This reversal of policy went far to undermine labor support for the regime.

Meanwhile, the army had never been pleased with Perón's favoritism toward labor and had gone along with, rather than supported enthusiastically, his policies. As time went on, anti-Perón feelings within the armed forces were stimulated by compulsory courses in *Justicialismo* for officers and the mandatory oath of loyalty to the person of Perón (this was especially resented in the navy). A military revolt was attempted in 1951. It failed, mainly for two reasons. First, many noncoms and enlisted men refused to follow the orders of disloyal officers (a sure sign of Perón's continuing hold on the lower classes). Second, there was a lack of planning and agreement among the plotters. Once again, the incompetence of his enemies strengthened Perón's hand. Unsuccessful as it was, the attempted coup heralded the accelerating movement of the officer corps away from Perón.

It was trouble with the Catholic church, however, that finally brought the dictator down. The Catholic church has never been very effective or active in Argentine politics, nor did it lend its official support to Perón in his early days in power. Under Perón, as under nearly all preceding regimes, the Argentine church was content to render unto Caesar in return for support, material and symbolic, from the state. By 1950, however, a rift had opened between Perón and the church hierarchy, first over Perón's insistence on legalizing divorce and prostitution, and later over his attempts to substitute Peronism for Catholicism in the schools. For reasons that remain obscure, the Peronists opened up a real assault on the church in 1955. The 1943 law making religious instruction in all schools compulsory was repealed in April, Catholic publications were muzzled, and Catholic radio broadcasts were prohibited. The regime also threatened to remove the church's tax-exempt status and even to separate church and state. After his expulsion of two bishops, Perón was excommunicated by the Vatican on June 16, 1955. Peronista thugs thereupon sacked and burned churches in Buenos Aires.

The struggle with the church was to prove fatal for Perón. Devoutly Catholic officers now joined liberal or simply anti-Peronist elements in the military. With the economy in a long-term state of disarray, with open war between the regime and the church, the armed forces moved in a more determined fashion than in 1951. One revolt in June 1955 was put down, but another, in the following September, succeeded. Perón fled for refuge to his fellow dictator, General Stroessner of Paraguay.

After 1955 politics in Argentina became a struggle between the loyal supporters of the ousted dictator and the elements he had defeated in the elections of 1946 and 1951, with the army often tilting the balance to the latter and occasionally taking power for itself. Years of exile only improved the image of Perón, the man who had brought the working class into politics and raised its standard of living to one of the highest in the world. This was especially so as one post-Peronist regime after another, military or civilian, failed to bring political and economic stability to the country after 1955. Perón's extraordinary hold upon the masses was demonstrated in 1973; the army capitulated, allowed their erstwhile enemy to return home after eighteen years of exile and run for president. Perón won with a huge majority and had only just begun a program of pacification when death came to him at the age of seventy-nine.

* * *

The rise and fall of Juan Perón reverberated everywhere in Latin America, perhaps nowhere more clearly than at the other end of the continent, in Colombia. There a long entrenched civilian elite had dominated a country that had long avoided the plague of military dictatorship. In 1953, aware that the society that had nourished and preserved it was growing restless, the Colombian elite sought to protect itself from violent disintegration by installing General Gustavo Rojas Pinilla as dictator-president. To the distress of his supporters, Rojas soon began to enunciate a program of serious social reform; even worse, he sought support for this program from the CNT (National Confederation of Labor), a workers' umbrella organization with ties to the Peronist Latin American labor movement. The overthrow of Perón (1955) did not seem to dampen Rojas's reforming ardor. Civilian groups, however, were stimulated to take action while still possible, and Rojas—still seeking to mobilize all potential support—was put out of office in a bloodless coup in 1957. Thus, a Colombian variant of Peronism was scotched only just in time. The specter of Rojas, however, would haunt Colombian politics for nearly two decades; in 1970, in a free election, Rojas was almost elected president of Colombia (some observers, including many in Colombia, believe that Rojas actually won but was counted out). Meanwhile, the large shadow of Peronism— reforming militarists allied with restless labor against foreign exploiters and their domestic lackeys—continued to fall over the whole continent. To several Latin American armies, it was either intriguing or alarming but in any case compelling.

12. Ghana: An African Variant

Men's worth—like fruit—has its season.
—La Rochefoucauld

African Socialism

There seems to be a definite congruence between fascist style, forms, and ideology and many of traditional society's deeply rooted practices and beliefs. Traditional society can understand corporatism—an ongoing commitment to the harmonization of group interests and to the consequent survival of some groups that might not otherwise survive— much more easily than it can understand liberal competition and individualism or Marxist class war. It is generally at home with the notion of hierarchy and the principle of leadership, but it may well find that the loyal opposition, the inalienable rights of the individual, and the dictatorship of the proletariat seem odd, meaningless, or irrelevant. Especially in this day of rampant nationalism, a large number of Third World countries apparently find that fascism, in a word, fits.

This congruence becomes apparent when one considers the ideas of regimes that proclaimed their commitment to "African socialism." Consider two well-known exponents of this philosophy, from opposite ends of the continent, Leopold Senghor of Senegal and Julius Nyerere of Tanzania.

Curiously for a socialist (as this term is commonly misunderstood), Senghor specifically denies the reality or value of the class struggle in Africa; for him, "the nation is the primary reality of the twentieth century." From his definition of the single party as the consciousness of the nation emerge elitism, statism, and his defense of the strong state as necessary to protect that same nation. In the tradition of Sorel, political consciousness and the attraction of myth are held to be vastly more powerful than so-called objective economic forces.

Julius Nyerere organized the Tanganyika African National Union (TANU), won control of the colonial legislature, and became first prime minister and then president of independent Tanzania. Nyerere defends the one-party state he erected with a revealing argument. Parties are either mere factions signifying nothing much, or they represent opposed segments of the nation. If the former, they are superfluous and potentially harmful; if the latter, the people can be divided only if injustice is being perpetrated by one segment upon another. Once this injustice is removed, once the opposing segments are reconciled, the need for more than one party—the party of all the nation—disappears.

One of the most interesting arenas in which to observe the congruence between classic fascist doctrine and practice and the political needs of emergent peoples is the Ghana of Kwame Nkrumah. Especially fruitful are brief examinations of Nkrumah's ideology, the nature of his single party, the question of repression, and the foundations of Nkrumah's foreign policy.

The Ideology of Nkrumah

In the last days of Nkrumah's power, Ghana was a training ground for "African freedom fighters" under Russian and Chinese experts. In January 1964, the semiofficial *Ghanaian Times* claimed that Ghana was striving to build a "revolutionary democracy headed by a revolutionary proletariat."

All this sounds very communistic—until one recalls Mussolini's denunciations of the Western powers as "plutodemocracies" bent on keeping "proletarian Italy" subservient. Nkrumah's positions—like those of Nasser—

can be attributed to anti-Westernism rather than procommunism. Nkrumah had many foreign advisors, not just communists, and the latter were restricted to security areas. And a few months after the editorial cited above, Nkrumah announced that cabinet members need to become better versed in "Nkrumahism" (not communism)—and then called for more Western investment in Ghana "in the spirit of partnership." Even during the most "socialist" years, roughly 85 percent of all investments in Ghana came from Great Britain, West Germany, the United States, and France. At any rate, it was clear that by 1965 the Soviets had lost interest in Ghana.

In his earlier years, Nkrumah had certainly not given any signs of being a crypto-communist. In February 1954 he announced that no communist was eligible for state employment, and shortly before that he observed that Ghana was not about to "exchange British masters for Russian masters." Distinguished students of African affairs have insisted that Nkrumah's Pan-Africanism was fundamentally incompatible with Leninism, that Nkrumah was a socialist rather than a communist, and that his theories were eclectic. For Nkrumah, socialism meant building up the economy to achieve economic independence. "Throughout the Nkrumah period, Ghanaian journalists and ideologues showed greater familiarity with the King James Version than with the works of Karl Marx." Unwilling to swallow an ideology whole, Nkrumah was "very willing to extract lines and phrases that appeared useful."[1] Indeed, a celebrated passage in his autobiography cites the influence on his intellectual development of the works of "Hannibal, Cromwell, Napoleon, Lenin, Mazzini, Gandhi, Mussolini, and Hitler."

The 1960 constitution, written at Nkrumah's direction, protected private property, religion, and access to the courts. There was no reference to any class struggle; indeed, Nkrumah himself was Ghana's chief capitalist, with many investments at home and abroad.

The philosophical grounding of Nkrumah's regime was "that form of populism in which the few speak in the name of the many." Nkrumah envisioned not a country torn by class struggle, but a nation on the march, in which "the whole nation from President downwards will form one regiment of disciplined citizens." Of his Convention People's Party, Nkrumah said that "we had excluded no one for, if national movements are to succeed, every man and woman of goodwill must be allowed to play a part." Not only national unity and discipline were emphasized; as in Mussolini's ideology, the key to national regeneration was not redistribution but increased productivity. This belief was expressed by the chairman of the National Economic Planning Commission, Kofi Baako, one of Nkrumah's chief ideologists and an expert on "Nkrumahism": "Our planning must aim at a two-fold purpose: to increase productivity and to accumulate capital for . . . industrialization. . . . It does not mean that every advance in productivity will lead to an immediate enhancement of standards of living. . . . The socialist objective implies the overall good of the nation."[2]

The Single Party

Nkrumah headed a seemingly powerful mass party, the CPP (Convention People's Party), which won clear, even lopsided, victories over its opponents in British-supervised elections in the Gold Coast (Ghana's pre-independence name) in 1951, 1954, and 1956. CPP majorities in the urban, sophisticated south, along with minority votes in the center and north, provided comfortable majorities in parliament. In the decisive eve-of-independence election of 1957, the CPP won 55 percent of the vote, and the rest was divided among several groups.

But these figures are deceptive. In 1957, for instance, although the CPP did win a majority of votes cast, this majority represented only 32 percent of the registered voters and a mere 16 percent of those old enough to have voted. Nor is it clear that all those CPP votes were firm votes. The state-run Cocoa Purchasing Board, which played a major role in the life of the small farmer, was a powerful instrument of patronage and punishment in CPP hands. Organized labor had once played a prominent role in the CPP, but relations with the regime turned sour: "the workers were expected to subordinate their needs to those of the national economic plan. The unions lost their independence and were integrated into the party apparatus." Union support all but disappeared when the regime broke the 1961 railwaymen's strike.

Apparent security in power hastened the disintegration of the CPP. The party had been primarily a vote-gathering machine, and when the single-party system put an end to contested elections, the party began to rust away. "It had no body of cadres at the grass roots" but learned to rely on "patronage and coercion." By 1965, "the party consisted of vast networks of committees which did not meet, organizations which failed to function, and personal manipulations which aroused mutual suspicion, mistrust, and recrimination."[3]

Then there is the question of electoral fraud. In 1963 the plebiscite on the one-party state produced 2,773,920 votes in favor and less than 2,500 against. This seems implausible. Even the judicious Austin holds that this and the overwhelming majority in favor of the republic in 1960 are unacceptable. Bretton also suggests widespread irregularities in the 1956 elections, and Finch charges vote-buying on a large scale as early as 1954. Peter Omari accepts the existence of CPP vote frauds but holds them to have been unnecessary until the very last years, for Nkrumah had enough popular support to have won even completely clean contests. Renzo de Felice, it should be noted, makes the same judgment on the 1924 elections (under the "Acerbo Law") in Italy; despite the presence of threats and violence, he believes, the fascists and their allies won a genuine triumph.

Nkrumah's Foreign Policy

Nkrumah's will began "I, Kwame Nkrumah of Africa," and he was "more than ready to fill the role of an African Tsar." Mussolini saw a revived Italy as the nucleus of a revived Roman Empire: "today Italy, tomorrow the Mediterranean." Nkrumah likewise saw Ghana as only the germ of a much greater African state, with himself as leader.

Nkrumah feared the permanent Balkanization of Africa.

As he said in Addis Ababa in May 1963, "There is hardly any African state without a frontier problem with its neighbors. . . . This fatal relic of colonialism will drive us to war against one another . . . unless we succeed in arresting the dangers through mutual understanding on fundamental issues and through African unity, which will render existing boundaries obsolete and superfluous."[4]

For Nkrumah, heads of state in neighboring countries who would not surrender sovereignty to a Greater Ghana were no different than the stubborn and dangerous tribal leaders with whom he was so bitterly embroiled.

Nkrumah's Pan-Africanist policies failed for a number of reasons. Unlike Egypt, which successfully mobilized a Pan-Arab movement behind itself, Ghana was small in area and population, and not strategically located. Nor was the foreign ministry up to the job. There were few trained personnel, poor communications between capital and ambassadors, and general disorganization. "That the most radical and ambitious panafricanist should have the Gold Coast as his base was almost as if Bela Kun's revolution had survived in Hungary, rather than Lenin's in Russia."[5]

Like Mussolini, Nkrumah allowed his growing preoccupation with wider international affairs to blind him to slow deterioration at home, both in the economy and the party. His "increasing irritation with those Ghanaian political problems which he regarded as essentially provincial" led him to appoint a party hack as general secretary of the CPP. Indeed, the greatest irony of the whole Nkrumah regime (and a telling commentary on how far out of balance Nkrumah's priorities and perceptions had become) is that he was deposed by a bloodless army coup while he was flying to Peking to "mediate" the Vietnam war.

Nkrumah and the Opposition

Benito Mussolini came to power—March on Rome or no—in a constitutional manner: he was appointed premier by the monarch and accepted by parliament. All the important steps that turned Italy into a one-party dictatorship (decree powers granted to the cabinet, changes in the electoral law, censorship of the press) were also taken according to the letter of the constitution. Nkrumah did likewise. Lawfully in control of the legislature when the British departed, he used this compliant body to dismantle guarantees of civil rights and to concentrate power in his own hands.

Why did Nkrumah want to do this? Some have blamed "human weakness" and "the corrupting tendencies of power." No doubt there is truth in this explanation. But much of the impetus behind the transformation of Ghana from a parliamentary democracy into a one-party dictatorship came from the political environment with which Nkrumah had to deal.

The leaders of the CPP inherited a harsh view of power from colonial days. Furthermore, as a newly arrived ruling group without the backing of tradition, they were insecure in their power. Finally they were well aware that the CPP did not enjoy the backing of a majority of the adult population. Things went well in the early days, with the heady enjoyment of independence and rising cocoa prices, which allowed a vastly increased civil service and grandiose plans for public works with important increases in taxation. But after 1960, the economic situation began to deteriorate, and along with it the CPP's tolerance of opposition.

Nkrumah's views on the nature of political power were not conducive to the evolution of democracy. His vision for Ghana consisted primarily of self-government, national unity, and support for Pan-Africanism. As the newly independent Ghana lacked unifying political or cultural symbols, Nkrumah himself would become such a symbol, the embodiment of the national state. Well aware that many in Ghana did not share his views, Nkrumah moved quickly to the concept that new states needed strong governments, which could best be provided by concentrating authority in one party. Indeed, such single-party rule was in Nkrumah's mind a natural development from African society. Never shy about giving nature a firm shove in the right direction, he wrote in his autobiography (indicatively entitled *Ghana*) that "even a system based on social justice and a democratic constitution may need backing up, during the period following independence, by emergency measures of a totalitarian kind. Without discipline, true freedom cannot survive."[6]

The nature of the opposition invited applications of "discipline." Urban intellectual opposition spoke through the United Gold Coast Convention (UGCC), its leader the distinguished Dr. Busia. Knowing that his party would lose the election of 1956, Busia asked a few weeks before those elections, "How could any self-respecting movement accept such an election victory [of the CPP] and not appeal to law, justice, and equity?" It is not clear what this means, but it does not sound very democratic. Having lost control of the colonial legislature to the CPP, Busia made a last-minute trip to London to beg the government not to grant independence to his country; he and his lieutenants also accused Nkrumah of being a communist. Nkrumah wrote, "There can be few, if any, governments in the world who have exercised so much tolerance and devoted so much valuable time to considering the whims of such an uncooperative minority as my government did in those years."[7]

The intellectuals of the UGCC were unable to mobilize the masses. Out of this weakness was born the bizarre alliance between the city intellectuals and the tribal chiefs. The opposition to the CPP was based on tribal and religious grounds—red flags to the nationalist CPP bull.

Hostility between the CPP and tribalists, especially in the Ashanti areas of central Ghana, led to violence. There had been Ashanti attacks on CPP members as early as January 1955. Later the principal Ashanti party, the National Liberation Movement, proclaimed that "the Ashanti Nation is at war with Kwame Nkrumah and his Convention People's Party." The CPP had always been weak in rural areas, and it was not easy for the government to protect CPP voters and leaders in hostile regions. In Nkrumah's words, "a campaign of violence developed in Ashanti where the situation became so desperate that hundreds of Ashanti CPP men and women were forced to leave their homes and seek refuge in other parts of the country." Austin writes, "The [opposition] leaders afforded the CPP every excuse to challenge their position on the grounds that they were deliberately promoting 'tribal and subversive' elements." And David Apter has observed that "The opposition position was awkwardly untenable, given its relative impotence—hence its irresponsibility. Threats of civil war were the last-ditch stand of a completely frustrated political opposition. But to Nkrumah, with his devotion to Ghana and African nationalism, the prospect of civil war and its consequences, which he could observe elsewhere in almost every other newly independent state, called for stern measures."[8]

In 1957 a secessionist rebellion broke out in certain southeastern areas as well, and persons convicted of inciting riots were released at the same time on legal technicalities. Nkrumah's critics concede that opposition violence had got out of hand. Nkrumah asked parliament for and got the Preventive Detention Act of 1958, which allowed Nkrumah to put anybody he wanted in jail and keep him there indefinitely. After that, large-scale organized opposition to the regime began to disappear, to be replaced by assassination attempts.

In 1962 a bomb thrown at Nkrumah killed four persons; a month later, another killed several children. Four others were killed in a hand grenade attack in January 1963, and a policeman fired his rifle at Nkrumah and killed his bodyguard in January 1964. Many of Nkrumah's enemies launched plots against him out of Lomé, the capital of neighboring Togo; indeed, Africa in the mid-1960s was becoming a scene of military coups and assassination plots against governments from one end to the other. In spite of all these provocations, Henry Bretton, perhaps the most vociferous of Nkrumah's non-Ghanaian critics, points out that there were no political executions by the Ghanaian government from 1957 to 1966, an unusual display of self-restraint on the part of a government so harassed. (It is true that a bitter foe of Nkrumah, Dr. Danquah, died in prison from physical weakness.)

Summary

In many respects, the regimes of Mussolini and Nkrumah are similar in both style and substance. There was a concern for outward legalities, a step-by-step approach to complete power, which suggests the absence of a well-laid plan. Both dictators won praise for their public works programs, which spurred economic development. Growing corruption spread cynicism and sapped vitality. In the end, both regimes collapsed with a suddenness and completeness that astonished friends and enemies.

More fundamentally, both dictators were deeply concerned with the magnitude and urgency of problems of economic development. For both, it was essential that these problems be overcome so that the country (and they themselves) could play a role in international politics. This grand design required disciplined mobilization of national energies. Neither Mussolini nor Nkrumah could be sure of controlling parliament through free elections and for long enough to finish the job. Moreover, each viewed the major opposition elements (Ashanti and other ethnic groups in Ghana, the socialists in Italy) as not only antiregime but antinational as well. Thus in both countries the established liberal order was gradually dismantled and replaced by an authoritarian regime seeking national regeneration and expansion through class cooperation and increased production.

13. Egypt: The Army and the Radical Revolution

And one sees, on the other hand, that when princes think more of a luxury than of wars, they lose their state.
—Machiavelli

The decisive year in modern Egyptian politics was 1952, when the coup of the Free Officers toppled the decadent Farouk monarchy and set the stage for the Nasser era.

In 1952 about 21,000,000 Egyptians (since drastically increased to 34,000,000) lived in a country of 360,000 square miles, the size of Texas and New Mexico combined. Most of this territory was inhabited only sparsely, if at all. The great majority of the population was (and is) concentrated in the roughly 15,000 square miles of the Nile Valley. This area is extremely overpopulated, with consequent pressure on the land and maldistribution of resources.

Pre-1952 Political Structure

Most of the precious arable land was in the hands of a few landowners, who rented tiny plots to the teeming peasantry and thus controlled economic and political life. This elite control of the country was supported by an equally small industrial and banking class in the great cities and by the Islamic clergy, who feared the secularism that must inevitably follow any significant modernization in the countryside.

To a surprising degree, the landlord-businessman-banker clique that dominated the social order of Egypt was of foreign origin, or even foreign born: the upper classes were more Turkish, Jewish, Lebanese, and Greek than Egyptian.

Many did not even speak Arabic. Beneath this foreign-flavored ruling class and the state apparatus that enforced its will was the peasant. Heavily taxed, unbelievably poor, terribly sick, and with only the hope of heaven to sustain him, the humble *fellah* provided the underpinning for the high living of the sophisticated set in Cairo and received nothing, less than nothing, from the state. There was no less a gulf between the poor of the villages and the poor of the cities, whose life patterns, though equally bitter, were radically different. The urban poor were in turn deeply divided among themselves: as in most Middle Eastern cities, the masses were extremely conscious of castelike distinctions based upon religious, ethnic, and occupational lines. Pre-1952 Egyptian society resembled one of the great pyramids: a collection of separate objects rather than an organic whole.

Unifying tendencies, however, were at work. The most important and explosive was anti-British nationalism, which emerged as an important force in the cities after World War I and helped forge an alliance between the swarming poor of the cities and the new middle and expanding upper classes. After 1918, hostility to British occupation and influence and the consequent reaction toward the idea of the Egyptian nation were to be the most important sources of energy behind the 1952 revolution.

The Egypt that existed before the explosion of 1952 was a fragmented society with a weak state and subordinate to the power of the landed oligarchy, religious loyalties, and family ties. Although there was a Western-style constitution, most of the time after 1923 the country was ruled by decree of the royal cabinet under conditions of martial law enforced by the army. The army itself was very small, completely bound to the support of the established order, and totally without any "glorious" traditions. But its less than impressive strength was enough to prop up the status quo.

In 1948 King Farouk made the error that was to topple his throne and unleash powerful, but hitherto unseen, forces inside his country. Seeking to capitalize on growing antiforeign sentiment in the cities, Farouk committed the Egyptian army to the war in Palestine—against the advice of senior military advisers. The Israelis utterly humiliated the Egyptian army; the Egyptian officer corps felt that its incompetence (and worse) had made it the object of worldwide derision. Soon after the conclusion of hostilities, charges of fraud concerning supplies for the army were widely circulated and believed. The army had been sent into the fray with shoddy and inadequate material; the national honor had been betrayed by thieves and traitors in the very highest positions! The life-style of His Majesty, meanwhile, was becoming more and more scandalous, and the person of the king less royal, more grotesque, and less loyalty-inspiring with every passing month. The willingness of the officer corps to shore up the rotting regime was rapidly evaporating.

Meanwhile, the officer corps itself had been undergoing serious changes. In 1936, sons of the lower classes were permitted to enter the military academy for the first time. Because of both their social origin and their nationalistic political aspirations, the younger element of the officer corps felt less and less willing to be the buttress of a foreign-toned upper class. Many of these younger men came together to form an association known as the Free Officers, vaguely modernizing, proud and deeply serious in their vocation in arms, and sensitive about their humble origins and the unexalted position of their country in the world order. The Free Officers organized the move against the king, and with the exception of the nominal leader, General Naguib, the conspirators were all under forty years of age and mostly of lower-middle-class background.

The long-simmering discontent of the Free Officers broke out on the night of July 22-23, 1952, when in a bloodless coup the Farouk regime was replaced by a military dictatorship. Shorn of its army support, the Egyptian monarchy and the system it represented—weak, discredited, and decadent—collapsed soundlessly into a heap of sand.

The Revolution and Its Policies

The Free Officers moved rapidly to consolidate their power. This they did in several phases. First, they eliminated

all possible rallying points for opposition to a radical regime
of modernization and nationalism. The king was exiled; the
monarchy was abolished; the politicians of the Farouk era
were put on trial, discredited, and jailed, and their political
parties were made illegal. The lands of the royal family and
of many great landowners were seized; this was both an easy
and a popular move, since these groups had had no real
support in the country except the army, which had now
turned decisively against them. The Communist party and
the fanatical Muslim Brotherhood, each the potential
nucleus of a mass movement uncontrolled by the army, were
effectively broken up. Within a brief period, the army had
removed all possible power rivals from the scene. In an
equally significant move, moderate forces within the army
were dealt a decisive blow by the displacement of General
Naguib as head of the Revolutionary Command Council
(RCC). His successor was the much more radical Gamal
Abdel Nasser. This change, in the words of one observer,
"signalled the definitive rejection of parliamentary institutions."

Having cleared the stage of competition, the RCC set out
to mobilize and mold public opinion in its favor. Urban
labor was organized, controlled, and pampered. Leading
Free Officers took great pains to appear as devout Muslims as
publicly and as often as possible, hoping to win the support
of the religious establishment and thereby the acquiescence
of great numbers of peasants. A much-vaunted land reform
was undertaken. The conception and execution of this
program left something to be desired, but the RCC's
proclaimed intentions and efforts in this area were certainly
effective in attaching the peasantry to the regime.

It was in foreign affairs, however, notably in the first years
of the revolution, that the new regime (especially after
Nasser solidified his control in 1954) made its most
distinguishing marks. Nationalism was the banner to which
elements from every segment of Egyptian society could rally;
it was also the banner most congenial to the army, which was
running the country. Nationalism is by far the most potent
religion in Egypt and, indeed, in the whole Third World. Its

attractions to Egyptians of all classes were magnified by the convenient presence of two foreign enemies that could be used to stir up paroxysms of nationalist (and pro-government) fervor: the British and the Israelis. The outlines of the RCC foreign policy soon became quite clear and probably did more to win over public opinion to the new regime than anything else. RCC foreign policy consisted of three main planks, all interconnected: (1) terminate Britain's military presence in the Suez Canal area; (2) take the leadership in an Arab unity movement inspired by hostility to Israel; (3) prepare for the inevitable consequences thereof by a rapid buildup and modernization of the country's armed forces. It would be easy (and unfortunate) to forget how important anti-British sentiment was for the development of Egyptian nationalism. Indeed, in the regime's early years, hostility to Britain played at least as great a role in Egyptian politics as opposition to Israel, and "it was Britain's promotion of the Baghdad Pact and of Iraq's Arab leadership in it in 1955 that pushed Egypt and the USSR together."

Foreign policy was also to be the scene of Nasser's most glaring failures—failures so great that the government would surely have toppled a number of times had there been any plausible alternative to it. In 1956 Nasser's diplomacy involved Egypt in a war against Israel, Britain, and France; Egypt was saved from utter catastrophe only by the rocket-rattling intervention of another newcomer on the world stage, Nikita Khrushchev. In the early 1960s, there was the embarrassing collapse of the short-lived union with Syria ("United Arab Republic"), and then the seemingly endless, expensive, and unsuccessful war in the Yemen, a sort of Egyptian Vietnam. In 1967, a decade and a half of military buildup, millenial oratory, and the intoxication of diplomatic maneuvering on a grand scale culminated, of course, in the colossal humiliation of the Six Day War. For the third time in a generation, Egyptian arms were defeated by the small but potent neighbor to the northeast. That Nasser was able to survive these setbacks is testimony to his own charisma, the tight control his supporters exercised over the levers of Egyptian power, and the utter incompetence of his enemies, both domestic and foreign.

The Egyptian Single Party

In 1956 a new constitution was promulgated. It created a strong presidency responsible to an elected parliament; neither in theory nor in practice, however, did this inhibit Nasser's power. That is, members of parliament were to be nominated by a newly created single party, the National Union, established by Article 192 of the constitution; and the party head, who controlled its nomination processes, was none other than Nasser himself.

For the next several years, the party suffered through many vicissitudes, including reorganization and a change of name (it was renamed the Socialist Union). It never became really institutionalized. It was never able to take hold of the Egyptians and be accepted as valuable and permanent. It never began to play a role in Egypt comparable to that of Guinea's PDG, the Indian Congress Party, or Tito's League of Communists. Its problems were various, but they all boiled down to its patent artificiality. As Leonard Binder wrote in 1966:

> There is no revolutionary aura about it. Loyalty to the state cannot be equated with loyalty to a party which did not create that state but is its creation. The mass party may be changed at will, and it has been changed at times significantly. Its members approach it pragmatically. For those who are not on the inside, membership or, better still, holding office in the mass party is the only way of making one's voice heard. It is not a very effective way but it is worth a try. For local dignitaries, officeholding is a necessity if they are to retain their local prestige and function of seeking redress for their aggrieved neighbors. But when none of the really important members of the regime is willing to give the organization much time, when others become suspicious that the party may be used as a means of building an independent power base, when the benefits the regime gets from the party fall below the favors that must be done, or when a new political crisis requires a renewal of enthusiasm, then the whole ceremony of establishing a mass popular political organiza-

tion may be repeated. If a popular organization is to be the repository of legitimacy, such an organization cannot be frequently or radically changed without mitigating its legitimizing effect. Finally, a mass political organization cannot serve as a legitimizing symbol without also serving as an effective means of popular political participation.[1]

The weakness of this organization for the "mobilization of the Egyptian people" has had two important consequences. First, because the party has had no real roots, the people who have risen to its top have turned out, as one would expect, to be the wealthier elements in the countryside and the professional class in the cities. The peasant mass has remained more or less disenfranchised. Second, and even more important, because the mass party has been so shallow and hollow, no political institution has been able to compete with the army for influence. The army has remained what it was in the beginning, the principal locus of power. Egyptian political leadership has been recruited largely from it.

The Army in Control

Immediately after the 1952 takeover, army officers took the key posts in security, diplomacy, education, and social and economic policy making. The military held and increased its stranglehold on power. After the 1956 constitution was proclaimed, most leading officers in key government positions remained at their posts; they merely changed into civilian clothes. As one observer has understated the case, "while the uniforms of a junta that constitutes a government leave no doubt of its military quality, the switch to mufti and even the formal surrender of commissions do not necessarily herald the civilianization of a military political regime." In 1961, for example, of 4,100 employees in the interior ministry, 3,400 were active officers or men who had resigned their commissions after transferring into the ministry. As late as 1964, a dozen years after the revolution, of twenty-six provincial governors, at least twenty-two were active or retired officers.

Egypt has thus remained a state run largely by its military.

The consequences of this have not been entirely negative by any means. However, the huge expenditures on defense, especially the importation of foreign arms, may well have seriously impeded economic growth. (One authority states that in 1966 almost 13 percent of the GNP was spent on arms.) It is often claimed that armies confer many benefits on modernizing economies, such as teaching conscripts to read and equipping them with mechanical skills. But it seems that after many newly literate ex-draftees return to their villages, their skills have no use and are soon lost. At any rate, it is clear that the army will continue to be the dominant institution in Egypt until and unless countervailing institutions come into being; the most likely challenge to the army's power, the single mass party, has so far been a failure.

Since the revolution in 1952, Egyptians have been too busy building up their country and fighting wars to have much time for philosophizing. Ideological statements by Nasser and others have tended to be elliptical, expounding a philosophy usually referred to as Arab Socialism, which might be described as an aspiration to instant modernization. The elements in this philosphy seem to be Islam, militarism, nationalism, harmony among the classes in the interest of national unity, a single party that all are invited to join, and state direction of the economy. The National Charter of 1962 rejected exploitative capitalism and the class war, proclaimed faith in "God, His Prophets and His Sacred Messages"; and seats in the Grand National Union Congress were to be apportioned according to social classes, with special preferences given to industry, the professions, and the bureaucracy.

We have encountered this combination of ideas and tendencies before; they are basic elements of what can best be described as the fascist model of modernization.

14. Brazil: The Army and the Conservative Revolution

*Cruelties ill committed are those which,
although few at first, increase rather
than diminish with time.*
—Machiavelli

Everything in Brazil is big: an area of over three million square miles (larger than the continental United States); a population approaching one hundred million; the largest Portuguese-speaking population in the world; the largest coffee exports in the world; the greatest river (the Amazon); the largest Roman Catholic population—and perhaps the greatest potential of any underdeveloped society in the world. Since 1964, Brazil has been ruled by a military-technocratic fascist regime, a regime whose origins reveal a great deal about the relationship among democracy, fascism, and economic development in the Third World.

Until 1822 Brazil was part of the Portuguese empire. In dramatic contrast to its Spanish-speaking neighbors, Brazil achieved independence peacefully and eschewed republicanism in favor of an imperial constitution with a member of the Portuguese royal house as emperor (Dom Pedro I). Despite its vast size and heterogeneous and scattered population, Brazil did not fragment into a number of independent and competitive states the way Spanish America did. It survived powerful centrifugal tendencies largely thanks to its imperial constitution: the emperor, with his prestige and his enormous appointive powers (all cabinet ministers, senators, bishops, and provincial governors), held Portuguese America together. Other legacies of the empire were less beneficial, such as the practice of "managed" elections. In most countries with a parliamentary system, elections are held, and the winners organize the new cabinet; but in imperial Brazil, the emperor usually appointed a new cabinet, which proceeded to hold (and win) elections. This tradition, in which the central executive "manages" the outcome of theoretically free elections, has survived, with a few twists, into our own day.

From Empire to Republic

Slavery was an important element in the Brazilian economy under the empire. After the U.S. Civil war, antislavery increased, and slavery was gradually eliminated until in 1888 all remaining slaves were freed without compensation to their owners.

The abolition of slavery helped undermine the empire. Abolitionists were convinced that the aging Emperor Pedro II could have done much more to bring about its demise much sooner. But the great landowners, the traditional props of the empire, felt betrayed by the emperor's failure to stem or at least dealy the abolitionist tide. Politically embittered and economically hard-hit, many conservatives withdrew from the political arena, leaving support for the throne mainly in the hands of an army whose loyalty was being ravaged by the spread of positivist doctrines and republican propaganda. In 1889, a bloodless revolution, in which army officers were prominent, abolished the empire an proclaimed the Republic of Brazil.

With the demise of the empire, Brazilian politics entered the period of the Old Republic (1889-1930). Political power was dispersed among a number of state bosses, who manipulated election returns within their bailiwicks, and who allocated the presidency of the republic by means of electoral deals among themselves. Thus, they carried on the traditional tampering with the ballot box. The vacuum left by the departed emperor was filled, at least in the army's mind, by the army; it would henceforth provide stability and legitimacy.

The boss system of the Old Republic became more and more outdated and distorted as Brazil's population increased in size and complexity. Finally, in 1930, a last attempt by an alliance of bosses to impose their candidate on the country resulted in armed rebellion. A coalition of landowners, rising industrialists, army officers, and liberal reformers rose up under the leadership of Getulio Vargas. Governor of the state of Rio Grande do Sul, Vargas had been "defeated" by the bosses in the recent presidential contest. His installation as revolutionary president in 1930 marked the end of the Old Republic, and his name and policies were to dominate Brazilian politics for more than three and a half decades.

Vargas

Vargas held the presidency from 1930 to 1945. During his long rule, centrifugal and diffuse Old Republican practices were reversed. Many functions of the states were transferred to Rio, and the federal government began to assume important responsibilities in the fields of industrial development and social welfare. Vargas's policies were a variation on the corporatist theme: the Brazilian government had something for everybody who would cooperate. Money, protection, promotion, contracts, attention, and more symbolic gratifications were directed especially toward the coffee barons, the industrialists, and the army. All significant groups became the beneficiaries of the state. This was especially true for a small but growing element: organized labor. As in most Latin countries (and indeed in most of the Third World), organized labor grew up as the favored child of the regime. Brazilian labor was organized from the top down, with the government paying special attention to skilled and semiskilled workers.

Economic developmentalism and national self-assertion was combined with centralization and authoritarianism. (This heady formula would reappear later, in surprising circumstances.) Suspicions arose that Vargas was preparing organized labor as a base of support for an indefinite continuation of his rule and as a counterweight to the army. This form of politics, an alliance between the president-protector and organized labor, was then being perfected in neighboring Argentina by Juan Perón. But before Vargas was able to bring his alleged plans to fruition, his enemies struck. Concentrated in the middle classes and the officer corps, desirous of free election (which Vargas kept postponing), and increasingly hostile to the social-welfare tendencies of the Vargas regime, they took advantage of the apparent world defeat of fascism in 1945 to put the semifascist Vargas regime out of power in a bloodless coup like that which had ended the empire half a century previously. Vargas retired to his ranch in Rio Grande do Sul—for a while. Civic virtue and economic liberalism had—apparently—triumphed at last.

Vargas was out of power, but his numerous and loyal supporters were still cohesive. Politics entered an era of fairly free elections, but the dominant issue remained Vargas, and the country began to polarize into fairly distinct pro- and anti-Vargas coalitions. Much to the disgust of middle-class constitutionalist elements, Vargas managed to win a plurality in the 1950 presidential election. Probably nothing did more to undermine the faith of anti-Vargas elements in electoral democracy as a system than the electoral triumph of their arch enemy, the corruptor himself. As his administration wore on, Vargas more and more openly assumed a laborist, nationalist (and anti-American) posture; moderate and conservative elements grew alarmed at the influence exerted in the administration by such sinister (to them) figures as Labor Minister "Jango" Goulart. Violence became common; Brazilian politics became constantly more hysterical. In 1954, for the second time in less than a decade, the army intervened to remove Vargas from the presidency— whereupon he committed suicide.

If anyone believed that these distressing events had ended the Vargas era once and for all, he was soon undeceived by the presidential elections of 1955; except for the physical absence of Vargas, they were a replay of 1950. The Vargas coalition, grouped around Juscelino Kubitschek, again won a plurality of the vote against a divided opposition. On the surface, the Kubitschek era (1955-1960) was prosperous: economic growth was the highest in Latin America, and the symbol of Brazil's self-confidence and growing power was rising, tangible and majestic, in the new capital of Brasilia. Under the surface, the portents were less favorable. Inflation, with all its social, political, and economic distortions and aggravations, was reaching unprecedented heights. For many, Kubitschek remained a living link with Vargas, especially since his vice-president was none other than Vargas's former Labor Minister Jango Goulart. Institutionally, Brazil's political development was simply not keeping pace with its economic and social progress. The presidency appeared to be firmly and permanently in the hands of representatives of urban populism, and the Congress, owing to voting restrictions and districting techniques, appeared equally firmly and permanently under to domination of a rural conservative, even feudal, majority. The Old Republic had collapsed because it no longer could cope with the changes taking place in the Brazil of the 1920s. Post-Vargas political institutions were proving themselves inadequate to the political tasks of the 1950s.

The anti-Vargas coalition (based on urban middle-class and upper-class groups) was at last able to defeat the heirs of Vargas in the presidential election of 1960; a "new man," Janio Quadros, won the greatest electoral mandate in Brazilian history. It appeared that Brazilian politics was going to emerge from its rut and advance with new men and new ideas into a new decade. But the quixotic resignation of Quadros in the summer of 1961 and the ascension to the presidency of the very symbol of Vargas populist rabble-rousing—Vice-President Jango Goulart—dashed all these expectations. (President and vice-president were elected separately; the Vargas coalition could not stop Quadros but was strong enough to hoist Goulart into a second term as vice-president over a divided opposition.)

Goulart carried the stigma of radical Vargasism and was thus probably doomed from the start. Unfortunately, he was also inexperienced (never a governor nor a member of Congress), incompetent, and his coterie of radical advisors and relatives struck real fear into the hearts of many, especially in the armed forces. In March 1964 apprehensions about the direction in which the Goulart administration was heading reached a crisis stage, and once again the army removed a constitutionally elected Brazilian president from office. However, 1964 was not to be a repeat of 1945 or 1954. The army had twice before removed the Vargas coalition from power only to see it return through the ballot box (1950, 1955) and by accident (1961). The decisive elements in the army now concluded that their only course was to hold on to supreme power indefinitely and to clean house, restoring power to a "cleansed" civilian political class at some time in the indefinite future. The military has been in power ever since.

Italian Parallels

Modern Brazilian politics calls to mind Mussolini's rise to power. Italian fascism was able to seize power in part because allegedly democratic political institutions were not performing their functions properly. Analogous situations existed in Brazil not once, but twice. In 1930 the Old Republic was cast aside by Vargas and his followers, and in 1964 the post-Vargas constitutional regime was to fall before a disenchanted army backed by important civilian groups. Especially striking are the similarities between Brazil's political development between 1945 and 1964—the fall of Vargas to the overthrow of Goulart—and that of pre-Mussolini Italy. In both countries, parliamentary structures provided a facade—which probably fooled very few—for rule by an oligarchy of professional politicians and landed aristocrats. In both countries, the "dual society syndrome"—modernized sectors existing side by side with the most backward imaginable—was particularly visible. Finally, in both countries, a prematurely aroused urban working class, representing a small minority of the population and captained by inexperienced and self-intoxicated rhetoriticians, was utterly overwhelmed by a counterrevolution supported by a heterogeneous and quite numerous coalition. The program of this coalition, in Brazil as in Italy, has been national regeneration through increased production and "discipline" now, with more attention to distribution presumably to follow.

Since taking power, the Brazilian army has purged the old civilian political class, stripping even ex-presidents of the republic of civil rights. "Institutional acts" have increasingly concentrated all effective power in the hands of the military through the office of the president. Two tame political parties, one representing the opposition and both controlled indirectly by the military, carry on electoral contests, the results of which have often been annulled by the regime.

"Stability and economic development"—ironically the formula of Vargas (and of Mussolini)—might be the motto of Brazilian military fascism. Serious attempts to open up and exploit the vast Amazon Basin are the most spectacular, but not the only, indicators of the government's commitment to development. In the past ten years, Brazil's rate of increase in GNP has often been the highest in all Latin America. More and more power is shared with civilian technocrats, who seem to find the present political setup much more amenable to their administrative and economic rationalization programs than any messy democratic system could ever be.

The Brazilian model of fascism has had at least two significant advantages over that of Mussolini: Brazil is bursting with natural wealth, and it has not been called upon to squander resources in the game of great powers. Furthermore, many aspects of the Brazilian model have been adopted by the Peruvian military, especially the concept of a developing corporatism under army supervision. It will be interesting to see if certain unforeseen consequences of the Brazilian model also appear in the Peruvian system. First, battles over resource allocation, priorities, goals, and foreign relations, once fought out in Congress, among other places, are now fought out inside the army, the only institution with real power. Consequently, army unity, never firm, has to a certain extent disintegrated. Second, the longer the army stays in power and shows itself determined to hold on to it, the more are determined opponents of the regime driven to desperate measures to express their opposition, and the more the army turns to brutal repression. The treatment of political prisoners, including terrorists, has been one of the chief factors in the growing rift between the regime and (of all things) the Brazilian Catholic hierarchy, and Pope Paul VI pointedly displayed his distress with the course of events by canceling his scheduled visit to Brasilia in 1970. The army has got itself inside a box: the longer it holds power, the more unpopular it becomes, the more isolated it is from its originally wide civilian support, and the more it leans on open repression. Fearing reprisals for its repression, the army fears to withdraw from control. Under General Geisel, inaugurated president in 1974, some steps have been taken toward a loosening up of the system, and perhaps—eventually—the army will withdraw, after so many years, from the presidential palace back to the barracks. The army has gambled that its economic strategies will pay off in time to enable its retreat from power to be orderly and graceful. It has been a fateful gamble.

15. Peru: The Army and the Moderate Revolution

The history of man is the history of the continuous replacement of elites.
—Pareto

"An important experiment is underway in Peru," writes Abraham F. Lowenthal. "It tests whether soldiers as rulers can use their power to implement major structural changes sufficient to open the way to equitable and integrated national development, without turning to repression, closing off participation, or merely replacing a civilian 'oligarchy' with one in uniform."[1]

The Peruvian Background

Peru, with a population of about fourteen million (nearly half of which is Indian), is roughly the size of Alaska. Most of the population lives in the western half of the country, and for 40 percent of these, Spanish is not the main language. Unlike many other Latin American nations, Peru has long had a diversified economy, including agriculture, mining, industry, and commerce. In other ways, however, the country is almost a caricature of the stereotypical Latin dictatorship. Before the military coup of 1968, the country was run by and for a small minority—the landed aristocracy, business leaders, and the highest figures of the army and the church—and the Indian half of the population was steeped in ignorance and misery. Since the middle of the last century, the domination of the "forty families" as been protected by a series of army dictators. Most presidents in the nineteenth century were military men, the honesty of Peruvian national

elections "remained dubious through the presidential
elections of 1962," and, indeed, "there have never been two
successive presidential elections in this century which
peacefully determined the transfer of power."

The contrast between constitutional stipulations (Peru
and most other Latin American republics require free
popular elections for president), on the one hand, and the
frequency of coups that bring a presidential term to an
abrupt halt, on the other, usually evokes consternation or
amused contempt among Anglo-Saxons. This reaction is
unwarranted. Latin American constitutions and political
practices can best be understood by viewing them as a
variation on British practice. In Britain, the prime minister
serves as long as, and only as long as, he enjoys the support of
the country's relevant political actors, the men of the House
of Commons. When his support in the House of Commons
diminishes or evaporates, his term of office comes to an end.
So it is in Peru and many other Latin states. When the
constitution states that the president shall serve for four
years, for example, it can be interpreted to mean that he will
serve *up to* four years unless he loses the support and
confidence of the country's relevant political actors; in Peru,
as elsewhere, that means the army, the church, and various
civilian elite groups. A prime minister who suffers defeat in a
vote of confidence instead of resigning beforehand is looked
upon either as a martyr or an incompetent; the same applies
to a Latin American president who allows himself to be
removed by an army coup (the equivalent of losing a vote of
confidence) instead of gracefully resigning.

The Army as Party

The leading Peruvian interest group is the army. The
right of civilians to occupy the presidential office was not
even recognized until 1872, and to be a principal actor in
Peruvian politics is "a prerogative that the Peruvian
military has never relinquished." The army, in effect, is and
always has been a party-in-arms and thus the "majority" party. Relatively speaking, the army has not made too bad a record in politics. "In all, military regimes since 1933 have a far

better record than so-called democratic governments in instituting social-welfare legislation."

The APRA

Though it has existed outside the charmed circle of power since its foundation and has been forcibly excluded from power all of its life, opposition politics in Peru has largely been monopolized by a remarkable institution known as the American Popular Revolutionary Alliance (APRA). Part political party, part conspiracy, and part army, the APRA was founded—typically—by a Peruvian exile living in Mexico, Víctor Haya de la Torre, one of the most influential and best-known Latin American politicians of this century. Haya led the APRA for nearly four decades and was its presidential candidate in 1931, 1962, and 1963.

Originally designed to appeal to white-collar workers, students, and other elements seeking political reform, the APRA began during the 1930s to attract growing worker and peasant support. Marxist in its early years, the party later became bitterly anticommunist. Haya de la Torre and his lieutenants lacked the pragmatic touch in politics: they managed simultaneously to antagonize the military, the church, foreign business interests, landowners, and the government bureaucracy. In consequence of having marshalled such an impressive array of enemies, the party was often outlawed.

Opinion about the character and meaning of APRA varies as widely among non-Peruvian scholars as it does inside Peru. The early party has been described as "a blend of old-world socialism, warmed-over Marxism (without the Lenin concept of a trained elite), a genuine concern for the conditions of the American Indian, and an amorphous anti-imperialist orientation," a party that "merely suggested a rigorous control of foreign capital while it recognized the necessity of foreign capital for development and the universality of the profit motive." In this view, "in a real sense the APRA has been Peru's social conscience for more than three decades."[2]

A contrasting view of APRA is offered by the distin-

guished historian Frederick B. Pike, who views the early party as anticapitalist, anti-imperialist, and middle-class-
oriented, but anticlerical, anti-Hispanic, and given to violence and messianism as well. For Pike, Haya de la Torre was
indeed a Leninist sort of elitist, who thought only
enlightened intellectuals could lead the masses. Honestly
defeated for president in 1931, Haya could not accept the
results and plunged Peru into widespread fighting. Indeed,
APRA violence and tendencies to violence were so marked
that even gradualists and moderate reformers were eventually frightened into supporting the status quo in preference to
the bloody specter of APRA rule. By the 1940s, Peruvian
politics had become distorted by *"Aprista* lust for unlimited
power" on the part of a party "motivated mainly by
opportunism."[3]

Whatever one's view, nevertheless it seems safe to say that
the APRA has at least been a main force in keeping the
Communist party in Peru weak and isolated. The *"Apristas*
have kept the labor unions in general leftist though anti-
Communist," thus isolating the communists from their
natural base in the industrial proletariat. Even here, critics of
APRA hesitate to give the APRA any credit: for Pike, for
instance, the principal source of communist weakness in the
country has been the association of the Communist party
with ideas of *indigenismo* and bloody revolution by the
submerged Indians of the Sierra, which have repelled both
the middle class and the proletariat of the great coastal
centers.

Modern Peruvian politics is the struggle between the army
and its sworn enemy, the APRA. The army hates APRA
because of APRA's antimilitarism, its frequent attempts (not
always completely unsuccessful) to infiltrate and subvert the
officer corps, and its tendency to resort to insurrection. The
army also fears that once in power, APRA will exact grim
vengeance for all the years it has been kept from power by the
army and for such incidents as the army massacre of more
than 2,000 *Apristas* in 1932. By the late 1950s, the APRA had
evolved from a more or less revolutionary grouping "into a
staunch defender of capitalism and had lost much of its

reformist zeal"; thus, "the continued military opposition to APRA now appears to be based almost solely on institutional factors rather than economic considerations."[4] The army vetoed Haya in 1962, and APRA had been outlawed for most of its life: from 1932 to 1945 and again from 1948 to 1956. Many commentators attribute the 1968 coup solely or primarily to the army's fear that APRA would win the upcoming presidential elections.[5]

Events Leading Up to the 1968 Coup

In 1945, when José Bustamante, a moderate reformer, was elected president, the APRA was legalized and brought into the cabinet. Subsequently, however, Bustamante broke with the party, which was again outlawed. An ill-fated *Aprista* revolt provided the army under General Manuel Odría with an excuse to remove Bustamante from power. Odría, a sort of small-bore Mussolini, occupied the presidential palace from 1948 to 1956 (during most of this time, APRA founder and leader Haya was ensconced inside the Colombian embassy).

Odría consented reluctantly to relatively free elections in 1956, and former president Manuel Prado, with the endorsement of the illegal APRA, was again elected chief executive and served until 1962. He legalized the *Apristas* and received support from their substantial faction in the congress.

In 1962, there were three principal candidates: the former president-dictator General Odría, Haya of the APRA, and Fernando Belaúnde-Terry running on a platform of democracy and reform. (Belaúnde was professor of architecture and scion of a politically prominent family; Prado had defeated him in 1956.) Haya came in first but lacked the constitutionally required one-third of the vote. Odría swept the slums of Lima (as another former general-president-dictator would sweep the slums of Colombia's great cities in 1970). Constitutionally, it fell to congress to choose the president. Following a brief period of disorder, deals, and confusion, during which Haya and the APRA offered the presidential election to their former persecutor, General Odría, the army stepped in to establish a provisional junta.

Elections were scheduled for the following year, and the same three candidates ran again. This time, Belaúnde, having picked up the support of many groups including the Christian Democrats, enjoyed a comfortable lead over Haya.

Belaúnde established a record as a moderate nationalist and progressive (in the Peruvian context). But because of trouble with guerrilla bands and mounting evidence that the APRA would probably win the 1969 presidential contest, the army ousted Belaúnde in October 1968, on the pretext that Belaúnde had sold out to U.S. oil interests. (The International Petroleum Company had been quite influential in Peruvian politics for many years, and accusations of oil dealing against prominent politicians were a normal feature of the Peruvian scene.) Shortly thereafter General Juan Velasco Alvarado assumed the presidency. (He fell in 1975.) As time and events would show, the 1968 coup was not to fall into the pattern of 1962 and 1948. The army had come back to stay. (The parallels with the Brazilian coup of 1964 are striking: the Peruvian army was to the APRA as the Brazilian army was to the Vargas coalition.)

The Policies of the Velasco Government

During its first year in power, the Velasco-led junta that ran Peru was preoccupied with problems of oil and land reform and with asserting the nation's dignity in international affairs. Then followed efforts at tax reform, programs to raise productivity in many fields and to reduce the more glaring inequalities of life in the urban sector. During all this, the regime continually referred to itself as revolutionary.

In recent years, the "revolution" seems to be groping its way toward institutionalizing itself. It is the army that controls, initiates, and executes, and it appears that "a great majority" of Peruvians "feel left out of the revolution."[6] No serious attempt has so far been made to remedy this situation in the classic manner of creating a mass party to support the regime; the army no doubt fears that such a party may acquire ends and means of its own. Apart from this danger, the army may view a mass party as basically unnecessary;

after all, is not the army itself, as it always has been, the country's strongest, best-organized political party? And if the aims of the army, as some observers believe, are not properly revolutionary in a social, as opposed to a political, sense, then a party of mass mobilization becomes irrelevant. "All available evidence tends to show," according to two Latin American scholars, that the Velasco policies did not aim to "sanction a drastic redistribution of social, economic, and political power. They did legitimize adjustments to the status quo that would make Peru a modern and stable society, while ensuring the survival of the military establishment as one of the deciding factors in national politics."[7] That is, as the army has acted in the past to protect the status quo from the attacks of such as the *Apristas*, it now acts to break up some of the more obviously outmoded structural impediments to bringing the bulk of the non-Indian population into the mid-twentieth century. Thus, according to one student, the salient characteristics of the present regime are "solidarity," nationalism, authoritarianism, "blatant instances of censorship," and corporatism—which he describes as "an attempt to harmonize all interests perceived by the regime as legitimate."[8]

Some Tentative Conclusions

Authentic and self-proclaimed fascist parties and groups appeared in Peru during the 1930s and 1940s, but remained very minor affairs; this is not hard to understand in view of the main outlines and actors in Peruvian politics for the past four decades.

The APRA, which has usually passed for the "left" in Peru, especially if the small and hapless communist groupings are ignored, has stood for elitism, vehement nationalism, a readiness to resort to violence as a matter of policy, and a program of radical reform. In a word, it has been the perfect example in a Latin context of "anti-establishment fascism."

The army, the other major political force and the APRA's great antagonist, was long the bulwark of a very reasonable facsimile of "defensive" or conservative fascism: the army, almost any army, is by definition the representative of such values as order, hierarchy, nationalism, elitism, and the appeal to arms as the *ultima ratio* of politics. During its tenure in power since 1968, it has gradually added on to these values a significant program of serious and even radical reform in many areas of national life, along openly corporatist lines. The army of Peru, that is, has expressly embarked upon a course of economic modernization without revolution from below. This is the classic Mussolinian formula.

Peru and Brazil are two Latin nations in which a functioning civilian constitutional regime has been replaced by military men with fascist programs. Outside observers tend to characterize the Peruvian dictatorship as "progressive" or "leftist" and the Brazilian dictatorship as "conservative" or "rightist." This helps to underline the important fact that fascist regimes, including those in which the military is the dominant element, should not be conceived of in stereotyped fashion. It is certain basic concepts and assumptions, combined with a certain style, that make a fascist regime what it is, not any *particular policy*.

16. Conclusions

Equal cooperation is much more difficult than
despotism, and much less in line with instinct.
— Bertrand Russell

We have seen how diverse are the situations and backgrounds—economic, political, cultural—from which fascistic regimes have emerged. The fascist solution to the problems of economic frustration and political instability seems to "fit" in many cases. A formula of nationalism, corporatism, and elitism, originally concocted in a European "great power" environment, has been adopted at various times from Lima to Accra, and from Cairo to Tokyo.

Now let us review some general points, offer some tentative conclusions, and hazard a few cautious predictions.

Fascism and the "Right"

There have been many instances—especially Mussolini's Italy—in which fascists and conservatives have cooperated. For the fascists, such cooperation was politically necessary if they were to get into power. As for the conservatives, most supported fascism at one time or another. But this does not make fascism conservative. It shows only that conservatives disliked the alternatives to fascism even more than fascism itself, that they were shortsighted or merely stupid.

Yet because of this collaboration, fascism is often referred to as being "on the right," as an extremist form of conservatism. This is regrettable, for it is quite clear that in today's Brazil, as in yesterday's Spain, Hungary, Rumania, and Argentina, fascism is on anything but good terms with conservative social forces. The political history of France and Germany is replete with conversions from communism to fascism and from fascism to communism, indicating that to many political activists, the two "opposite extremes" were congenial. Mussolini made the transition from revolutionary socialist to founder of fascism with little trouble.

If fascism, moreover, is the "extreme right" and communism the "extreme left," if they are complete opposites, then it would follow that whatever is characteristic of the one should be completely absent in the other. Thus, if fascism represses human liberty and dignity, communism must exalt them; if fascism is all bad, communism is all good. Clearly, this view is unacceptable. The problem arises from the continued use of the terms *Left* and *Right*, which came into existence to describe a world that no longer exists. It would be more than helpful for dealing with the real world if those terms were jettisoned, since they have become a substitute for thought and an obstacle to analysis. As Clinton Rossiter suggested, we might well conceive of the political spectrum not as a straight line but as a circle. The two end points of the straight line—"extreme left" and "extreme right"—would then become contiguous, graphically illustrating what everybody already knows: that fascism and communism look very much alike to the committed democrat because they *are* very much alike, separated by the mere thickness of a prison wall.

Fascism and Capitalism

Much of the difficulty in coming to grips with the relationship between fascism and capitalism (aside from obsolete Marxian incantations) stems from Mussolini's willingness to allow foreigners to portray him as the savior of Italian capitalism. After all, in the simplistic logic of the 1920s, the man "who stopped the Bolsheviks" could *by definition* be no other. But the presence of capitalists in fascist Italy did not make that country capitalist any more than the presence of Roman Catholics in the United States makes that country Roman Catholic. That some Italian capitalists benefited from fascism does not mean that they

"caused" it. In communist regimes, the principal benefi-
ciary is the bureaucracy, but this does not mean that the
purpose of communism is to make life pleasant for hordes of
bureaucrats. To label Nazi Germany a capitalist society is
even more grotesquely distorting. If Nazi Germany was
capitalist because some Germans had more access to, and
control over, material goods and money than others, then by
the same measure the USSR today is capitalist.

The important question is the relationship between the
state and the citizens. A capitalist society is one in which the
powers of the state are limited by private groups—capitalists
especially but not only—in the economic sphere. Where
there are no such limits on the power of the state, there is no
capitalist society, there is only wealth in private hands,
which the state can expropriate at any moment. This was the
case in fascist Italy.

Fascism, Communism, and Modernization

There is a widespread assumption even among distinguished scholars that fascism is a slower (and therefore less
attractive) path to modernization than communism. This
assumption is faulty. It arises from an unfair comparison
between Italy and Spain, on one hand, and the Soviet Union
on the other. Spain, it has been argued in this book, can
hardly be called fascist. Although fascists have played and do
play a role in that country, they have never played a leading
role. More importantly, the resources available to Lenin and
Stalin simply dwarfed those available to Mussolini. And
those Russian resources—human and material—were
wasted on a scale that challenges the imagination.

There is no doubt that the main attraction of communism
in today's Third World lies not in its musty Marxism but in
its promise to break up age-old obstacles to modernization
through authoritarian mobilization. But this has also been
the program of many fascist movements, to which the
fascists have added an unabashed appeal to nationalism.

There are many indications that the fascist formula is
politically more "natural" than the communist formula.
International communism long ago dissolved into national

components: e.g., the Cuban "road to socialism," the Chinese, the Yugoslavian. There have even been bloody clashes between "fraternal" communist states, and there may be more—and worse—in the future. Concomitantly, one authority has identified "the tendency, manifested by other 'regimes of development' with growing frequency, to copy the organizational forms of central investment planning, and even the one-party state, but to reject Communist ideology in favor of an eclectic combination of nationalist and socialist ideas with native traditions while deliberately limiting their practical program to the modernization of their country."[1] This "tendency" is the tendency toward fascism.

It may well be that orthodox communism is too much of a cold bath for all but a very few societies—too shocking to the system, in view of that tenacious survivability of tradition that is only recently being recognized. Fascism does not demand such a sharp, total, visible break with all that preceded it. Perhaps it is well past time to reevaluate the attractive power—to countries anxious for economic and social development—of the fascist formula.

Fascism and Militarism

Although fascism today wears a much more pronounced military look than a generation ago, it is possible to make too much of this. Mussolini's movement, for instance, owed a great deal to the support of veterans (especially ex-officers) and to the overt sympathy and cooperation of the regular army both before and after the March on Rome.

Mussolini organized a civilian political party because, as an outsider in a system dominated by civilians, he could hope to come to power only in this way. Along with its poverty, however, most of the Third World is dominated politically by the army—which is traditional in Latin America and becoming so in Africa and the Middle East. Army hierarchies in these areas are insiders par excellence and do not need a party to bring them to power (though they may want one afterward—as in Argentina, Egypt, and Brazil).

Military governments are the rule in the Third World, and powerful forces operate to turn many of these onto the fascist path. As is well known, career officers tend to view class and party struggles as dangerously divisive. Hence, they see both democracy and communism as undesirable. At the same time, they know that an effective program of social and economic modernization is needed to erase the shame of backwardness and vindicate the national dignity. The officer elite—the essence of the nation—has the duty and the means to impose its authority on the nation for the realization of these goals. Hierarchy, unity, discipline, patriotism— fundamental military values—must become the values of the whole country. The citizens must be mobilized, production must be increased, consumption controlled, group conflict suppressed. Thus, in Turkey in the 1920s, Egypt in the 1950s, and Peru and Brazil in the 1970s, the army becomes the party of fascist modernization.

Sometimes military fascism produces a charismatic leader (Perón, Nasser), sometimes it does not (Japan, Peru, Brazil). This difference is probably due to cultural influences or mere chance; it does not make a regime any less fascist. (The charismatic leader as a hallmark of fascism is perhaps overemphasized; after all, communism and democracy also have had charismatic figures. Leading Italian fascists such as Grandi were able to believe themselves perfectly good fascists without admiring or trusting Mussolini.)

Modernization and Democracy

In gentler days, many hoped that a democratic constitution and rising living standards could turn almost any country into a democracy. In one generation, however, the anticipated world triumph of democracy has turned into a global retreat, and the number of stable democracies (or unstable ones, for that matter) continues to decrease.

This vastly disappointing denouement is partly explained by the fact that every society is a blend of the old and the new; many peculiarities of a country's historical development can be ignored but not erased. Western democracy is to a large degree the result of Calvinist Protestantism superimposed on medieval church-state dualism resting on a foundation of Greek rationalism—a complex, peculiar, and venerable mixture, one that is hardly exportable. Besides, most stable democracies—the Anglo-Saxon and the Low countries, Scandinavia, and Switzerland—were established as such long before the rise of communism or fascism.

To many in the Third World, anxious to attack ancient roadblocks to a better life, totalitarian ideologies seem so much more realistic and sacrifice-inspiring, so much more motivating than insipid, egoistic, blathering, time-consuming democracy. Nationalism is now the great religion of this world—along with the authoritarian solutions that flow logically from it. Nationalism has been around for a long time, but in our day it unfolds against a backdrop of mass politicization and the frenzied demand for rapid economic transformation. But what is nationalism but self-love dressed up as altruism? And how can democracy— rationalist, neither hot nor cold—compete with that? (We have it on the very highest authority that by their fruits we shall know them. The gigantic efforts to build a new world of brotherhood through violence produced the barbarism of Stalin. The appeals of solidarity and community brought forth the unspeakable infamies of Hitler. Apologies for democracy are no doubt dull; they do not make the blood course through the veins. Neither do they make blood course through the streets.)[2]

The Varieties of Fascism

It was once customary to consider fascism an aberration. If a country developed a powerful fascist movement or if it fell under fascist control, it was going off the track owing to peculiar circumstances. Today it is clear that fascism has come to power unaided in more countries than has Leninism; indeed, the appearance of fascism from Italy to Argentina, from Germany to Peru, from Japan to Brazil, from the 1920s to the 1970s, suggests that fascism cannot be viewed as merely an exceptional development.

It used to be fashionable to "explain," for instance, the rise of Nazism in terms of "Versailles and Moscow"; that is, in terms of defeat in the World War and fear of a Kremlin-masterminded revolution. But Italy was victorious in the war; and in Japan, Argentina, and Rumania, powerful fascist currents surfaced that can be explained neither by wartime defeat nor by communist agitation, for these were absent. That liberal Italy, at odds with Catholicism and despised by the working class, succumbed to fascism is no surprise. But Nazism rose to power in a society where a democratic constitution was vigorously supported by the Catholic church and the working class. Fascism has arisen under the most diverse circumstances; everything seems to be grist for the fascist mill.

In the Third World, fascism is in large part the result of the convergence of three key factors.

First, the pressures arising from modernization. The breakdown of traditional mores and restraints, the fevers of nationalist exaltation, and the thirst for economic development here and now—all demand a strong state armed with an ideology that can forcefully respond to these pressures.

Second, the congruence of many fascist conceptions with traditional norms and practices. Some forms of fascism are mere updatings, with microphones and mass parades, of ancient practices. Mussolini was striking a more profound pose than perhaps he realized when he presented his regime as the new Roman Empire. In any event, we may safely say that forms of authority and notions of legitimacy in traditional societies, no matter how heterogeneous they may be, usually come much closer to fascism than to Westminster-type democracy.

Third, in a bizarre twist to the notion of the "advantages of backwardness," would-be messiahs and their followers have a number of fascist models on which to pattern themselves. Thus, Perón studied Italian fascism, and Rojas sought to copy Perón.

Italy's descent into fascism was prepared in part by the existence of disaffected minorities and by the violence and bitterness provoked by the rise of millenial doctrines. These conditions now help shape the political struggle from Chile to India. Similarly, one scholar is convinced that:

the factors at work in prewar Eastern Europe seem tragically in the process of being duplicated in many of the developing nations: the drive by minorities for ethnic determination, the unsuccessful effort by newly established states to establish their own economic and political viability, the inability of states to establish integration without obliterating cultures— and often peoples—through assimilation, population transfers or genocide, and, finally, the efforts of larger, more powerful states to establish control or absorb unintegrated, fragile political systems.[3]

Today's Third World reproduces many of the political and social maladies of yesterday's Europe and can therefore be expected to reproduce some of Europe's "remedies."

Fascism: So What?

Suppose we all agree that fascism is again appearing and has a bright future. What of it? Where does it all get us? As a matter of fact, the rise of contemporary fascism has a number of practical consequences.

First of all, the application of fascist categories to the developing nations helps us recall that there are really very few discontinuities in the human experience; events in Italy or Japan in one generation find analogues in Brazil or Egypt in another. We like to think of our generation or decade as being quite distinct from all that went before, but perhaps it is not. Moreover, the search to understand the roots of Argentine or Peruvian fascism will perhaps shed some light on how fascism came to power in Italy or Japan: the present illuminates the past. Similarly, the once-disturbing paradox of "national communism" becomes less strange; Cuba or Yugoslavia are very different from Argentina or Italy in some ways, not so different in others.

It is clear that to the extent fascism flourishes there, the Balkanization of the African continent will become permanent. The same applies to other areas of the globe: fascism and internationalism are not friends. Fascist nationalism will certainly impede the erection of that rational world economic order so long sought by the United States. In other ways, too, the multiplication of fascist governments will make things difficult. U.S. relations with Juan Perón, for example, were usually quite strained, and the greatest war the United States ever fought was, of course, against an alliance of fascists.

Is Fascism Forever?

The principal fascist regimes of the twentieth century—Germany, Italy, and Japan—were destroyed by defeat in war. But fascism may also be modified or even totally altered by internal forces. The excesses of Peronism led to its overthrow. Changes in Egypt seem to promise that by 1980 many of the rigidities of the Nasser era will have been relaxed. The dictatorships in Peru and Brazil, by building up the middle sectors, lessening enormous class differences, and laying the groundwork for a more humane economic life, may be preparing the soil—at very long range—for the eventual emergence of something like democracy. (Barrington Moore in his influential *Social Origins of Dictatorship and Democracy* posited a "thoroughgoing bourgeois revolution" against feudalism as a prerequisite for stable democracy. This era's modernizing military may be the surrogate of the bourgeoisie. Cromwell, after all, helped prepare the way for Gladstone.)

If fascism can ever yield to some form of democracy, it is because of its coalitionist nature. Where communism comes into control, all forces that might compete for power—military, property, religion, ethnic and professional groupings—are either totally destroyed or totally absorbed by the party. Society is leveled, the party towers over it. In fascist regimes (at least the ones with which we are familiar), power is shared among fascist and nonfascist groups. This sharing of power varies in extent, from relatively little in Nazi Germany to a great deal in fascist Italy. In Brazil, the opposition is permitted a public, if circumscribed, existence; in Spain, the fascists were only a junior partner in running the country.

Contemporary military fascism is a coalition in several respects: within the army; among the fascists, conservatives, and moderates; and between the army on one hand, and the bureaucracy and other civilian groups on the other. In this distribution of power lies the hope for the emergence of a more humane polity.

Mussolini coined the term *totalitarianism* to describe his regime, but Italian fascism never approached totalitarianism. *Totalitarian* means not total control of everything and everybody by the state (impossible except in the Orwellian imagination), but the refusal to recognize any *limits* on what the state may attempt to do. Mussolini's freedom of action was openly limited by the crown, the church, the army, and big business. This is one reason why, for more than a quarter of a century, a vigorous pluralist democracy has flourished in the former cradle of fascism. In this sense, perhaps the only truly totalitarian society in the world has been Soviet Russia.

Traditional government—based on authority and hierarchy—is the political organization mankind has lived with longest and seems most to understand and therefore accept. Fascism is the modern form of such political organization, and it is coming to power in more and more countries. Communism, in contrast, has triumphed only under extraordinary circumstances. Future historians may well write of the last quarter of the twentieth century as the Golden Age of Fascism.

Whether communism or fascism turns out to be the "wave of the future," it will certainly not be democracy as we understand it. However regrettable all this may be, we will have to cope with it. We have had our crusades, from Woodrow Wilson to Lyndon Johnson, to make the world safe for democracy. Perhaps the best thing we can do now is make democracy safe in America.

Appendix A
Fascism and Big Business

It has long been a fashion to "explain" fascism, especially in Italy, as being hardly more than the paid bodyguard of capitalism. It no doubt has become evident that such single-factor explanations are hardly adequate. One can, however, learn much about the nature of power in its various forms by examining the relationship between the fascist party, before and after it came to power, and Italian big business. Fortunately, Roland Sarti, in his *Fascism and the Industrial Leadership in Italy,* has provided us with a great deal of information and insight on the subject. This appendix considers the main points made by Sarti.

Marxist demonology posits an aggressive, powerful, and optimistic bourgeoisie, but this was far from true of the pre-Mussolini Italian bourgeoisie, especially in their self-evaluation:

> Italian industrialists have always felt politically vulnerable. Confronted in the course of history by economically conservative and politically influential agricultural inter-ests, aggressive labor unions, strong political parties ideologically committed to the liquidation of capitalism, and governments responsive to a variety of pressures, Italian industrialists developed a sacrificial-lamb complex.... Their sense of frustration was understandable. While entrepreneurs in the more advanced Western nations were able to face the pressures one by one, or over the span of several generations,

Italian industrialists had to deal with them simultaneously. That is the price paid by latecomers to the industrial revolution.

By 1919, several tendencies were converging within the industrial leadership group. First, there was the exaggerated, but nevertheless real, fear of imminent social revolution as in Petrograd. This fear sharpened the political sensitivity of the industrial leaders. Second, there was a growing belief in the superior skills, managerial and technological, of the industrial class: the industrialists both knew better than others what Italy really needed, and knew better than others how to provide it. Both factors—fear of revolution by economically illiterate socialists who would ruin the country and an increasing belief in their own unique abilities to provide the nation with a better life—combined to enkindle in many businessmen the determination to "restore the social order and make the government more responsive to the needs of industrial production." Partially as a result of these growing feelings, the General Confederation of Italian Industry *(Confindustria)* was founded (April 1919) to coordinate the resistance of the managerial class to what were seen as irresponsible union demands and the threat of social upheaval. Thus, "it would be misleading to think of the industrialists as a reactionary group," writes Sarti. "They accepted fascism not only because it helped restore law and order, but also because it promised to cut through many ideological Gordian knots and rapidly reform the apparatus of government." (In the same way, French technocrats and industrialists would welcome the opportunity provided by the Vichy regime to transform many aspects of French economic life and practice.)

Mussolini's Economic Views and Policies

In Sarti's view, the disaster at Caporetto turned Mussolini toward the doctrine of "productionism." The war could be won, and Italy's age-old economic difficulties and the attendant social unrest could then be solved, Mussolini believed, only through planned efforts to expand production, not through the redistribution of the all too meager national "wealth."

> Productivism marks Mussolini's transition from his own original revolutionary radicalism to his subsequent stand as the man of law and order. As a productivist he claimed that anyone who really wanted to raise the general standard of living could not in good conscience condone radical economic and social experiments that threatened to disrupt production. By accepting productivism, he could move in the direction of capital (the constructive "captain of industry" eventually became one of the heroic figures of fascist mythology) without turning against labor.

Thus the war taught Mussolini not only that nationalism was stronger than "international proletarian solidarity" but also that production, rather than revolution, was the key to a new world for the Italians. The search was henceforth for the proper mix of policies and men to maximize production.

Mussolini, once in power, appointed as minister of finance Alberto De Stefani, an out-and-out advocate of laissez-faire economics (October 1922). Theoretically, De Stefani's ideas were quite acceptable to Italian big business. "Public enterprise was to give way to private initiative wherever possible" on the grounds that this was the surest way to increase general productivity. As it turned out, however, De Stefani took laissez-faire "more seriously than many businessmen who were always ready to pay lip service to the doctrine but who were more interested in securing high protective tariffs, concluding agreements in restraint of trade, and obtaining government contracts." So pure was De Stefani's faith in liberal economics that under his direction fascist Italy recognized Leninist Russia in 1924 and concluded a commercial treaty with it. Business before ideology! Eventually, De Stefani had to go (July 1925), driven from office by business resentment of his fiscal policies and his opposition to protectionism and also by Mussolini's growing doubts about the efficacy of laissez-faire. Mussolini, the former socialist firebrand, was never comfortable with doctrinaire capitalism. "Mussolini attacked the socialist party for its continued polemic against the war, for its internationalism, and for its political tactics at home, but he usually professed sympathy for programs of social reform. There is good reason to believe that both before and after the March on Rome he would have welcomed the cooperation of the moderate, reformist wing of the Socialist party." The De Stefani episode represents not confusion or absence of doctrine but an empirical search for the right combination of means and men.

Sarti describes how actual economic exigencies interfered with the operations of the vaunted fascist "corporate state," which in practice meant the self-regulation of big business. The rise of protectionist policies all over the world during the Great Depression had serious repercussions on Italy's always fragile economy; so did the sanctions imposed by the League of Nations as a result of the invasion of Ethiopia. These developments forced the regime into a policy of autarky—economic self-sufficiency. But the state's pursuit of economic independence means by definition a deep and continuous interference in the affairs of big business, thus undermining the basic operations of corporatism.

The Industrialists View Fascism

"There were many Fascisms in Italy and every man could choose the one he liked," writes Sarti about the movement's multifaceted nature, which had been such a source of strength to it on the road to power and its greatest handicap once it arrived there. Fascist labor leaders, for example, were constantly torn between what they saw as their duty to the party and nationalism, on the one hand, and what they saw as their duty to labor on the other. The various, even mutually hostile, elements within the fascist party required constant reconciliation, and consequently Mussolini "behaved essentially as a political mediator devoted to preserving the balance of forces that supported his regime."

Astute Italian conservatives never evaluated fascism as a totally, or even predominantly, conservative movement, and neither should we. Even though fascism fought and destroyed revolutionary socialism, it was not necessarily conservative, but it was only rejecting what it understood socialism to be. To reject the changes that socialism advocated in 1914-1922 is by no means to endorse the status quo wholly or even in large part. Many fascists saw themselves as real revolutionaries bent on cleaning up the decadence brought about by throne, church, and bourgeoisie.

This heterogeneous nature of fascism, as well as its onetime rabble-rousing proclivities, colored the relations between Mussolini and the great industrialists.

> The self-styled revolutionaries within Fascism, and the political instability they imparted to the Fascist movement, preoccupied the industrial leaders. Unlike many anti-Fascists who called Fascism a socially conservative or even reactionary phenomenon, the industrialists never took Fascist conservatism for granted. And, because they never took that conservatism for granted, they were able, with the help of other vested interests like the Monarchy, the Church, the army and the civil service, to prolong the life of the existing social system with minimal change.

Fascism and Big Business

In Leninist and Stalinist Russia, political and economic control were vested in a single leadership group. In Germany and Japan, the political or military leadership could impose its will fairly easily on industry. But in Italy, "the industrial leadership was still sufficiently independent of party and government to bargain with them from a position of relative power," and thus it could thwart the designs of the social-revolutionary element within the fascist party.

By 1921, Mussolini had begun to receive rather heavy subsidies from certain industrial interests. "Venality was not one of Mussolini's weaknesses, but, practical politician that he was, he understood the importance of money for political success." However Mussolini was in no sense the industrialists' "puppet"; indeed, the relationship between fascism and industry, once fascism had ensconced itself in power, is quite revealing of the real, that is, the complex nature of the regime. "Although fascism claimed to be monolithic and totalitarian, it was really a most accommodating political regime. It carried on the practice of *trasformismo* which was well-rooted in Italian politics before fascism came to power. The industrialists were more interested in the details of economic and social policy than in the grand lines of political conduct. Their influence on foreign policy was always limited and they were not too unhappy with this arrangement."

Italian industry heartily disliked and feared Nazi Germany and the German alliance, for some very tangible reasons. The *Anschluss*, for example, severely hurt the trade of Trieste and helped that of Hamburg.

The complex and ambiguous nature of corporatism during most of Mussolini's rule can be more clearly explained if it is kept in mind that corporatist policy was to a great extent the product of an elaborate and protracted tug-of-war between the party-state and the leaders of *Confindustria*. Industry's retention of its distinct organization was advantageous to it in the long run as well: since it was not too closely associated with the regime on a purely political plane, *Confindustria* was able to divorce itself from the fate of the fascist regime (as the monarchy was not); "the political purge which followed World War II had few repercussions in entrepreneurial and managerial circles."

* * *

Big business benefited from fascism in a number of very important ways. Corporatism gave the industrialists access to the public power and the public treasury in ways only dreamed of previously; the political power of organized labor was tamed; corporatist cartelization favored the already large firms in the allocation of scarce resources. Nevertheless, Sarti has concluded that (1) "the relationship between industry and fascism defied simple, mechanical cause-and-effect explanation," and (2) "it makes as much sense to say that Mussolini made use of the industrialists as it does to say that the industrialists manipulated Mussolini."

Appendix B
A Closer Look at Corporatism

The term *corporatism* usually brings to mind the corporate state of Italian fascism. Indeed, *corporatism* and *fascism* are often used as if they were synonyms. This identification between the two terms has some foundation in experience and is not completely erroneous. However, corporatism can be understood quite independently of any regime or ideology. Corporatism antedates fascism; indeed, it has no necessary connection with fascism (as the latter term is used in this book).

Corporatism is usually seen as a middle way between two other models of society, the liberal and the Marxist. To understand corporatism, therefore, it is necessary to consider these models. The liberal model posits pluralism (the existence in society of diverse groups—economic, religious, and ethnic). It further posits that these groups will have diverse, frequently contradictory, aims. Group conflict is natural and is not dangerous as long as it does not get out of hand (into violence, for instance, or into the complete exploitation of some groups by others). The purpose of the state is primarily to regulate group conflict and enforce the rules of the game. Individuals within (or outside) various groups may and will pursue their particular goals also. They must not be hindered in this pursuit of happiness, however defined, as long as they do not interfere with the rights of other individuals.

The Marxist model divides existing society into two basic groups, the exploiters and the exploited. The social dynamic at any one time consists in the struggle of the exploited to break the bonds that hold them in artificial subjection to an obsolete exploiting class. The highest form of the social struggle takes place in industrial society, in which the protagonists are the exploiting capitalists and the exploited proletariat. Three essential notions of this model are: (1) conflict takes place between the "good" and the "bad," (2) the conflict thus will become violent, and (3) the violent conflict will end in the complete displacement of one group (class) by its adversary. Ultimately, society will be classless.

Both the liberal and Marxist models of society view change as inevitable and desirable. Both are future-oriented and optimistic; both see social conflict as progressive and creative. Corporatism, on the other hand, emphasizes the benefits of stability, is pessimistic and skeptical about "progress," looks to experience as enshrined in tradition and custom, and regards group conflict as harmful to society, which is conceived of as organic. Rejecting liberal egoism and competitiveness and Marxist classism and violence, corporatist models view group conflict as neither inevitable, legitimate, nor beneficial.

The characteristic structures of liberal democracy are not found in the corporatist model. Legislative assemblies based on geographical divisions, representing changing numerical majorities composed of individual citizens, and organized by competitive and potentially divisive political parties are rejected as artificial. Citizens are organized and represented instead by the hierarchically structured, noncompetitive, and compulsory groups ("corporations") that are "found in the natural order." These corporations are mostly vocational in nature (e.g., farming, industry, the professions). Relations among them are regulated by the state (whose role is not necessarily unlimited) according to canons of distributive justice (not necessarily egalitarian). The state has the important task of overseeing the selection of leaders within each corporation. The state guarantees that no corporation violates the rules of the game. The state may even have been the creator and organizer of the corporations. It by no means follows, nevertheless, that the state must or should come to dominate or absorb society. Society, properly organized into its "natural" components, will to a large degree run itself. The dominant values of the corporatist model are harmony among groups leading to the harmonious development of a society conceived of as an organic, living entity with a moral dimension. Every group—every corporation—has its place, its duties, and its right to survive.

Because of the close historical identification of corporatist ideas with regimes regarded as fascist, it should be stressed that corporatism can be either democratic or authoritarian. Decisions within each corporation, as well as decisions among the corporations as a group, can be reached after free discussion and even majority voting. Nor does corporatism necessarily imply a virulent nationalism, emphasis on increased production for the struggle among nations, and the omnicompetence of the state. Thus one might advocate a corporate structuring of society that would lack what have been posited as absolutely essential aspects of fascism. (In today's major industrialized nations, labor-capital relations are moving rapidly toward the corporate model. In Britain, for instance, negotiations on a national level between unions and industry are commonplace, with the government acting as referee.)

On the other hand, fascist ideology necessarily includes fundamental aspects of corporatist thought. The rejection of the Marxist class war, the rejection of the liberals' individualism and group competition and conflict, and the urgency of organizing society for effective international competition—these are at the heart of fascism. These fundamental notions demand a corporatist-type model, with this special feature—that the regulatory power of the elitist party-state knows no bounds. All corporatists are not fascists, but all fascists are corporatists.

Corporatism as it operated in fascist Italy makes it easier to understand why Marxists, and especially communists, claim to view fascism as nothing more than an attempt to suppress the working class in the interest of the wealthy. Non-communist industrial society is by definition (of communists) built on exploitation of the proletariat. The only remedy for this exploitation is the communist state and the expropriation of the exploiting class. When corporatists preach and practice class cooperation, they do so, in communist eyes, in order to freeze a social system that is by definition unjust. Class cooperation is for Marxists the cooperation of the rapacious capitalist wolf and the proletarian lamb. The fact that most Westerners tend to view fascism as some sort of capitalist (or at least anti-working class) conspiracy demonstrates how successful Marxists have been in imposing their particular interpretations of politics and history on those who share neither their premises nor their goals.

Notes

Chapter 1
General Considerations on the Subject of Fascism

1. A. James Gregor, "African Socialism, Socialism, and Fascism: An Appraisal," *Review of Politics* 19 (July 1967): 353; John Weiss, *The Fascist Tradition* (New York: Harper and Row, 1967), p. 129; A. F. K. Organski, *The Stages of Political Development* (New York: Knopf, 1965), p. 179.

2. Henry Turner, "Fascism and Modernization," *World Politics* 24 (July 1972): 564.

3. A. James Gregor, *Fascism: The Classic Interpretations of the Interwar Period* (New York: General Learning Press, 1973). All subsequent quotations from Gregor in this chapter are from the work cited.

Chapter 3
The Ideology of Fascism

1. A. James Gregor, *The Ideology of Fascism* (New York: Free Press, 1969), p. 98.

2. Ernst Nolte, *Three Faces of Fascism* (New York: Holt, Rinehart, Winston, 1963), p. 151.

3. Gaetano Mosca, *The Ruling Class* (New York: McGraw-Hill, 1939), p. 50.

4. Ibid., p. 478.

5. H. Stuart Hughes, *Consciousness and Society* (New York: Vintage, 1958), p. 251.

6. Ibid., p. 78.

7. This section relies mainly on Hughes, *Consciousness and Society;* Irving L. Horowitz, *Radicalism and the Revolt Against*

Reason (New York: Humanities, 1961); Gregor, *Ideology of Fascism;* and Georges Sorel, *Reflections on Violence* (New York: P. Smith, 1941).

8. Horowitz, *Radicalism and the Revolt Against Reason*, p. 118.

9. Gregor, *Ideology of Fascism*, p. 71.

10. Christopher Seton-Watson, *Italy from Liberalism to Fascism* (London: Methuen, 1967), p. 352.

11. Nolte, *Three Faces of Fascism*, p. 151.

12. Herbert W. Schneider, *Making the Fascist State* (New York: Fertig, 1968) p. 109.

Chapter 4
The Mussolini Regime

1. Sigmund Freud sent Mussolini one of his books in 1933 inscribed "To Benito Mussolini from an old man who greets in the ruler the Hero of Culture," and Gandhi publicly proclaimed Mussolini "the savior of Italy and—I hope—the world."

Chapter 5
European Variants: Spain

1. J. H. Elliott, *Imperial Spain, 1469-1716* (New York: St. Martin's, 1963).

Chapter 6
European Variants: Eastern Europe

1. Norman Kogan, "Fascism as a Political System," in *The Nature of Fascism*, ed. S. J. Woolf (New York: Vintage, 1969), p. 116.

2. Eugen Weber, *Varieties of Fascism* (Princeton, N.J.: Van Nostrand, 1964), p. 64.

3. Eugen Weber, "The Men of the Archangel," in *International Fascism 1920-1945*, ed. Walter Laqueur and George Mosse (New York: Harper and Row, 1966), pp. 103-104.

Chapter 7
Modernization: The Challenge

1. C. E. Black, *The Dynamics of Modernization* (New York: Harper, 1967), p. 7.

2. Samuel P. Huntington, "The Change to Change," *Comparative Politics* 3 (April, 1971): 298.

3. John Lynch, *The Spanish American Revolutions* (New York:

Norton, 1973), p. 24.

4. Black, *Dynamics of Modernization*, p. 19.

5. Samuel P. Huntington, *Political Order in Changing Societies* (New Haven: Yale University Press, 1968), p. 5.

6. Ibid., p. 1.

Chapter 8
Militarism: The Response

1. Huntington, *Political Order*, p. 194.

2. Ibid.

3. John J. Johnson, *The Military and Society in Latin America* (Stanford: Stanford University Press, 1964).

4. Charles W. Anderson, *Politics and Economic Change in Latin America* (New York: Litton, 1967).

5. Huntington, *Political Order*, p. 220.

6. Dankwart A. Rustow, "Turkey," in *Political Modernization in Japan and Turkey*, ed. Robert E. Ward and Dankwart A. Rustow (Princeton, N.J.: Princetown University Press, 1964), p. 352.

7. Ibid., p. 365.

8. James Thomas Flexner, *George Washington in the American Revolution* (Boston: Little, Brown, 1967), p. 273.

Chapter 9
Communism and Modernization

1. Black, *Dynamics of Modernization*, p. 65.

2. C. E. Black et al., *The Modernization of Japan and Russia* (New York: Free Press, 1975).

Chapter 10
Japan: An Asian Road to Fascism

1. Chitoshi Yanaga, *Japan Since Perry* (New York: McGraw-Hill, 1949), p. vii.

Chapter 12
Ghana: An African Variant

1. W. Scott Thompson, *Ghana's Foreign Policy 1957-1966* (Princeton, N.J.: Princeton University Press, 1969), pp. 112, 421.

2. T. Peter Omari, *Kwame Nkrumah* (New York: Africana, 1970), p. 200.

3. David Apter, *Ghana in Transition* (Princeton, N.J.: Princeton University Press, 1972), pp. 377-378.

4. T. Howell and J. P. Rajascoria, *Ghana and Nkrumah* (New

York: Facts on File, 1972), p. 96.

5. Thompson, *Ghana's Foreign Policy*, p. 9.

6. Kwame Nkrumah, *Ghana: The Autobiography of Kwame Nkrumah* (New York: International, 1971), p. x.

7. Ibid., p. 280.

8. Apter, *Ghana in Transition*, p. xii.

Chapter 13
Egypt: The Army and the Radical Revolution

1. Leonard Binder, "Political Recruitment and Participation in Egypt," in *Political Parties and Political Development*, ed. Joseph La Palombara and Myron Weiner (Princeton, N.J.: Princeton University Press, 1966), p. 228.

Chapter 15
Peru: The Army and the Moderate Revolution

1. Abraham F. Lowenthal, "Peru's Ambiguous Revolution," *Foreign Affairs* 52 (July 1974): 817.

2. Peter Ranis, *Five Latin American Nations* (New York: Macmillan, 1971), pp. 74, 215.

3. Fredrick B. Pike, *The Modern History of Peru* (New York: Praeger, 1967), pp. 243, 261, 281.

4. Stephen L. Rozman, "The Evolution of the Political Role of the Peruvian Military," *Journal of Inter-American Studies and World Affairs* 12 (October 1970): 557.

5. For examples, see Marvin Aliskey, "Peru," in *Political Forces in Latin America*, ed. Ben G. Burnett and Kenneth F. Johnson (Belmont, Calif.: Wadsworth, 1971), p. 382; and Rozman, "Political Role of the Peruvian Military," pp. 561-562.

6. Lowenthal, "Peru's Ambiguous Revolution," p. 817.

7. Carlos A. Astiz and José Z. Garcia, "The Peruvian Military: Achievement Orientation, Training and Political Tendencies," *Western Political Quarterly* 25 (December 1972): 680.

8. Lowenthal, "Peru's Ambiguous Revolution," p. 803.

Chapter 16
Conclusions

1. Richard Lowenthal, as cited in *The Developing Nations*, ed. Frank Tachau (New York: Dodd, Mead, 1972), p. 162.

2. For patient efforts to implant this simple but profound truth into his semi-impermeable head, the author is indebted to Professor Elwyn F. Chase, Jr., of St. Joseph's College.

3. Myron Weiner, "Political Integration and Political Development," in Tachau, *The Developing Nations,* p. 66.

Bibliography

This chapter-by-chapter bibliography consists of works in the English language. Those who read other languages will find many helpful bibliographies in the works cited here. Those who read Italian could do no better than to explore Renzo De Felice's massive, masterful, multivolume life of Mussolini (Turin: Einaudi); the truly relentless will tackle Mussolini's collected works (Florence: La Fenice, 1951-1962).

Chapter 1: *General Works on Fascism*

Drucker, Peter. *The End of Economic Man*. New York: Harper and Row, 1969.

Gregor, A. James. *The Fascist Persuasion in Radical Politics*. Princeton, N.J.: Princeton University Press, 1974.

Joes, Anthony James. "Fascism: The Past and the Future." *Comparative Political Studies* 7 (1974).

___ . On the Modernity of Fascism: Notes from Two Worlds." *Comparative Political Studies* 10 (1977).

Kornhauser, William. *The Politics of Mass Society*. New York: Free Press, 1959.

Laqueur, W., and Mosse, G., eds. *International Fascism, 1920-1945*. New York: Harper and Row, 1966.

Nolte, Ernst. *Three Faces of Fascism*. New York: Holt, Rinehart, Winston, 1963.

Rogger, H., and Weber, E. *The European Right*. Berkeley: University of California Press, 1965.

Turner, H. "Fascism and Modernization." *World Politics* 24 (1972).

Weber, Eugen. *Varieties of Fascism.* Princeton, N.J.: Van Nostrand, 1964.

Weiss, John. *The Fascist Tradition.* New York: Harper and Row, 1967.

Woolf, S. J., ed. *The Nature of Fascism.* New York: Vintage, 1969.

Chapter 2: *Italy Before Mussolini*

Albrecht-Carrié, René. *Italy from Napoleon to Mussolini.* New York: Columbia University Press, 1964.

Clough, Shepard B. *The Economic History of Modern Italy.* New York: Columbia University Press, 1950.

Croce, Benedetto. *A History of Italy, 1870-1915.* New York: Russell and Russell, 1963.

Jemolo, A. C. *Church and State in Italy, 1850-1950.* Oxford: Blackwell, 1960.

Salomone, A. W. *Italy in the Giolittian Era.* Philadelphia: University of Pennsylvania Press, 1945.

——, ed. *Italy from the Risorgimento to Fascism.* New York: Anchor, 1970.

Seton-Watson, Christopher. *Italy from Liberalism to Fascism.* London: Methuen, 1967.

Smith, Denis Mack. *Italy: A Modern History.* 2 ed. Ann Arbor, Mich.: University of Michigan Press, 1965.

Sprigge, C. J. *The Development of Modern Italy.* New York: Howard Fertig, 1969.

Thayer, John A. *Italy and the Great War.* Madison: University of Wisconsin Press, 1964.

Whyte, A. J. *The Evolution of Modern Italy.* New York: Norton, 1965.

Chapter 3: *The Ideology of Fascism*

Gregor, A. James. *Contemporary Radical Ideologies.* New York: Random House, 1968.

——. *Fascism: The Classical Interpretations of the Interwar Years.* Morristown, N.J.: General Learning, 1973.

——. *The Fascist Persuasion in Radical Politics.* Princeton, N.J.: Princeton University Press, 1974.

——. *The Ideology of Fascism.* New York: Free Press, 1969.

Harris, Henry S. *The Social Philosophy of Giovanni Gentile.* Urbana, Ill.: University of Illinois Press, 1960.

Horowitz, Irving. *Radicalism and the Revolt Against Reason.* New York: Humanities, 1961.

Hughes, H. Stuart. *Consciousness and Society*. New York: Vintage, 1958.

Michels, Roberto. *Political Parties*. New York: Free Press, 1962.

Mosca, Gaetano. *The Ruling Class*. New York: McGraw-Hill, 1939.

Nolte, Ernst. *Three Faces of Fascism*. New York: Holt, Rinehart and Winston, 1966.

Pareto, Vilfredo. *The Rise and Fall of the Elites*. Totowa, N.J.: Bedminster, 1968.

Sorel, Georges. *Reflections on Violence*. New York: P. Smith, 1941.

Weber, Eugen. *Varieties of Fascism*. Princeton, N.J.: Van Nostrand, 1964.

Chapter 4: *Italian Fascism*

Borgese, G. *Goliath: The March of Fascism*. New York: Viking, 1938.

Cassels, Alan. *Fascist Italy*. New York: Crowell, 1968.

_____ . *Mussolini's Early Diplomacy*. Princeton, N.J.: Princeton University Press, 1970.

Chabod, Federico. *History of Italian Fascism*. London: Weidenfeld and Nicolson, 1963.

Derkin, F. W. *The Brutal Friendship*. New York: Harper and Row, 1962.

Delzell, Charles F. *Mussolini's Enemies*. Princeton, N.J.: Princeton University Press, 1961.

Fermi, Laura. *Mussolini*. Chicago: University of Chicago Press, 1961.

Finer, Herman. *Mussolini's Italy*. New York: Universal Library, 1965.

Germino, Dante. *The Italian Fascist Party in Power*. Minneapolis: University of Minnesota Press, 1959.

Halperin, S. William. *Mussolini and Italian Fascism*. Princeton, N.J.: Van Nostrand, 1964.

Hughes, H. Stuart. *The United States and Italy*. Rev. ed. Cambridge, Mass.: Harvard University Press, 1965.

Kirkpatrick, Ivone. *Mussolini: A Study in Power*. New York: Hawthorne, 1964.

Levi, Carlo. *Christ Stopped at Eboli*. New York: Grosset, 1947.

Megaro, Gaudens. *Mussolini in the Making*. Boston: Houghton Mifflin, 1938.

Salvemini, G. *Under the Ax of Fascism*. New York: Fertig, 1969.

Sarti, Roland. *Fascism and the Industrial Leadership in Italy, 1919-1940.* Berkeley: University of California Press, 1971.

———. ed. *The Ax Within.* New York: New Viewpoints, 1974.

Schmidt, Carlo T. *The Plough and the Sword.* New York: Columbia University Press, 1938.

Schneider, Herbert W. *Making the Fascist State.* New York: Fertig, 1968.

Silone, Ignazio. *Fontemara.* New York: Atheneum, 1960.

Sturzo, Luigi. *Italy and Fascismo.* New York: Harcourt, Brace, 1926.

Tannenbaum, Edward R. *The Fascist Experience.* New York: Basic Books, 1972.

Tasca, A. *The Rise of Italian Fascism, 1918-1922.* New York: Fertig, 1966.

Villari, Luigi. *Italian Foreign Policy Under Mussolini.* New York: Devin-Adair, 1956.

Webster, Richard A. *The Cross and the Fasces.* Stanford: Stanford University Press, 1960.

Wiskemann, Elizabeth. *The Rome-Berlin Axis.* London: Collins, 1966.

Chapter 5: *Spain*

Borkenau, Franz. *The Spanish Cockpit.* Ann Arbor, Mich.: University of Michigan Press, 1963.

Brennan, Gerald. *The Spanish Labyrinth.* Cambridge: Cambridge University Press, 1967.

Elliott, J. H. *Imperial Spain, 1469-1716.* New York: St. Martin's, 1964.

Jackson, Gabriel. *The Spanish Republic and the Civil War.* Princeton, N.J.: Princeton University Press, 1965.

Linz, Juan. "The Party Systems of Spain: Past and Future." In *Party Systems and Voter Alignments,* edited by S. M. Lipset and S. Rokkan. New York: Free Press, 1967.

Madariaga, Salvador de. *Spain: A Modern History.* New York: Praeger, 1958.

Malefakis, Edward E. *Agrarian Reform and Peasant Revolution in Spain: Origins of the Civil War.* New Haven: Yale University Press, 1970.

Payne, Stanley. *Falange: A History of Spanish Fascism.* Stanford: Stanford University Press, 1961.

———. *Politics and the Military in Modern Spain.* Stanford·

Stanford University Press, 1967.

Peers, E. A. *The Spanish Tragedy*. New York: Oxford University Press, 1936.

Souchere, E. de la. *An Explanation of Spain*. New York: Random House, 1964.

Thomas, Hugh. *The Spanish Civil War*. New York: Harper and Row, 1961.

Chapter 6: *Eastern Europe*

Barbu, Z. "Rumania." In *European Fascism*. New York: Vintage, 1969.

Deak, I. "Hungary." In *The European Right*, edited by Hans Rogger and Eugen Weber. Berkeley: University of California Press, 1965.

Horthy, Nicholas. *Memoirs*. New York: Robert Speller, 1957.

Janos, A. "The One-Party State and Social Mobilization: Eastern Europe Between the Wars." In *Authoritarian Politics in Modern Society*, edited by Samuel P. Huntington and C. Moore. New York: Basic Books, 1970.

Macartney, C. A. *Hungary*. London: Ernest Benn, 1934.

Seton-Watson, Hugh. *The East European Revolution*. New York: Praeger, 1956.

____ . *Eastern Europe Between the Wars, 1918-1940*. Cambridge: Cambridge University Press, 1945.

Weber, Eugen. "The Men of the Archangel." In *International Fascism, 1920-1945*, edited by Walter Laqueur and George Mosse. New York: Harper and Row, 1966.

____ . *Varieties of Fascism*. Princeton, N.J.: Van Nostrand, 1964.

Chapter 7: *Modernization*

Apter, David. *The Politics of Modernization*. Chicago: University of Chicago Press, 1965.

Black, C. E. *The Dynamics of Modernization*. New York: Harper and Row, 1967.

Black, C. E., et al. *The Modernization of Japan and Russia.* New York: Free Press, 1975.

Emerson, Rupert. *From Empire to Nation*. Cambridge, Mass.: Harvard University Press, 1960.

Huntington, Samuel P. *Political Order in Changing Societies*. New Haven: Yale University Press, 1968.

Kautsky, John H. *The Political Consequences of Modernization*. New York: Wiley, 1972.

Bibliography

Lynch, John. *The Spanish American Revolutions.* New York: Norton, 1973.

Marx, Karl, and Engels, F. *Manifesto of the Communist Party.* In *The Marx-Engels Reader,* edited by Robert C. Tucker. New York: Norton, 1972.

Moore, Barrington. *Social Origins of Dictatorship and Democracy.* Boston: Beacon, 1966.

Myrdal, Gunnar. *Asian Drama: An Inquiry into the Poverty of Nations.* Abridged by Seth King. New York: Pantheon, 1971.

Organski, A. F. K. *The Stages of Political Development.* New York: Knopf, 1965.

Rostow, W. W. *Politics and the Stages of Growth.* Cambridge: Cambridge University Press, 1971.

Rudolph, I., and Rudolph, S. *The Modernity of Tradition.* Chicago: University of Chicago Press, 1967.

Tachau, Frank, ed. *The Developing Nations.* New York: Dodd, Mead, 1972.

Tucker, Robert C. *The Marxian Revolutionary Idea.* New York: Norton, 1969.

Chapter 8: *Militarism*

Anderson, Charles W. *Politics and Economic Change in Latin America.* New York: Litton, 1967.

Bienen, Henry, ed. *The Military and Modernization.* Chicago: Aldine-Atherton, 1971.

First, Ruth. *Power in Africa.* Baltimore: Penguin, 1971.

Fluharty, Vernon Lee. *Dance of the Millions.* Pittsburgh: University of Pittsburgh Press, 1957.

Huntington, Samuel P. *Political Order in Changing Societies.* New Haven: Yale University Press, 1968.

Johnson, John J. *The Military and Society in Latin America.* Stanford: Stanford University Press, 1964.

Kinross, Lord. *Atatürk.* New York: Morrow, 1965.

Lerner, Daniel and Robinson, Richard D. "Swords and Ploughshares: The Turkish Army as a Modernizing Force." *World Politics* 13 (1960).

McWilliams, W. C. *Garrisons and Governments.* San Francisco: Chandler, 1967.

Robinson, Richard. *The First Turkish Republic.* Cambridge, Mass.: Harvard University Press, 1963.

Ward, Robert E. and Rustow, Dankwart, eds. *Political Moderniza-*

tion in Japan and Turkey. Princeton, N.J.: Princeton University Press, 1964.

Chapter 10: *Japan*

Beasley, W. G. *The Meiji Restoration*. Stanford: Stanford University Press, 1972.

_____ . *The Modern History of Japan*. New York: Praeger, 1973.

Black, C. E. *The Modernization of Japan and Russia*. New York: Free Press, 1975.

Borton, Hugh. *Japan's Modern Century.* New York: Ronald, 1970.

Hackett, Roger F. *Yamagata Aritomo in the Rise of Modern Japan*. Cambridge, Mass.: Harvard University Press, 1971.

Hellman, Donald C. *Japan and East Asia*. New York: Praeger, 1972.

Reischauer, Edwin O. *Japan: Past and Present*. New York: Knopf, 1963.

_____ . *The United States and Japan*. Cambridge, Mass.: Harvard University Press, 1965.

Scalapino, Robert A. *Democracy and the Party Movement in Pre-War Japan*. Berkeley: University of California Press, 1967.

Ward, Robert E., ed. *Political Development in Modern Japan*. Princeton N.J.: Princeton University Press, 1968.

Ward, Robert E., and Rustow, Dankwart, eds. *Political Modernization in Japan and Turkey*. Princeton, N.J.: Princeton University Press, 1964.

Yanaga, Chitoshi. *Japan Since Perry*. New York: McGraw-Hill, 1949.

Chapter 11: *Argentina*

Barager, J., ed. *Why Perón Came to Power*. New York: Knopf, 1968.

Blanksten, G. *Perón's Argentina*. New York: Russell and Russell, 1953.

Ferns, H. S. *Argentina*. New York: Praeger, 1969.

Kennedy, John J. *Catholicism, Nationalism, and Democracy in Argentina*. South Bend, Ind.: Notre Dame University Press, 1958.

Lieuwen, Edwin. *Generals vs. Presidents*. New York: Praeger, 1964.

Snow, Peter G. *Political Forces in Argentina*. Boston: Allyn and Bacon, 1971.

Whitaker, Arthur P. *The United States and Argentina*. Cambridge,

Mass.: Harvard University Press, 1954.

Chapter 12: *Ghana*

Apter, David. *Ghana in Transition.* New York: Atheneum, 1963.

Austin, Dennis. *Politics in Ghana, 1946-1960.* London: Oxford University Press, 1964.

Bretton, Henry L. *The Rise and Fall of Kwame Nkrumah.* New York: Praeger, 1966.

First, Ruth. *Power in Africa.* Baltimore: Penguin, 1971.

Fitch, Bob, and Oppenheimer, M. *Ghana: End of An Illusion.* New York: Monthly Review Press, 1966.

Gregor, A. James. "African Socialism, Socialism, and Fascism." *Review of Politics* 29 (1967).

Grundy, Kenneth W. "Nkrumah's Theory of Underdevelopment: An Analysis of Recurrent Themes." *World Politics* 15 (1963).

Howell, T., and Rajasooria, J. *Ghana and Nkrumah.* New York: Facts on File, 1972.

Kraus, J. "Arms and Politics in Ghana." In *Soldier and State in Africa,* edited by Claude Welch. Evanston, Ill.: Northwestern University Press, 1970.

Maloney, William P. "Nkrumah in Retrospect." *Review of Politics* 30 (1968).

Nkrumah, Kwame. *Ghana: The Autobiography of Kwame Nkrumah.* New York: International Publishers, 1971.

Omari, T. Peter. *Kwame Nkrumah.* New York: Africana Publishing, 1970.

Price, R. M. "Military Officers and Political Leadership: The Ghanaian Case." *Comparative Politics* 3 (1971).

Thompson, W. Scott. *Ghana's Foreign Policy, 1957-1966.* Princeton, N.J.: Princeton University Press, 1969.

Chapter 13: *Egypt*

Abdel-Malek, Anouar. *Egypt: Military Society.* New York: Random House, 1968.

Binder, Leonard. "Political Recruitment and Participation in Egypt." In *Political Parties and Political Development,* edited by Joseph La Palombara and Myron Weiner. Princeton, N.J.: Princeton University Press, 1966.

Hurewitz, J. C. *Middle East Politics: The Military Dimension.*

New York: Praeger, 1969.

Janowitz, Morris. *The Military in the Political Development of New Nations.* Chicago: University of Chicago Press, 1964.

Nasser, Gamal Abdel. *Egypt's Liberation: The Philosophy of the Revolution.* Washington, D.C.: Public Affairs, 1958.

Stephens, Robert. *Nasser: A Political Biography.* New York: Simon and Shuster, 1971.

Vatikiosis, P. J. *The Egyptian Army in Politics.* Bloomington: University of Indiana Press, 1961.

___ . *Egypt Since the Revolution.* New York: Praeger, 1960.

___ . *The Modern History of Egypt.* New York: Praeger, 1969.

Chapter 14: *Brazil*

Dulles, John F. W. *Vargas of Brazil.* Austin: University of Texas Press, 1967.

Fishlow, Albert. "Brazil's Economic Miracle." *The World Today.* November 1973.

Flynn, Peter. "The Brazilian Developmental Model: The Political Dimension." *The World Today,* November 1973.

Lowenstein, Karl. *Brazil under Vargas.* New York: Macmillan, 1942.

Schneider, Ronald M. *The Political System of Brazil.* New York: Columbia University Press, 1971.

Skidmore, Thomas E. *Politics in Brazil, 1930-1964.* New York: Oxford University Press, 1967.

Stepan, Alfred. *The Military in Politics: Changing Patterns in Brazil.* Princeton, N.J.: Princeton University Press, 1971.

___ . ed. *Authoritarian Brazil.* New Haven: Yale University Press, 1973.

Chapter 15: *Peru*

Aliskey, Marvin. "Peru." In *Political Forces in Latin America,* edited by Ben G. Burnett and K. F. Johnson.

Astiz, Carlos A. and Garcia, José. "The Peruvian Military: Achievement Orientation, Training, and Political Tendencies." *Western Political Quarterly* 25 (1972).

Bourricaud, F. *Power and Society in Contemporary Peru.* New York: Praeger, 1970.

Chaplin, David. "Peru's Postponed Revolution." *World Politics*

20 (1968).

Collier, David. *Squatters and Oligarchs.* Baltimore: Johns Hopkins Press, 1976.

Lowenthal, Abraham F. "Peru's Ambiguous Revolution." *Foreign Affairs* 52 (1974).

_____ . *The Peruvian Experiment.* Princeton, N.J.: Princeton University Press, 1975.

Malloy, James M. "Authoritarianism, Corporatism, and Mobilization in Peru." *Review of Politics* 36 (1974).

Paquette, James S. "Revolution by Fiat: The Context of Policy Making in Peru." *Western Political Quarterly* 25 (1972).

Pike, Frederick B. *The Modern History of Peru.* New York: Praeger, 1967.

Rozman, Stephen L. "The Evolution of the Political Role of the Peruvian Military." *Journal of Inter-American Studies and World Affairs* 12 (1970).

Appendix B: *Corporatism*

Beer, Samuel H. *British Politics in the Collectivist Age.* New York: Alfred Knopf, 1966.

Newton, Ronald C. "Natural Corporatism and the Passing of Populism in Spanish America." *Review of Politics* 36 (1974).

Schmitter, P. C. "Still the Century of Corporatism?" *Review of Politics* 36 (1974).

Shonfield, Andrew. *Modern Capitalism.* New York: Oxford University Press, 1965.

Wiarda, Howard J. "Corporatism and Development in the Iberic-Latin World: Persistent Strains and New Variations." *Review of Politics* 36 (1974).

_____ . *Corporatism and Development: The Portuguese Experience.* Amherst, Mass.: University of Massachusetts Press, 1977.

_____ . "Toward a Framework for the Study of Political Change in the Iberic-Latin Tradition: The Corporate Model." *World Politics* 25 (1973).

Index

and Italian power groups, 65-
66
and knowledge of politics, 55
and legality of power, 64-65
and nationalism, 57-59
and Nkrumah, 167, 169, 170,
174
and Pareto, 49
and Perón, 159, 160
and phases of rule, 63
and racism, 61, 70
and road to power, 38-41, 43, 44
and Socialist origins, 28, 45-46
and Sorel, 51

Naguib, General Mohammed,
177, 178
Napoleon III, 23, 24, 115
Nasser, Gamal Abdel, 56, 129,
178-180, 203
ideology of, 182
Nathan, Peter, 8
Nationalism, Italian, 52-54
Nazism and Nazi Germany, 3, 4,
61, 74, 204, 205, 207, 214
Nehru, Jawaharlal, 139
Neitzsche, F. W., 54
Nkrumah, Kwame
attempted assassinations of,
173
compared to Mussolini, 174
foreign policy of, 169-170
ideology of, 166-168
Nolte, Ernst, 5, 46, 55
Nyerere, Julius, 165-166

Odría, Manuel, 126, 139, 195
Omari, Peter, 169
Organski, A. F. K., 4, 5, 110
Ortega y Gasset, José, 10

Palme Dutt, R., 12, 13
Palazzo Chigi and Palazzo Vi-
doni, Agreements of, 68
Pareto, Vilfredo, 43, 46, 48, 49, 53

Paul VI, 190
Pedro II, 125, 126, 184
Perón, Juan, 157-164, 203, 205
and Brazil, 184
and the Church, 162-163
and Italy, 159
and *Justicialismo*, 161
takes power, 158-159
Perry, Commodore, 147
Pike, Frederick B., 194
Pius IX, 21, 22, 24, 25
Pius X, 28
Pius XI, 36, 65, 66
Popular Party and *popolari*, 35,
36, 37, 39, 40, 59
Prado, Manuel, 195
Primo de Rivera, José Antonio,
84
Primo de Rivera, Miguel, 79-81

Quadros, Janio, 187

Racism, 61, 70
Reich, Wilhelm, 8
Reischauer, Edwin, 149
Robespierre, M., 139
Rojas Pinilla, Gustavo, 93, 126,
139, 164, 205
Roman question, 24-26, 35, 66
Roosevelt and the New Deal, 67
Rosas, Juan, 157
Rossiter, Clinton, 200

Salandra, Antonio, 30, 32, 33
Salò, 60
Salomone, A. W., 39
Sarti, Roland, 12, 209, 210, 212,
214
Satsuma Rebellion, 148
Scalapino, Robert, 150
Senghor, Leopold, 165
Smith, Adam, 20